DRAWING, 1809
Esther Yoder (1780–1871).
Somerset County, Pennsylvania. 7¹/₂ × 7¹/₂.

Esther Yoder I am named
Up in Heaven is my real Homeland
Five fingers have I on one hand
How frail is luck and glass.

Courtesy Ezra and Orpha Hershberger.

Amish Roots

A TREASURY OF
HISTORY, WISDOM,
AND LORE

edited by
John A. Hostetler

The Johns Hopkins University Press
BALTIMORE AND LONDON

for Elizabeth and Jonathan

© 1989 The Johns Hopkins University Press
All rights reserved. Published 1989
Printed in the United States of America on acid-free paper

Johns Hopkins Paperbacks edition, 1992
06 05 04 03 02 01 00 99 98   6 5 4 3 2

The Johns Hopkins University Press
2715 North Charles Street
Baltimore, Maryland 21218-4319
The Johns Hopkins Press Ltd., London

Library of Congress Cataloging-in-Publication Data
Amish roots: a treasury of history, wisdom, and lore / [edited by]
  John A. Hostetler.
    p.   cm.
    Bibliography: p.
    Includes index.
    ISBN 0-8018-3769-3 (alk. paper) 0-8018-4402-9 (pbk.)
    1. Amish—History. 2. Amish—Doctrines 3. Amish—Social life
and customs.   I. Hostetler, John Andrew
  BX8129.A5A45   1989
  289.7′09—dc19   88-31688

Acknowledgments and Permissions (pp. 305–6) constitute a
continuation of the copyright page.

CONTENTS

CONTENTS

CONTENTS

CONTENTS

CONTENTS

PREFACE

he primary aim of this book is to enable the reader to comprehend the lifeways of the Amish people. Reading the literary works of the Amish instead of the generalizations made by others about them has its rewards.

This collection was inspired by Edwin S. Gaustad's two-volume work *A Documentary History of Religion in America* (1982). Citing the prize-winning historian Barbara Tuchman as exemplary, Gaustad notes that "with documents close at hand, it is possible for every man and woman to be his or her own historian." This book, like Gaustad's work, enables the amateur to reconstruct the ethos of the Amish people with the essential building blocks.

Not every voice from the past has been included here. Nor have all the documents been uncovered. No claim is made that the selections are representative. But without some criterion, an anthology would be a literary jungle. Surviving records are not spread equally across the span of time. It is neither possible nor feasible to give equal time to all "actors" on the stage of Amish history, but an effort was made to be faithful to the variety of known literary and archival sources.

Assembling an anthology of Amish writings has its surprises and disappointments. The scholar who is wholly dependent on literary texts has reason to become discouraged with their sparsity. In respect to writings and records left behind, the literary productivity of the Amish contrasts sharply with that of their predecessors, the Anabaptists. The Amish religion did not originate in the context of the great theological debates of the sixteenth century. Several Swiss and Dutch Anabaptist leaders knew Greek, Latin, and Hebrew as well as the common speech of their day. They included men such as Conrad Grebel, Baltzer Hubmaier, Jacob Hutter, Felix Manz, Dirk Philips, Michael Sattler, and Menno Simons. Some left behind voluminous works.

The Amish emerged 168 years after the founding of the Swiss Anabaptists, and in the social context of decadent Swiss congregations that were surviving in remote rural areas. Jacob Ammann's confrontations with fellow elders called for greater separation from the world, more stringent dress and grooming practices, and the expulsion of apostate members. No record is left of any Amish leaders who had ever attended university or had ever been pastors in state churches. The leaders were farmers and craftsmen who lived in the hinterlands with the Bible, the hymn book, and the martyr book as their main sources of inspiration.

The literary character of writings by the Amish is influenced by their cultural values: doing rather than saying, becoming rather than achieving, humility rather than aggressiveness. Their nonverbal stance and guarded use of speech for 250 years in America has left an impact. It follows that the Amish have written more about problem areas of life than about nonproblem ones. Thus, they have written less about agriculture, gardening, nature, birth, family, old age, and death, and more about "right living," proper attitudes, and issues that bring them into conflict with the world, such as conscientious objection to war, control over education, and symbolic identification with worldly people and worldly behavior. Birth and death are not viewed as problems, hence little is written about them. In addition, most Amish are not comfortable writing about themselves.

The constant stress on self-yieldedness, as well as unity in family, church, and brotherhood, has ironically resulted in a body of knowledge about church divisions. The earliest Amish writings were letters (1693–1711) pertaining to the division among the Swiss Brethren. Other subdivisions have occurred in America, leaving a record of partisanship and dissension over the search for the "proper" discipline. In disputes between progressive and traditional factions, it is typically the progressive party that will write an account of the division. The traditional faction, not given to literary expression, would rather withdraw and quietly disassociate itself from contention.

The Amish have produced few statements for the public, the outer world, and then only where their religious freedom was in jeopardy. Their writings are primarily directed to their own members, to their immediate family, and to the community of faith.

In making selections for this book, I gave strong consideration to personal and passionate voices within the Amish community, some never before published. Rules, resolutions, and pronouncements, which by their very nature are impersonal and platitudinous, are not ignored but are given less prominence.

Most selections are those written by the Amish themselves, or, if not by them, by those who spoke for them in appropriate times and in sensitive areas. Some selections were written by people who, although not Amish, understood their feelings and culture in remarkable ways. Light editing was considered essential in some selections. Alterations involved punctuation, uniform spelling, sentence completion, and arrangement of the material into paragraphs. Some titles of the selections are those of the authors, whereas I have supplied others. Changes made in the original sources were submitted to all living authors who could be located. My words or phrases are indicated by brackets. Omission of material is indicated by ellipses.

NOTE ON THE PLATES

The illustrations in this book were made by the Amish; minor exceptions are noted. All of the illustrations were made by or for the Amish; minor exceptions are noted. All of the illustrations were made in Pennsylvania. The earliest Amish drawing is dated 1795. There are drawings with representations of animals, birds, trees, flowers, and plants. page in the front of a book, which frequently gives the name of the owner and a short narrative with embellishments. Bookplates often appear in treasured or highly valued books, such as the New Testament, a hymn book, or a prayer book.

The texts in Amish bookplates and other embellished drawings are brief when compared to *Fraktur* (illuminated manuscripts) made by other German-speaking groups in Pennsylvania. The groups that speak Pennsylvania German, known as the "church people" (Lutheran and Reformed German denominations), are famed for their use of *Fraktur,* including bookplates and baptismal certificates *(Taufschein).* The birth certificates of Lutherans and Reformed Germans (both of whom practiced infant baptism) frequently contained lengthy biblical passages in fine handwriting. "Professionals," especially schoolmasters among them, made stylized birth certificates. The Amish baptized adults and did not customarily use decorative certificates associated with birth and baptism. Births were regularly recorded on the flyleaf of the family Bible during the eighteenth century.

Compared to the bookplates made by the Pennsylvania Germans, including the Mennonites, or those attributed to Christopher Dock, Amish bookplates are simple, decorative, and original. Their embellishments reflect the personal expressions of the artist and do not follow a rigid pattern. The Amish drawings were gifts, given to one relative or another, or given as tokens of friendship among friends. Bookplates were seldom made by the owner. The artists usually drew the owner's name, and sometimes his or her own name or initials, on the bookplate. The artists were frequently between the ages of about thirteen to early adulthood. Some handicapped people spent their time making decorative arts. Two of the most well-known artists in the Lancaster County Amish community were Barbara Ebersol (1846–1922), who was a dwarf, and Henry Lapp (1862–1904), who had speech and hearing impediments. Amish artists worked without the constraint of deadlines and did not attempt to imitate popular styles from the outside world, although they did copy the designs of others.

The legend of each illustration provides several kinds of information. Every illustration has a descriptive name and a date. The artist's name is given, and also his or her dates (if known). Each work is also identified by medium, as well as the Pennsylvania county in which it was made. When known, size is given in inches, width by height. German texts have been translated into English. Family names are spelled as they appear in the illustration. Some explanatory notes of general interest are given.

INTRODUCTION TO
A WAY OF LIFE

The Amish, who emigrated two and a half centuries ago from German-speaking countries in Europe, have survived in America in small, viable, and distinctive communities. As a "quiet people in the land," the Amish today resemble a little commonwealth. Their members claim to be ruled by the laws of brotherhood and redemption. The social bonds that unite them are many.

Having disassociated themselves from state and territorial churches, including Catholic, Lutheran, and Reformed ones, all Anabaptist (including Amish) groups suffered for their stand. They held, based on their study of the Bible, that membership in the Christian church should be voluntary, that church and state should be separate, and that believers are required to practice the teachings and example of Christ in a disciplined community. Their reforms were considered heretical, and, being pacifists, the Anabaptists suffered severely at the hands of the church and state. Many were burned at the stake. Some were placed in sacks and thrown into rivers. Others were tortured in different ways, as described in their book of martyrs, the *Martyrs Mirror*.

The Amish have survived in America, considered the "melting pot" of the world, but have completely disappeared from their European homeland. They do not live in colonies, villages, or compounds, but for the most part live in the countryside, around small rural towns and interspersed among non-Amish, or "English," families.

Together with other German-speaking people, the Amish came to American shores during the eighteenth century from about 1727 to 1790, and during the nineteenth century from about 1815 to 1860. The original Amish immigrants settled in Berks, Chester, and Lancaster counties in southeastern Pennsylvania. They moved westward—to Ohio in 1808, to Indiana in 1839, and to Iowa in 1840.

Today the Amish people live in at least twenty U.S. states and one Canadian province, Ontario. There are over 750 congregations, with a total population of over 130,000. Ohio has more Amish than any other state, followed by Pennsylvania and Indiana. Amish also live in Delaware, Florida, Illinois, Iowa, Kansas, Kentucky, Maryland, Michigan, Minnesota, Missouri, New York, Oklahoma, Tennessee, Texas, and Wisconsin. They have large families, a low rate of infant mortality, and prohibitions against birth control. Like other people, they live longer than in years past. The average number of live births per family is seven. Despite the number of children who do not join the church of their parents, or who leave and become "English," the Amish are not declining in membership.

The Amish migrate readily within America, and therefore there is a considerable number of extinct communities, and new communities are constantly being formed.

There are several groups of Amish today, just as there are many Mennonite groups, whose practices range from the orthodox to the modern. As used in this introduction, "Amish" refers to the Old Order Amish, as distinguished from related Amish groups, called Amish-Mennonite or sometimes by localized names.

The Old Order Amish are distinguished by several shared values and characteristics, in contrast to "new," or more progressive, congregations. The Old Order Amish meet for worship in their rural farm homes. They attempt to maintain an agricultural way of life, a horse-and-buggy culture, the use of the Pennsylvania German dialect, and plain grooming and attire, all of which are specified by church rules. With few exceptions, they have no meeting houses and do not send their offspring to secondary schools or colleges. They do not conduct organized missionary activities or feel compelled to evangelize others to their way of life. Their *Ordnung,* or church rules, restrain members from adopting aspects of technology which would erode the social bonds of family and community. Humility, simplicity, sharing, and sacrifice for the welfare of a community are emphasized.

The major technological inventions and social customs that radically changed American life in the nineteenth century did not affect the Amish in the same way. Those Amish who resisted modern fashions and more consistently retained their community self-sufficiency acquired the name "Old Order," whereas those Amish who adopted many of the prevailing economic and social changes were by contrast called "New Amish."

Innovations that the Old Order Amish resisted in the past, and that some Amish groups have unsuccessfully resisted, include the following: buttons on coats and vests, the mustache, men's suspenders in various forms, hats for women, store-bought clothes, detachable collars, modern styles of underwear, patterned dress material, fine shoes, low shoes, women's high-heeled shoes, parted hair, church houses, four-part singing, hymn books with printed musical notes, laypeople's use of Bibles at meeting, Sunday schools, revival meetings, secondary education, central-heating furnaces, carpets, window curtains, storm windows and screens, writing desks, upholstered furniture, brightly painted farm machinery, "falling" top buggies, rubber-tired buggies, buggy steps, whip sockets, dashboards, lawn mowers, bicycles, tractors with tires, tractors for field work, elaborately decorated harnesses, musical instruments, commercial electricity, automobiles, and telephones.

Opposing positions taken by local congregations on controversial issues resulted in numerous divisions. Not only were there individuals and their families who adopted prevailing changes, but also many congregations became affiliated with Mennonite groups and no longer considered themselves Amish. After their arrival in America, many nineteenth-century immigrant Amish affiliated with Mennonite denominations.

Amish and Mennonite groups, diverse as they are, have an affinity for each other. They all teach and profess nonresistance in time of war. In time of natural disaster (such as floods or tornadoes) or national crisis, Amish and Mennonite groups cooperate in helping their neighbors, faraway refugees, or other people in desperation. The Amish have always regarded the Mennonites as more worldly than themselves, too deeply involved in higher education and in the organizational scale of modern life. The Mennonites have frequently looked upon the Amish as backward and crude. But despite a kind of love-hate relationship between the Amish and the Mennonites, the Amish people are remarkably free of judgmental attitudes toward those outside their faith.

During the nineteenth century, the population of the Amish grew at a slow rate. This rate can be attributed to proselytizing groups and to Amish congregations who wished to modernize. In the twentieth century, the Amish population has doubled every twenty-two years. Many people, including demographers and sociologists who predicted the eventual assimilation of the

Amish, are astonished at this increase. They ask, "What is the secret of their survival?" Without going into either great statistical or philosophical detail, I shall discuss several factors important to Amish survival and viability.

Amish Survival Patterns

As demonstrated by the Amish people, the creation of a loving brotherhood includes the following key values: (1) the maintenance of a redemptive community; (2) the functional uses of tradition; (3) the uses of appropriate technology; (4) strong family ties, combined with training in the practical arts; and (5) widespread use of nonverbal discourse. Each of these elements has an important function in maintaining an integrated society.

Maintaining a Redemptive Community

The Amish view themselves as a Christian body suspended in a tension field between obedience and disobedience to an all-knowing and all-powerful Creator. Central to the Amish view is the story of Creation in Genesis. Through the Fall, humanity became heir to a disobedient nature, bringing with it a curse. Man therefore must live "by the sweat of his brow." But there is hope for those who accept the gift and provision of God. The Amish people view themselves as recipients of an undeserved gift. Thus they live in a moral predicament, for they must prove worthy, faithful, grateful, and humble. In return for the hope of redemption, the Amish reciprocate by living in brotherly communion and community.

The gift offered to God is a corporate "body," a community incarnated with Christ-like sacrificial suffering, obedience, submission, humility, and nonresistance. As a corporate offering, this body must be "without spot or blemish" (Eph. 5:27), existing in a state of brotherly love and union, in readiness, and in constant struggle to be worthy as "a bride for the groom" (Rev. 21:2). Two of the more important metaphors illustrate the acceptable models of behavior: humility versus pride, and love versus alienation.

Pride leads to a form of knowledge which erodes a person's knowledge of God. The knowledge that comes from disobedience is from "the evil one" and will lead to the broad path of destruction. The knowledge of God, in contrast, comes from obedience, which yields humility and leads to the narrow path of redemption. The Amish educational goals for their children, and their antipathy toward human speculation and worldly knowledge, are grounded in these beliefs.

4

The Functional Uses of Tradition

Sociologists today can offer the Amish little or no improvement for transmitting their values to the young. The Amish have no techniques that others, such as the Essenes, Orthodox Jews, and monastic orders, have not used. The Amish simply make tradition functional in a wide range of human activities. The Amish embrace a charter that requires a way of thinking distinguished from worldly thinking. They practice limited geographic isolation by living in rural areas.

Interpreting the essence of Christianity as a redeeming community is central to Anabaptism. The establishment of this concept cost the Amish and their ancestors, the Swiss Anabaptists of the sixteenth century, great sacrifice. It meant severing their relationships with the state church reformers, specifically the Reformed church of Ulrich Zwingli, disfranchisement of themselves as citizens, and ultimately deportation.

Although highly valued as skillful farmers in Germanic countries, the Amish were denied the rights of ownership and were totally dependent on the goodwill of lesser rulers for their existence. Only after immigrating to America did the Amish have the opportunity to buy land and organize unique communities never realized in the Old World.

The Amish maintain that separation exists between the obedient and the disobedient. There is a continuous tension between the two spheres. Believers are mandated to live apart from the "blind, perverted world" and to have no relationship with the "unfruitful works of darkness" (Phil. 2:15). The Amish are "in the world but not of it" and hence claim the status of "strangers" and "pilgrims" (1 Pet. 2:11). To hold public office or function in wider political spheres would be unthinkable. A separate language, as well as separate dress and grooming practices, supports the prescribed community boundaries. In addition, the Amish manage to keep the past alive in their present. An example of the latter is the singing of sixteenth-century hymns, whose meaning is comprehensible only to the insider.

Appropriate Technology

Because it was created by God in the Garden, soil has a spiritual significance for the Amish. In support of their obligation to care for the land, Amish ministers quote Genesis 2:15: "God took the man, and put him into the garden of Eden to dress and keep it." Humanity must keep the garden and protect it from exploitation. Stewardship is continuous and will terminate in a day of reckoning. This view of land implies not only sustenance for life but also keeping a place that is attractive and orderly. If treated violently or exploited selfishly, the land will yield poorly, leaving humankind in poverty. The Amish approach to land contrasts sharply with the so-called Western view, which sees humanity as exploiters of nature. To damage the earth means, for the Amish, to destroy one's own offspring.

The character of Amish society requires that members make their living from farming or, if not from farming, from occupations of a rural or semirural character. The Amish do not farm for monetary rewards. The joys of living together are not traded for "progress." The Amish will accept some progress but will not let it destroy their community life. Moderation is an important principle in social survival.

The Amish are selective in choosing the inventions and machines that will influence their lives. They see nothing inconsistent in writing with magic markers and driving a horse and carriage. Pocket calculators or battery-operated razors are no threat to family solidarity. They see no contradiction in forbidding a telephone in the home but permitting its use from a pay station. A person will not talk so long or so often at a pay booth down the road.

The use of electricity from public utilities is another matter. The Amish feel that, should they plug into an electrical socket, they will change their whole way of thinking and their relationship to nature, for with electric power will come all the conveniences that would wipe out simplicity, humility, and the institutions of communal dependence.

Amish thinking about the use of tools stands in sharp contrast to the metaphor of bigger and more efficient machines. The logic of bigger technology points toward infinite industrial growth and infinite energy consumption. The energy crisis for the Amish is not one of supply or of technology, but a question of morality.

In respect to energy, and the balancing of human life with machines, the Amish have mastered one of the contradictions so puzzling to modern society. Should they accept the large machines, the Amish feel they would lose their skills. This in turn would lead to the loss of stewardship, which would result in the loss of fellowship and community life. They would exile themselves from Creation and ally themselves with the forces of annihilation.

Practical Training in the Family Context

In the functioning of family, farm, and faith, social and work roles are clearly defined. The farm is the man's kingdom. His wife manages household affairs—cooking, cleaning, gardening, preserving food, and keeping up the appearance of the house and lawn. She also has primary care of the children. Personal relationships in Amish society are quiet and responsible, with respect as the norm of behavior. Family and home are effective socializing institutions, and children participate in work, play, and ceremony to the limit of their abilities.

Home forms the center of life and a place of belonging for all family members, including those who are handicapped or retarded. It is a place of security and the center of decision-making. Children are so reared that they never feel secure outside of the family and community—they not only anticipate rewards when they grow older but also share fully in rewards within the family.

Amish country schools prepare the young to live in community. For more than a century the Amish in America attended public schools but, when forced to attend consolidated schools in an environment hostile to humility, simplicity, and the fear of God, they felt threatened and formed their own one-room country schools.

Amish child-rearing emphasizes cooperation, responsibility, humility, and skills that are learned thoroughly. Schools are located in the Amish farm environment, taught by Amish people, and conducted in an atmosphere of trust. Many Amish schools use discarded books from the public schools. They favor old books because they have less science, less reference to television, and less discussion of ego-centered activities than do the latest textbooks. Books supporting conspicuous consumption, militaristic superiority, or sex education are avoided.

The schools fit the child to become a part of the community. Because the dignity of tradition rather than progress is emphasized, Amish schools function to prepare the young to live simply, with minimum reliance on the mass communication systems of modern society.

Silent Discourse

The Amish use their words sparingly. When people are deeply involved with each other, there is pervasive communication with a minimum use of words. Collective awareness develops to such an extent that it becomes a religious experience—an involvement that cannot be uttered in words. Silence functions as an effective conveyor of information.

Deep commitments to the faith tend to be silent rather than vocal. Prayers before and after meals are periods of uninterrupted silence. Sundays at home are spent in silence—hammering, building, and loud noises are not permitted. Silence is a defense against fright or the unknown. Silence is a way of living and forgiving, a way of embracing the community with charity. The member who confesses all before the church is forgiven, and the sin is never spoken of again.

Divisive topics of conversation which might provoke discord are avoided. Silence in the face of misbehaving young people permits the adults to absorb the faults of the immature. When the Amish are confounded by a bureaucrat, outwitted by a regulation, or cursed by an outsider, their answer is silence. Ultimate answers to questions are demonstrable in life, scarcely in words. The farm routine of feeding the animals and cultivating the soil is done methodically and quietly.

The individual in Amish society does not consciously need to order everything. Much is patterned and ordered covertly, and in silence there is room to work out contradictions. Many noises, including "needless words," are a displeasure to God, and once words are spoken they can never be taken back or stricken from the record. Evil words spoken by individuals will surface again on the Day of Judgment. A simple yes or no is sufficient. "Let every man . . . be slow to speak, slow to wrath" (James 1:19) is often quoted. There is the silence of turning the other cheek.

Amish sermons routinely stress biblical passages related to speech behavior; for example, "The tongue is an unruly evil, full of deadly poison" (James 3:8). Cleverness, long-windedness, eloquence, and wordiness belong to the proud and wicked.

Contributions to American Life

Within the American rural environment, the Amish found the freedom to develop their religious ideals. These ideals helped to shape the social, economic, and educational character of the community. Amish social networks resemble those of a little commonwealth. Commonwealth implies a place, a province, a domain sufficiently unified, both geographically and socially, to have a consciousness of its own. Its inhabitants feel comfortable with their own customs, and the "place" possesses a sense of distinction from other parts of the country. Members of a commonwealth are not footloose. They have a sense of productivity and accountability in a province where the general welfare is accepted as a day-to-day reality. Commonwealth has come to have an archaic meaning in today's world, because, when groups and institutions become too large, the sense of the common good is lost. Much of what is obsolescent in modern society remains functional in the Amish commonwealth.

It may be argued that the Amish have retained elements of wholesome provincialism, a saving power to which the world in the future will need more and more to appeal. Provincialism need not turn to ancient narrowness and ignorance, confines from which many have sought to escape. A sense of province, with its cherished love of people and self-conscious dignity, is a necessary basis for relating to the wider world community.

In the Old World the formation of community life was thwarted by the established system of landholding, by the limitation on association, and by compulsory territorial religion. Nonconformists such as the Amish were denied the rights of ownership. Individual families who fled from authorities rented land or sold their services to noblemen in exchange for protection. The extended family, rather than the community, was the dominant form of organization. In America, the Mennonites formed compact neighborhoods and geographic communities. Prior to the War of Independence, the Mennonites had purchased large blocks of land in Lancaster County. The Amish followed, with eight separate settlements in Pennsylvania.

In the New World the Anabaptist-related groups maintained a strong affinity for agriculture and manual skills. Tilling the soil was not one of the founding principles that gave rise to the Anabaptist movement but was an emphasis acquired during periods of persecution. It was in the hinterlands that the Amish developed unique skills of work incentives and crop production. The basic techniques devised in the Palatinate, Alsace, and elsewhere in Europe—such as rotation of crops, indoor feeding of cattle, meadow irrigation, the use of natural fertilizers, and the raising of clover and alfalfa as a means of restoring soil fertility—were applied in Pennsylvania. The Amish combined animal husbandry with intensive cultivation on rented land. The family occupied a farm, and the entire household worked together. Married children sometimes lived with the family in anticipation of renting the farm. The parents would retire early and help their children financially, spending their later years assisting the young couple to take over. In this manner all the generations of a farming family were integrated by agricultural labor. Improvement of the soil and the dwellings were made feasible by long-term leases. The principles of family occupancy, family entrepreneurship, continuity, and motivation for labor were combined in the management of the farms.

Those who came to Pennsylvania showed a strong preference for family-sized holdings on soil that was suited for intensive cultivation. Furthermore, they wanted to combine agriculture with a preferred way of life, and not farm primarily for commercial gain. They sought limestone soil, which they believed to be superior. Although the Amish located on large acreages, ranging from one hundred to four hundred acres at the outset, they gradually reduced their holdings to what could be managed with family labor. Plantations or large-scale farms did not interest them.

The agricultural practices of the two major immigrant groups of the colonial period—the British and the Swiss-Germans—were very different. The British were mobile, "forever changing," and were inclined to move to cheaper land. The Swiss-Germans, who settled in communities, soon made the land valuable. In 1785 Pennsylvania's famous physician and citizen Benjamin Rush observed that the German farms were "easily distinguishable from those of others, by good fences, the extent of orchards, the fertility of soil, productiveness of the fields, and the luxuriance of the meadows" (Rush 1875: 11). This observation is still fitting, because the Amish maintain these characteristics, as can be seen when driving through their settlements. Moreover, the Swiss-Germans tended to secure the farms of the British and to improve and restore depleted soils.

The Mennonites and Amish set high standards of work for themselves. Work patterns took on the characteristics of ritual. "To fear God, and to love work," wrote Rush, "are the first lessons the Pennsylvania Germans teach their children, preferring industrious habits to money itself" (Rush 1875: 11–12). Communities today differ, however, in the tempo of work and in motivation. Few will hire an outsider to do farm work. "Outsiders," they say, "do not know enough and they don't work hard enough."

As farmers in America, the Amish people might be classed as small-scale operators. Manual labor, frugality, industry, and honesty are valued, but such moral virtues do not give assurance of salvation. Wealth does not accrue to individuals for their enjoyment, or for the advancement of their social standing, but it enhances the well-being of the community. For example, the Amish are embarrassed by outward signs of social recognition. Similarly, their calling is not that of seeking worldly success, for neither the individual nor the family will depend on material acclaim for assurance of salvation. The ascetic limitations on consumption, combined with the necessity to save, make possible an economic base for a people who consider themselves "in the world, but not of it."

Diversity and cleavages are characteristic of American Mennonite and Amish groups. Their faith, in an environment of religious toleration, gave rise to many subgroups and social types. Yet these diverse groups are supportive of one another. Within diversity there is a degree of freedom. Sociologists have often drawn the premature conclusion that any change within a group results in assimilation into the larger society. In reality, a small-scale structure persists despite a flow of individuals across boundaries. Separate group identities are maintained by techniques of exclusion and not by lack of mobility. The functions of Amish signs and symbols are pervasive: the many colors and shapes of horse-drawn carriages (white, black, gray, or no tops), the varieties of suspenders and hats which distinguish one group from the other, and the variation in hymn tunes.

Amish communities have functioned as mediating structures within the many tensions that make a pluralistic society possible. Over the centuries, the communities have often seemed to thwart the objectives of the nation state. Though they have paid their taxes, they have consistently refused military service, public office, and trades or businesses that rely on manipulative, highly competitive, and questionable ethical practices. They have often rejected the notion of progress. Some people regarded the Amish as a stubborn sect living by oppressive customs. They have resisted the influence of the modernizing processes and industrialization, as well as modern secular schools. They do not train their members for upward mobility in the world of science or the intellectual professions. On matters of family, church, neighborhood, working place, and commitment, they have maintained a clear line of thinking within worlds of tension and worlds of meaning.

Amish communities have supported the individual in his or her private life against the impersonal bureaucracies of modern life (Kraybill 1989). The distrust of bureaucratic structures in industrialized societies is not without foundation. The proliferation of impersonal structures results in widespread alienation. Meaning and identity for the individual are thwarted. The loss of community and those trusting relationships nurtured in family, neighborhoods, church, and voluntary associations weakens the fabric of the larger society. By resisting industrializing influences and preserving their communities, the Amish have functioned as value-maintaining communities essential in the wider society.

Communities of preservation not only check the excesses of government but also expand familial love to a wider range of human groups. Healthy communities make members feel specifically bound and responsible to others. Instead of being a hindrance to the wider society, communities can be ennobling, strengthening, healing, and satisfying. Mediating human associations are roadblocks to totalitarian governments, whether socialist or capitalist, for they typically view ethnic and religious subcultures as narrow, disruptive, evil, irrational, and restrictive.

Like other ethnic groups, the Plain People run the risk of developing an inflated view of their own superiority. Excessive ethnocentrism can lead to nationalistic arrogance and racism. The checks against such excesses are not the destruction of the mother group but self-correction from within. One such restraint is the practice of humility and moderation as key values in human associations. Among the Amish people an old saying, "Self-praise stinks," has worked effectively in checking both individual and group arrogance.

Religious pluralism founded and practiced in Pennsylvania in a new way three centuries ago subsumes a healthy respect for differences. It subsumes the right not only to be a citizen of the world but also to retain one's own cultural integrity, to enable one's own children to join one's peoplehood, and to exercise creativity within one's tradition.

The Amish know they cannot halt industrialization. The most they can hope for is tolerance for their religious communities existing as pockets in rural America. They have no interest in allying themselves with an agrarian movement or a political party in order to restore the dignity of the small community. Their life seems precarious in a world enamored with the illusion of having power over nature. As the Amish view the general decay of sensibilities in the outside world of disobedience, they maintain a willingness to suffer for their redemption.

1

THE EUROPEAN CONNECTION

The Amish were among the early Germanic settlers in William Penn's woods, or Pennsylvania. They originated in the Anabaptist movement (1525–1536), which gave rise to several Christian communities that survive to this day, among them the Mennonites of the Netherlands, the Hutterites of Austria, and the Swiss Brethren. The Amish, an orthodox branch of the Swiss group, in 1693 took their name from Elder Jacob Ammann. He led a reform movement (1693–1697) among scattered Mennonites 168 years after the initial founding of the Anabaptist-Mennonite movement. Ammann represented older traditions and separation from the world to a greater extent than other Anabaptist-Mennonite groups.

All Anabaptist groups suffered martyrdom for their deviation from the established territorial state churches—Catholic, Lutheran, and Reformed. From a renewed study of the Bible, they held that membership in the Christian church should be voluntary (adult instead of infant baptism), that church and state should be separate, and that believers are required to practice the teaching and example of Christ in a disciplined community. Their reforms were greeted with death and deportation. They suffered as heretics at the hand of church and state, being burned at the stake and tied to wagon wheels. Many were placed in sacks and thrown into the river or tortured in other cruel ways, as described in their book of martyrs.

Today's Mennonites of Swiss origin come from the same seventeenth-century stock as the Amish, but they differ in the degree of modernity. The Amish have incorporated more of the past into their communities—in their manner of worship, simplicity, styles of dress, and high degrees of nonverbal and symbolic communication. They cherish personal relationships over organizational ones, and they maintain restraints on modern technology. Their early connection with the Anabaptist movement is essential for understanding their religious life.

>>>->>>->>>->>>->>>->>>->>>->>>

A Fresh and Radical Break

FRANKLIN H. LITTELL

*P*rofound social changes had been taking place in Europe long before the beginning of the Reformation in the sixteenth century. The large variety of counterculture groups in that century demonstrates the seriousness with which people sought solutions to a better life. Rebellion against traditional systems of authority gave rise to debates and wars. The peaceful Anabaptists introduced the biblical model of "a brotherly community."

Four and a half centuries ago [in Europe], little house-churches of earnest Christians began a spiritual emigration from Christendom. They were convinced that the world of nationalism and mindless technology which was emerging was hopelessly committed to war and violence. For Christians, perceiving the world's rush toward self-destruction, the only answer was to restore a True Church based on New Testament models. The Bible, long neglected, was again providing a way for those who took holy history seriously.

The leaders of the official churches had made themselves part of the problem by adding glosses and compromises to the Gospel. A True Church, as the Anabaptists saw it, had to break out in a fresh and radical way. . . .

At a time when large numbers of people are becoming aware that the dominant society is in fact hopelessly devoted to war and violence, the classical Anabaptist witness to the nature of the good Society has a chance at a wider hearing. For the Anabaptists were not a sectarian or self-consciously elite group: they believed that the Bible was relevant to continuing history, and that it provided clear guidance as to how God intended human beings to relate to each other.

Out of the experience of the Anabaptist counterculture, certain lessons emerged which apply well to the world at large. The Anabaptist vision of a pilgrim church now appeals to many who have grown up in the old traditions of coercive and established Christendom. The Anabaptist view of the nature of a just and limited state is also timely. For during these four and a half centuries of modern warring, of which the twentieth century is already the most murderous era, the nation-state has developed into the most demonic and destructive force of all. Not just the monstrous and dehumanizing acts of totalitarian governments, but also the illegal acts of legitimate governments have become a grievous burden to men and women of conscience. Indeed, the worst curse of the age has become the pattern of illegality and injustice of which the modern nation states are the chief instruments.

The Anabaptists had an answer to exploitation and de-humanization: mutual aid, practiced under the Christian rule of brotherhood love. But even the economic exploitation of less technologically advanced peoples—depressed minorities in Europe and North America, whole populations in Asia and Africa—can today continue only through the forceful misuse of power by the most powerful governments.

The Anabaptists were condemned and defamed by spokesmen of the sixteenth-century establishments because they refused to support the power-systems then emerging. The nation-states demanded that the church bless their ambitions and sanctify their warring. When the Anabaptists refused to repeat the feudal oath, refused to bear arms, and withdrew from participation in the legally privileged and controlled churches, they struck a radical blow for liberty, conscience and human dignity. Their devotion was directed toward true Christianity rather than social reform, but the secondary consequences of their spiritual emigration were also momentous.

Today we can see that the Anabaptist-Mennonite testimonies were very important for both church and state. While much of the teaching of the Roman Catholic and Protestant theologians of the sixteenth century is today unreal and irrelevant, what the Anabaptists taught about mutual aid, peace, discipline, religious liberty, lay witness, etc., is as fresh and important as it was fifteen generations ago.

Source: Littell (1971)

->>>->>>->>>->>>->>>->>>->>>->>>

The Anabaptists: Their Beliefs and Practices

JOHN C. WENGER

*M*ainline reformers and theologians *supported the state church system in Europe and suppressed the Mennonite emphasis on separation of church and state. John C. Wenger outlines some of the major emphases of the Anabaptist movement, as contrasted to those of modern Christianity.*

The Anabaptist-Mennonite understanding of the church differed from mainline reformers in certain respects. On the so-called major doctrines of the Christian faith: God, Christ, Holy Spirit, Man, Sin, Salvation, the Second Coming of Christ, and the like, Mennonites held the same doctrinal views as prevailed in Protestantism, especially as found in the Reformed faith. But there were certain distinctive emphases which taken together formed a constellation of beliefs which more or less marked off the Anabaptists and their modern descendants from much of Christendom.

1. The Anabaptists had a strong emphasis on the necessity of *conversion.* It was not enough, they said, to be baptized as an infant, to hold membership in the State Church, and to receive the sacraments. What God demands is holiness of heart and life, and inner "baptism" with the Holy Spirit. In order to be saved a sinner needs to heartily repent and to turn away from sin, and surrender to Christ. No Anabaptist would think of trusting in church membership as such for salvation. Neither did the Anabaptists believe that salvation was mediated by the sacraments. Only faith, they said, could lay hold on Christ for salvation. Conversion must be a reality, and not a theory. This emphasis on contrition, and continuing brokenness of spirit (called in German *Bussfertigkeit*) characterized the Anabaptists.

2. The Anabaptists stressed the necessity of not merely passively trusting in Christ, but of also becoming *committed disciples* of Christ. Each believer needs to take up the cross for himself. The Scriptures were given to be obeyed. This is one of the symbolisms of baptism. The disciple signified by being baptized his intention to live a life of holy commitment to Jesus Christ.

16

He is prepared to follow Christ at any cost. Coupled with this earnest ethical endeavor was a simple acceptance of the word of Christ at face value, regardless of how Christendom explained away any given commandment. The oath is a good illustration. No language could be plainer than that of Christ when He forbade any and all oaths on the grounds of the finiteness of humanity. The leading theologians, however, of the Reformation period held that it was only the abuse of the oath, a carelessness of truth which fortifies one's word by many oaths, which was condemned by our Lord.

It was because of this emphasis on the church's being composed of earnest disciples that the Anabaptists insisted on the practice of church discipline. Every effort must be made to bring each member to full maturity, spiritually and ethically, in Christ.

3. The Anabaptists held that there were *two kingdoms,* that of God, and that of Satan. These two kingdoms are in conflict and will be so until the return of Christ to raise the dead and judge the world on the Last Day. Therefore believers need to keep themselves separate from the sins of the world. As one martyr wrote to his daughter in 1572: "And read the Holy Scriptures, and when you have attained your years, consider and ponder it well; and pray the Lord for understanding then, and you shall be able to discern good from evil, lies from truth, the way of perdition, and the narrow way that leads unto eternal life. And when you then see pomp, boasting, dancing, lying, cheating, cursing, swearing, quarreling, fighting, and other wickedness, such as drinking to intoxication, . . . think then: 'This is not the right way, these are not the works of Christians, as the Holy Scriptures teach.' "

4. The Anabaptists stressed a *brotherhood church.* All too frequently it has been the case that in the congregations of Christendom such things as education, wealth, and ordination tend to stratify the members of the church into various levels of importance and status. In the Anabaptist-Mennonite tradition, the church shall be a brotherhood, with all titles omitted in the life of the church, and the members addressing one another as brother or sister. The church is to be a brotherhood of love. Indeed, this seems to have been precisely the emphasis of the Lord Jesus in John 13 when He taught His disciples that they ought to wash one another's feet. Each member, because he regards his brethren as sons of God, is willing to humble himself before them and render the most lowly service as a token of the Christian love which binds together the members of the body of Christ.

5. The Christian shall be a *nonresistant follower* of the Lord Jesus Christ. That is, he shall deliberately follow the royal law of love. This doctrine of not resisting an evil man, which is taught in the New Testament by Christ and the apostles, was taken in an absolute way by the Anabaptists. They could not bring themselves to have any part in the taking of human life. They

renounced absolutely the use of force and violence in human relations, and were prepared to suffer, if need be, rather than to inflict suffering on others. On this point, as on the oath, the Anabaptists believed that Jesus "fulfilled" the law of the Old Testament by lifting His followers to a higher level than God had required of his people prior to the coming into the world of the Son of God. The doctrine of nonresistance is perhaps the most distinctive emphasis of the Anabaptists.

6. The Anabaptists also had a strong emphasis on the church as a *missionary body*. In a day when leading theologians considered that the Great Commission had been fulfilled by the Apostolic Church in the first century, and was no longer binding upon the body of Christ, the Anabaptists quietly insisted that the entire New Testament was binding on every believer, and that the Christians ought to go everywhere making disciples for the Lord Jesus Christ. This attitude refused to recognize the polity which prevailed at that time in which the ruler of a given territory established the faith for his subjects, compelling them by law to conform. This was regarded by the Anabaptists as intolerable. The Anabaptists did not hold that there were no saved persons outside their fellowship. What they denied was that the rank and file of the population were born-again Christians, that the rulers had any right to determine the faith of anyone (for faith is a gift of Christ, and the conscience should not be coerced by any human being), and that any ruler had the right to forbid any believer to witness to his faith to those whom he encountered.

7. The Anabaptists also appealed to those passages in the New Testament which represent Christians as expecting to suffer for their faith in a hostile and sinful world. They therefore often referred to those passages of the New Testament on the necessity of entering into the kingdom of God through much suffering, of bearing the cross, and of being willing to witness to the truth with their blood. The original documents do not betray an undue desire for martyrdom, but they do reveal the expectation that being a real child of God will likely excite the opposition and hostility of a cruel world, so that fines, imprisonment, and even death will be all too common in the brotherhood.

Source: Wenger (1961): 11–13

-⫸-⫸-⫸-⫸-⫸-⫸-⫸-⫸-

Infant Baptism: An Abomination

CONRAD GREBEL

I*n 1524 Conrad Grebel, founder of Swiss Anabaptism in Zürich, at the age of twenty-six wrote this scathing denunciation of child baptism. Mennonites, including the Amish people, still reject the practice of infant baptism.*

All children who have not yet come to know the difference between good and evil, and have not yet eaten from the tree of knowledge, will certainly be saved through the suffering of Christ, the new Adam. He restored their life. If Christ had not suffered, they would have been subject to death and damnation. The children, not yet mature (grown up) enough to corrupt, prove to us that Christ had not suffered for the children. We exclude children from the requirement of having faith as the basis for salvation. We believe they will be saved without faith. And from the above mentioned verses and the description of baptism and the stories (according to which no children were baptized), likewise from other writings which do not refer to children, we conclude that infant baptism is a senseless, blasphemous abomination of Scripture.

Source: Grebel (1952): 13

-⫸-⫸-⫸-⫸-⫸-⫸-⫸-⫸-

The Founders Were Cursed and Slandered

HUTTERIAN BRETHREN

T*he authors of the great chronicle of the Hutterians describe the sacrifice of the early Anabaptist faithful ones.*

Many were tormented day and night with unheard-of tricks and cunning. Monks and priests came with smooth words, and scholars of Scripture with false teaching; they insulted and threatened, stormed and abused, with lies and horrible blasphemy. But this did not make the faithful lose heart.

Some of those who suffered such cruel imprisonment sang songs of praise to their God because they were full of joy.

Some did the same when taken from prison to the place of execution. They sang joyfully, their voices ringing out as if they were going to meet the bridegroom at a wedding. . . .

No human being and nothing on earth could steal the truth from their hearts anymore. They were such zealous lovers of God that his fire burned in them, and they would rather die the bitterest death, rather endure ten deaths, than forsake the truth they had recognized. They would accept neither glory nor kingdom nor all the world's pleasures and goods in exchange for their faith in Christ, in whom they had foundation and assurance.

From the shedding of such innocent blood, Christians arose everywhere. The number of believers increased in all those places. . . .

In some places the authorities filled all the prisons and dungeons (as was done by the Count Palatine on the Rhine), thinking to quench God's fire by violence. But the prisoners sang joyfully until their enemies outside (who had thought the prisoners would be terrified) were themselves more frightened than the prisoners and did not know what to do with them, for in many cases they realized that the believers were innocent. Many were kept in prisons and dungeons for a short time, some for many years, enduring every torture. Some had holes burned through their cheeks before being set free. Some obtained their freedom with God's help, often through his intervention in wonderful ways. They remained steadfast in faith until God took them to himself.

Those who escaped all this were hunted and driven from place to place and from land to land. They had to be like owls and night herons, not daring to appear by day, hiding among crags and crevices in the rocks, in wild woods, and in pits and holes. They were hunted by constables and dogs; snares were set to capture them like birds. All of this without any offense on their part—they were neither harmed nor wished to harm anyone.

Source: Hutterian Brethren (1987): 222–24

➤➤➤➤➤➤➤➤➤➤➤➤➤➤➤➤

The Reforms of Jacob Ammann

JACOB AMMANN

One hundred and sixty-eight years after the initial founding of the Swiss Anabaptist movement in 1525, Jacob Ammann led a reform (1693–1697) emphasizing simplicity of life, separation from the world, ceremonial foot-washing, and social avoidance of excommunicated members.

Little is known of the personal life of Elder Jacob Ammann, founder of the Amish, except that he was born in Switzerland and moved to the Alsace area to provide pastoral care for scattered Mennonite families. Ammann felt that the congregations in Switzerland became careless by not observing foot-washing and by not "avoiding" those who had been excommunicated from the church. Realizing that these practices were not uniformly observed, Ammann made a journey to Switzerland. At each assembly he pressed the pastors to declare their attitude on these points. John Reist, the senior elder of the Swiss churches, refused to attend Ammann's meetings. The biblical teaching of avoidance, he said, was never practiced by the Swiss, and furthermore the teaching meant that "fallen" or excluded members should not partake of communion. Ammann contended that the teaching applied to social avoidance, including not eating at the same table with apostate members (1 Cor. 5:11). At the conclusion of his journey, Ammann excommunicated Reist and six others, declaring them apostate.

The division affected the Mennonite churches in Switzerland, France, and Germany. Letters between the participants in the controversy have been preserved. The selections below represent the views of the two sides in the controversy; Ammann's views appear first.

The charges against John Reist are these:

First: I sent Nicholas Moser . . . to ask him (John Reist) whether expelled persons should be avoided in both natural and spiritual eating, to which he replied: "That which enters the mouth is not sin."

Second: I, Jacob Ammann myself, . . . went to him and asked him whether he could confess that the expelled should be avoided in natural and spiritual eating and drinking, but again he answered: "What enters the mouth is no sin, Christ also ate with publicans and sinners."

I also asked him if known liars should be expelled from the church, but he would not confess it . . . a reputed liar who had conceived falsehoods in her own heart, . . . admitted her untruth, yet he refused to expel her from the church.

Third: I sent John Gerber and Peter Zimmerman to John Reist to demand his confession that the expelled be avoided, but he would not answer them. Then he wrote a letter stating that he would not adopt this commandment to avoid the expelled in both natural and spiritual eating. In the letter he also wrote that in matters concerning doctrines and ceremonies not too much attention should be paid to the younger men . . . why did he circulate this letter among ministers and bishops, warning them to disregard the teachings of young ministers?

John Reist himself also told me that his authority was above mine. Yet we are ordained to the identical ministry. Is this not spiritual pride? . . .

He also attributed salvation to the kindhearted persons, who do not conform to Christian faith and rituals, and who are not in accord with our mode of baptism and the observance of the Lord's Supper. These he consoles with salvation. . . .

I went to these afore-mentioned men to determine how we should further conduct ourselves toward John Reist, who has not confessed the faith with us, and has been careless. . . .

I asked Benedict Schneider whether he had been asked about the article of avoidance. He resisted violently. He also would not confess that known sinners would be expelled from the church. . . .

Apart from the Word of God no one can be saved. There is but one faith that counts with God. There is but one people who are the bride of Christ. Are we not among this people? Are we not traveling the narrow path? . . .

Our opponents would admit these kindhearted people by another way into the sheepfold, without this Christian ritual, without the cross, without tribulation. These are thieves and murderers, deceptive workers whom we shun because they preach their hearts' desire and not out of the mouth of the Lord. . . .

All excommunicants shall, without distinction, be shunned and avoided until the time of their repentance. . . .

Keeping house according to Christian rituals and the Word of God is my highest concern. . . .

It is not becoming for us to walk to strange preachers outside the church of God, as though light could be found among darkness, or truth among lies.

If anyone desires to conform to this world, by trimming the beard, by wearing long hair and attractive apparel, and will not confess that it is unrighteous, he shall be justly punished; for God is not pleased with the proud.

You have accused us, and in particular me, Jacob Ammann, of disciplining too strictly and for not yielding to appeals for patience and forbearance. This is not true. We extended more patience and toleration than the Scripture required of us. . . .

Those who were stubborn and would not confess I, Jacob Ammann, with the counsel of ministers and bishops, was obliged to expel from the communion of God . . . even though they are ministers and bishops, for faith has no respect of persons. The Word of God requires obedience of leaders as well as followers, of preachers as well as audiences.

It appears much as though you wished to gain lordship of our faith. You have dealt contrary to the Word of God, in that you instruct us to be reconciled with such unbelieving people.

Either confess with us, or inform us another and better way. . . .

But if you will not confess these contested articles of the Christian faith with us, and cannot inform us of another and better way, then you shall by us . . . be expelled, excluded, and placed under the ban as apostates and sectarians and as unhealthy members. You shall be shunned and avoided by all members of the church of God.

If there is anyone among you who does not wish to be included under this judgment it is his (or her) duty to report either in person or by writing. . . .

This document is made and finished this twenty-second day of November, in the year 1693.

Source: John B. Mast (1950): 28–48, 49

Reply to Jacob Ammann

JOHN REIST ET AL.

*J*ohn Reist, the senior elder of the Swiss Brethren in Switzerland, opposed Ammann's teaching. His reasons for this opposition, as well as those of others who concurred with him, appear in the following statements. Although the wearing of hooks-and-eyes on clothing was not an issue in the division, the Amish were called the Häftler (hook-and-eyers) and the Reist group was identified as Knöpfler (button people) for many years.

We, the undersigned, are unable to agree with Jacob Ammann. Our reasons are that he is introducing avoidance in natural eating and drinking, taking it from I Cor. 5. As we understand I Cor. 5, we do not concede that the apostle was referring to natural eating, but of eating the Passover. . . .

The Swiss Brethren have never used outward avoidance, and have maintained peace and harmony, also kept the church in restraint and order that I should desire nothing better than that God might give us grace that we could preserve ourselves and the church in peace and prosperity. . . .

Jacob Ammann summoned us. . . , wanting to hear the letters I had carried to Switzerland. So I read the one by Jacob Good first. Then he commenced speaking irreverently and called me a liar, . . . and had estranged the people from him. He warned me to leave off or he would take hold of the affair. . . .

Rudolph Huszer and I told him we were not alarmed, and would not forsake our ministry. He said we are false teachers, banished, lying men, the devil's servants. I said I had not yet perceived the false teaching; Jacob Ammann requested that I read the other letter (Jonas Lohr) to him also. Then I commenced reading, and . . . a quarrel began as fire entering straw, with scolding and scorning, the like of which I have never heard.

The legal claim to the church house was also disputed. He said the house belongs to them, for those who purchased it have the faith with him. Rudolph Huszer told him this was untrue, whereupon the argument ensued with scolding and contempt. I cannot express with writing how he scolded us as "lying grayheads" who should be ashamed to pastor a congregation. We told him . . . that he would not be the judge at the Last Day, but must await his verdict.

Jacob Ammann resolved to hold communion services twice a year.

We pleaded with Jacob Ammann, that . . . he should not bring about a division. Thereupon Ammann said: "John Reist has scorned the Word of God." Then he pulled out a letter on which were written six charges against John Reist. Jacob Ammann pronounced him expelled and banished from the Christian church. We were horrified that the meeting was not conducted in an orderly manner.

Source: John B. Mast (1950): 50, 58, 61–63

2

COMING TO AMERICA

The Amish as a whole were very reluctant to leave their native Swiss homeland. Swiss people were generally proud of their country. Those who severed their loyalties and moved away were frequently regarded as scoundrels. But the Anabaptists were harassed so severely that they had no other choice. The Amish came to America as part of a much larger movement of German-speaking people, including the Mennonites.

The ship *Adventure* (from Rotterdam) arrived in Philadelphia on October 2, 1727, and its passenger lists show several typical Amish names. No record of Amish immigrants has been found prior to this date. Ten years later, however, on October 8, 1737, the *Charming Nancy* brought numerous Amish families, whose names included Beiler, Herschberger, Hertzler, Kauffman, Kurtz, Lehman, and Mast. During their early period, the colonial era, the Amish formed settlements in Berks, Chester, and Lancaster counties, Pennsylvania.

The journey across the Atlantic Ocean was a dreaded ordeal. Passengers who kept diaries speak of numerous custom houses between Switzerland and the Netherlands, each involving a long delay and an additional expense. One person who made the trip in 1750 speaks of passengers packed as closely as herring into large boats. There was a stench from fumes, vomiting, dysentery, and scurvy. Filthy food and water were major sources of misery, as well as lice, disease, and severe storms. Overcrowding gave way to stealing, cheating, cursing, and bitter arguments between children and parents, and husbands and wives. Those who lacked the money to pay for their fare were auctioned off as "redemptioners" to the highest bidder. Ship captains were prone to entice passengers, including children, onto their vessels and sell their services once they reached the American shores. Many persons, especially children, died during the long voyage, which may have taken up to eighty days.

Our Voyage to America

HANS NUSSBAUM

An Amish leader who immigrated to America in 1818, Hans Nussbaum describes his transatlantic journey to his relatives who remained in Europe. Of special interest is his description of visits to Amish communities in America.

February 8, 1818—

On the Fourth of July, 1817, we (Nussbaum, Schrag, Augsburger, and Brand families) boarded a frigate at Amsterdam. Francia was the captain. He looked after us very well. But I would warn you of a certain Peter Ullerich of Amsterdam who is a "slave dealer." He transported three loads of Württembergers to America, treating them more like cattle than human beings. He packs them in boats like herrings.

As the wind was no good we could not sail until the 25th. By the 29th we had gotten only as far as we should have with one day's good wind. On the 3rd of August we stopped at Texel (Holland) to load food. We had to wait until the fifth sail. Then we had a good wind that gave us speed. On the same morning a young man from Baden died who had come aboard ill. He was buried at sea. On the 8th of August we could still see the English coast. For the next four days we had bad wind. The Captain decided to turn back and go completely around England through the North Sea.

On the 17th we were in an area as cold as Switzerland in winter. An old woman died on the 28th. On September 11th we had an ill wind that blew us back. On the 16th we came on a fishing bank. We saw seven fishing ships there. The captain went to one in a small boat and traded wine, cheese, and zwieback for fish. We saw the first land on October 5th and at the same time we got a pilot aboard. But shortly we got into the worst storm that we encountered . . . waves were as large as high mountains.

By the 9th the wind had abated enough for us to enter the Delaware River. Here we saw beautiful land on each side of us. This encouraged us greatly. And three o'clock in the afternoon we dropped anchor and nurses from the clinic came to give us a physical examination. As we were all well we could proceed to Philadelphia.

For our fortunate journey we had God to thank as well as our American captain. Many Germans came on board ship and gave us apples and bread. Other persons came to hire passengers to work for them. They paid them 5.040 bz. ($1,000) per year.

Dear friends, very likely you would like to know what our rations were while on board ship. Monday, one pound meal [per family]. Tuesday, one pound beef. Wednesday, one-half pound bacon and peas. Thursday, one pound beef and barley. Friday, one pound flour. Saturday, one-half pound bacon and sauerkraut. Each day we got two glasses of brandy and each week we got six pounds of bread.

Each day we got three and one-third liters of water. Each week we got one pound of butter, one pound of cheese. We received one and two-third liters of vinegar per week per four persons.

On the 16th of October we went 23 miles from Philadelphia to a settlement of five Amish families. On the 17th we then went to the Pequea. Here we stayed a week to get deloused. The brethren bestowed upon us food, including butter, meat, bread, and vegetables. From there they guided the way for us to Kalchlis (Kishacoquillas). There is also an Amish community at this place. We stayed another week here. We were given very kind treatment.

They guided us to Somerset County which was a nine-day journey. Here in the Klotz (Glades) is another Amish community. In all these places they gave us much to eat, and charged us nothing.

Jacob Schrag, who came in 1816, saw to it that each of our families had a place to stay over winter. The young people in our company went to work.

On the 27th (October, 1817) Schrag and I and his son went to Ohio to find a new fatherland. We went via Pittsburgh, New Washington, Steubenville, to Walnut Creek where there is also an Amish settlement. On the 6th of December we stayed overnight with a man named Stutzman who owns 900 acres of land. On December 9th we came to Wooster to an Amish community. The brethren here went with us to choose land. Schrag and I each chose 160 acres. We also chose land for the other families.

We waited here over winter. We had wished to go south of the Ohio River to choose land there, but the brethren advised against that as there is much disease and little good water. Here the land is fertile and level.

Anyone who wishes to make this journey should think twice. The trip is difficult, more difficult than dangerous, I again say that I advise no one to come who does not find pleasure in work. The sleepy and lazy may well stay at home.

Source: Gratz (1953): 137–38

⇛⇛⇛⇛⇛⇛⇛⇛⇛⇛⇛⇛⇛⇛⇛⇛

Property of Immigrants Confiscated

VIRGIL DETWEILER

Melchior Detweiler, age thirty-seven, *and his family landed in Philadelphia to face severe disappointment. Their goods had been seized by the customs officers and sold, and the money was forwarded to the British government. The family had traded their old utensils for better ones as they traveled on the Rhine to Rotterdam, and appear to have acquired large quantities of wares; for example, 20 iron pans, 30 stoves, 590 scythes, and, astonishingly, 8 flutes. It seems doubtful that the musical instruments had any significance other than their resale value.*

It was probably late June of 1736 that "One hundred and twelve foreigners from the Palatinate, and other places, who, with their families, making in all three hundred thirty persons . . ." boarded the ship "Princess Augusta" with Samuel Marchant as Master at the port city of Rotterdam.

This Palatinate group "being Protestants and subjects to the Emperor of Germany, and encouraged by the accounts that they had received from others of their countrymen in the province of Pennsylvania, of the great blessings of peace and liberty of conscience, enjoyed in the said province, under the protection of that gracious and mighty prince, King George the second, King of Great Britain and elector of Hanover, they thereupon, in the year of our Lord, One thousand seven hundred and thirty six, did transport themselves, with their families into this province; and having disposed of their old household goods and utensils, which were very bulky, at their coming down the Rhine, for very small quantity of new ones of the same kind, they were laden on board the ship Princess Augusta at Rotterdam.

And when the said ship made report of her landing at the port of Cowes, in Great Britain, the said household goods, utensils and other things belonging to your petitioners were freely exposed to the Officers of that Port, who suffered them to pass without molestation or requiring any rates, duty or customs for the proper use of your petitioners and not for sale.

But so it is, may it please your Honors, that upon the arrival of your petitioners in the said ship at Philadelphia she (the ship Princess Augusta), together with the said goods and utensils aforesaid was seized by the collector and Naval Officer of this port, or one of them, by which and the severity of the said Officers, your Petitioners were reduced to very great straits. And notwithstanding the said ship, upon a full hearing in the Court of Admiralty of this Province—was legally acquitted, yet the said goods were condemned as forfeited. . . ."

The "said goods" are listed as:

> Thirty Stoves, in the information exhibited called Chimney backs
> Five hundred and ninety-six Scythes
> One hundred and three large Iron Instruments called Straw-knives
> Fourteen Iron Instruments called Drawing knives
> Twenty-seven Iron stew pans
> Eighty-one Iron Ladles
> Five dozen and three Iron Shovels
> Twenty-seven Iron pot lids
> Twelve Iron dripping pans and frying pans
> Thirteen axes and one hatchet
> Three small and one large crosscut saws
> One gross of Shoemakers and two gross of Saddlers awls
> Six box Irons and six Chisels
> Six Iron baking stove pans
> Twenty-three dozen of clasp knives
> One dozen of Plyers and Hammers
> Six Iron Lamps
> Six Trowels
> One Spade
> One cask of nails and a Smith's Vice
> Fourteen copper kettles

Five copper stills
Two dozen scissors
One packet of sleeve buttons and studs
Four umbrellas
Four dozen and one half of Worsted Caps
Two dozen of printed linen Caps
Six pair of worsted stockings
Four pieces of striped cotton Handkerchiefs
Twenty-five pieces of Tape
Two dozen black Girdles
One piece of black Crepe
One piece of striped Cotton
Nineteen pieces of Bedtick
Two pieces of brown Linen
One piece of blue and white Linen
Two dozen of Ivory Combs
Two dozen and one half of tobacco Pipes with brass covers and a brass box
Two dozen of Ivory needle cases
Three handbrushes
Three dozen of Pewter spoons
Three dozen Spectacles
Eight looking glasses
Eight Flutes
Six wooden Clocks
One dozen of briarhood Sickles

All these goods were condemned and sold and the money was given to the English Government.

These German-Swiss were not English and not naturalized. The goods which they attempted to bring to this country were, therefore, subject to seizure as English law did not allow any goods, other than certain amounts of clothing and household goods, from any country except England to be brought into the American colonies.

It was with this calamity that Melchior Detweiler, age 37, and family were greeted on their arrival in Philadelphia on Sept. 16, 1736, on the ship "Princess Augusta." Melchior made his "X" mark on the shiplist as did many others.

Source: Detweiler (1984): 73–74

-≫≫-≫≫-≫≫-≫≫-≫≫-≫≫-≫≫-≫≫-

By Steamboat

DAVID LUTHY

The Amish immigrated to America during two periods, one in the eighteenth century (1727–1790) and the other in the nineteenth century (1815–1860). David Luthy describes some of the conditions and hazards.

Most of the settlers who came directly from Europe to central Illinois before 1840 arrived on the eastern coast of America at one of three ports: New York, Philadelphia, or Baltimore. There they left the sailing vessel and traveled overland to the closest Amish settlement—Lancaster County, Pennsylvania. They would spend a few weeks or months visiting with the brethren, relaxing for the journey to Illinois which lay ahead. They mended and greased their shoes or had new ones made, for portions of the trip would be made on foot. When the day came for them to begin their journey, they proceeded by horse and foot over the mountain passes of Pennsylvania to Pittsburgh (some 250 miles) where they boarded a flatboat on the Ohio River.

The flatboat, propelled by the river's current and a single oar or pole, would carry them down the winding Ohio River beneath the southern borders of three states: Ohio, Indiana, and Illinois. . . .

At Cairo, Illinois, the settlers would board a steamboat which, unlike a flatboat, could travel upstream as well as down. Up the river the steamboat traveled, stopping at St. Louis to unload much of its cargo and many of its passengers. There the settlers boarded another steamboat which would take them further up the Mississippi River and into the Illinois River and on to Peoria.

After 1840 the Amish who came from Europe to central Illinois no longer landed on the east coast. They discovered that they could avoid the long overland trip through Pennsylvania mountains by sailing to New Orleans as their port of entry. There at the mouth of the Mississippi River they could buy passage on a steamboat all the way to Peoria.

An Amish settler's first glimpse of a steamboat must have been breathtaking, for he knew of no such large and splendid boat in his native land. The three-story-high steamboat with its twin smokestacks rising high above it, its large paddle wheels on each side, its many balconies trimmed with jigsaw-designed woodwork and painted gleaming white must have been quite a marvelous sight for him to see.

But the Amish settlers did not experience the loveliest parts of the steamboat—the central parlor, dining room, and bedrooms. Those parts of the boat were reserved for the wealthy passengers. The Amish rode as deck passengers, having tickets which required them to remain on the main deck where they found whatever space they could among the piles of cotton bales and other cargo. They brought their own food aboard with them and were not invited into the luxurious dining room where Negro porters waited on wealthy passengers seated at tables covered with linen and set with crystal and silverware. Nor would they have a comfortable bed in one of the many staterooms which lined both sides of the upper decks. The settlers' beds would be the planks of the deck covered with blankets or cloaks. Some of the children might find a softer place by climbing on top of the cotton bales.

The settlers were not the only deck passengers by any means. Men who made their living by bringing cargo down the river on flatboats would return up the river by steamboat, having sold their flatboats in New Orleans for lumber. Also aboard were lumberjacks from the pine woods of Minnesota and Wisconsin who had floated down the river on huge rafts of logs which they sold at New Orleans. They would travel home by the easiest and quickest way—steamboat. Many of them were big, rough-featured fellows with shaggy hair, knives at their belts, and rifles over their shoulders. They swore and drank and gambled on the deck and were the least desirable of the passengers. Also aboard were peddlers with huge packs on their backs. They would sell their wares to the passengers and to the people who gathered at the wharves when the steamboat stopped on its trip upstream to take on fuel, cargo, or more passengers.

But most of the passengers on the deck were immigrants—quiet folk who kept to themselves and chatted in their native languages. They, like the Amish settlers, had come to America to find new homes and jobs somewhere up the great river in the Midwestern frontier.

Source: Luthy (1986): 77–78

➤➤➤-➤➤➤-➤➤➤-➤➤➤-➤➤➤-➤➤➤-➤➤➤-➤➤➤

Lewis Riehl Seized at Age Eight

DAVID LUTHY

Most of the Amish immigrants were poor. A few apparently brought with them tools and property. They bought land soon after their arrival. Lewis Riehl, a lad of eight, was brought to the New World against his wishes. The story, which has been told for generations, can be traced to Elias B. Riehl (1818-1901), his grandson.*

Lewis Riehl was born somewhere in Europe in the year 1746 and died in Mifflin County, Pa., May 5, 1806, aged 60 years. When about eight years old, he was stolen from his mother, brought to this country and bound to a certain man until of age. A man by the name of Kurtz persuaded him to get on board a vessel about to sail to America and when once on board, the boy in vain implored to go on shore but the vessel moved off and he was forced to remain on board and come to America.

It is commonly held that Lewis had a very rough life at the hands of the man he was bound to. This practice of being bound to a person was known as indentured service. It was taken advantage of by many early American immigrants. The person they were bound to paid their passage to America. Lewis had no bed and often slept with the pigs to keep warm in winter. The place where he served his indenture was in Chester County, Pennsylvania. It is not known if he lived near the Amish at Malvern in the same county. But it is said that after his term of service was over he found his first welcome home in America with the family of Christian Zook, an Amish minister in Chester County.

Lewis Riehl joined the Amish church and married an Amish girl, Veronica Fisher, daughter of Christian Fisher. It is not known for sure how many children they had, but there were at least seven, five boys and two girls. Lewis and his family moved to Mifflin County, where he died in 1806 and his wife in 1825. Some of Lewis's descendants migrated to Lancaster County where the "Riehl" name today is most commonly found among the Amish.

Source: Luthy (1972): 22

-->>--->>--->>--->>--->>--->>--->>--->>-

Wilhelm Bender

CHRISTIAN W. BENDER

Some Amish families in Europe sent their young men to America to avoid conscription and military service. Wilhelm Bender, one such young man, came to America at the age of fifteen.

Wilhelm, the oldest son of Daniel Bender and Elizabeth (Bauman), it was decided, should go to America before he reached the age when young men must enter military training. But the family was very poor. Passage to America was beyond their means, and Wilhelm became a redemptioner. Peter Kinsinger, an Amish friend who was coming to America, paid Wilhelm's passage. When they landed at Baltimore, they came in contact with the proprietor of a nursery who paid Kinsinger the amount of Wilhelm's passage, with the understanding that Wilhelm would stay as a redemptioner and work out the sum he had paid for him. Kinsinger came west on the "National Trail," now U.S. Route 40, and joined the Amish settlement in Somerset County, Pennsylvania, and Garrett County, Maryland, while Wilhelm, a boy about fifteen years of age, was left near Baltimore, a stranger in a strange land.

When Kinsinger arrived in Somerset County, and the brotherhood learned of Wilhelm in Baltimore, bound as a redemptioner, the Amish bishop, Benedict Miller, took steps to have him redeemed and brought to Somerset County. One of the daughters of Bishop Miller said, "That boy may become a husband for one of us." She spoke more truly than she knew. Miller went personally to Baltimore on horseback, paid the redemption money, and brought Wilhelm to his own home. About eight years later, in 1838, Wilhelm Bender and Katharine Miller (the girl who said the above) were married.

Source: Christian W. Bender (1948): 3

35

→→→-→→→-→→→-→→→-→→→-→→→-→→→-→→→

A Dog Comes to America

DAVID LUTHY

*C*hristian Beck brought with him on *his ocean crossing not only his wife and six children [in 1834] but also a ton of belongings which included his blacksmith and locksmith equipment. Even the family dog made the journey and later accompanied the Becks to Fulton County, Ohio. The Beck youngsters, like all children, had found it very difficult to even think of parting with their pet. Their father had allowed them to take it with them across France to the port but had then told them to get rid of it. The following story relates how the dog came to America.*

The eldest son was told to drown the dog, since a dog was not allowed on board the ship. She disappeared from sight. She had been their pet and a good watchdog. Unknown to his father, the son John had gotten the dog on board and hidden it in their room. All went well until a litter of pups born on ship could be kept hidden no longer. When one ran across the floor while the captain was in the room, the sky looked dark. He asked, "Have you any more? Bring them out." The boys brought out the five and with sinking hearts expected them to be thrown overboard. The captain looked at them and petted them, saying, "I would like this one." Reaching into his pocket, he handed John a silver dollar and a daguerreotype of himself (an early type of photograph). When the father heard about this, he took both the dollar and the picture from the boy. It was wrong to have the picture, according to Amish beliefs. The old dog later followed them all the way to German Township (Fulton County) beside the wagon while travelling and under it resting.

Source: Luthy (1986): 357

3

PIONEERING IN
THE AMERICAN WEST

During their first 150 years in America, Amish communities were small. There was no master plan of colonization or settlement. Each family moved or regrouped in keeping with its preference and opportunity. The Amish faced years of apprehension because of the War of Independence, attacks by Native Americans, and competition from proselytizing religious groups. A single bishop, traveling by foot and horseback, performed marriages and offered communion to scattered clusters of families. The communities grew from natural increase by having large families, as they still do. The three largest settlements to emerge were Lancaster and Chester counties in Pennsylvania, Holmes and Wayne counties in Ohio, and Elkhart and LaGrange counties in Indiana. From these three "mother" settlements, many smaller communities have been founded elsewhere.

Western "fever," or the urge to move westward, struck more than a few Amish during the late-nineteenth and early twentieth centuries. Some were more willing than others to leave their friends and well-established communities for the sake of pioneering and colonization. In some cases, church problems in their communities encouraged them to seek new territory. In addition to the desire to homestead and find cheaper land, there were other factors. A deep concern for the spiritual welfare of their children spurred them on to find a more tolerable place to live. Others wished to escape overcrowding and the regulations imposed on simple farming people.

Many of the western communities did not succeed. As nonresistant Christians, the Amish were ill-equipped to cope with frontier situations that required the use of force or coercion. Generally, the Amish were not the first to respond to westward movement. Following others who went before them, the Amish gardened and improved the soil. Amish settlers faced a variety of adversities. Dust storms and tornadoes appeared without warning. Periodic drought, hot winds, and blizzards were fierce, and prairie fires were a threat to their farm homes.

Amish life requires acreage that can be managed by the family and that is suited to scale for horse farming. The vast acreage on the plains was more suitable for single-crop production than for generalized farming. The Amish settlements in the west usually remained small, and they were frequently too inbred to permit the number of marriages necessary for the perpetuation of the community. Many families enjoyed pioneering during the child-rearing stage of family life. For others, life in the west was a financial disaster. Some Amish who remained in the west adopted mechanization and became members of Amish-Mennonite churches. The following selections illustrate some of the pioneering hazards and economic stresses.

❊❊❊❊❊❊❊❊

Nebraska Prairie Fire

DAVID LUTHY

T*he hazard of fire and the means of protection against it are described by Abe S. Yoder, a young man who experienced life on the plains.*

The area where the families settled could truly be called "the wide open prairie," for the land was very level with few trees growing anywhere except beside the creeks and rivers. While the settlers eventually built frame houses, their first homes were made of tough prairie sod. Following is a description of the one built by Moses E. Yoder as remembered by his son Abe:

> In the summer of 1889, father built a sod house on the north end of 320 acres, or on his share of about 106 acres. The sod house was built by first plowing the sod about $2^1/2$ inches deep and 12 inches wide. Prairie sod was nice and tough and not brittle. Then it was cut with a spade, twice the length of the width and laid up like brick—one crosswise and the next longways two beside each other. Thus a wall 24 inches thick was built which resembled our eastern stone dwellings. This was plastered on inside (and some dwellings on outside) right against the sod, making quite a comfortable abode.
>
> The roofing material created some problems. Father was permitted to cut some scrub timber poles for rafters in canyons a few miles west of us. He purchased boards to put on these pole rafters. A cast of tarpaper was put on the boards and covered with 3 inches of Nebraska soil. This made a rather flat roof, and I surmise the roof leaked during some welcome rains.

The Yoders built a one-and-a-half-story frame house about their fifth year in Nebraska. It was only sixteen by eighteen feet and during one very windy night it shook so much that Moses had to prop beams from his hay ladders against the south side to steady it. Likely the family's thoughts went back to their more primitive, yet more solid, sod house.

Another advantage of a sod house, besides being inexpensive and wind resistant, was it was basically fireproof. When the thick prairie grass was dried by the summer sun and winds, a spark could ignite it. When such a fire started and was fanned by the wind, it was very hard for the pioneers to stop. Jonas Yoder, bachelor brother of Moses E. Yoder, found that out the hard way. Following is an account of his prairie fire experience as related by his nephew Abe:

> In the early years when Uncle Jonas was herding hundreds of sheep on government land, he was the cause of a big prairie fire. He had built a corral of sod, three or four feet high. Early in the spring one year he thought it wise to set a match to the dead grass and have all clean new pasture for the sheep.
>
> But soon a brisk breeze came up and drove his fire northward out of control and sixteen miles to the Platte River. Then the wind turned and came from the north, driving the fire back and south along the east side of the already-burnt strip. I well remember it coming near our place one night. By then the air was quite calm and the men of the neighborhood brought it under control and were able to put it out close to the place where it had started. This was at the east and west road one mile south of us.
>
> I do not remember how many days and nights it had burned. We had only one horse then which was staked out, about a quarter of a mile from our sod house. His hair and especially his tail was quite scorched.
>
> To safeguard themselves from prairie fires, the people in the area would often plow a few furrows around their buildings and then burn the dead grass for quite

a strip beyond the furrow. This same fire burned a number of haystacks for a cattle man, which was a real loss to him.

Source: Luthy (1986): 271–72, based on Abe S. Yoder (1965): 2; (1968): 12

➤➤➤-➤➤➤-➤➤➤-➤➤➤-➤➤➤-➤➤➤-➤➤➤-➤➤➤

Oklahoma Living

ABRAHAM B. MILLER

One *of the earliest Amish settlers in Oklahoma (in 1893), Abraham B. Miller, describes the hardships of pioneering.*

Most of the first settlers were of the poorer class with very limited means. Many made dugouts to live in. Some of them were covered over with soil and had perhaps one or two half-windows and one door. Others made half-dugouts, that is, half in the ground and the other half above the ground with perhaps more windows but usually one door. . . .

Prairie chickens were so plentiful that they would destroy whole fields of grain if left in the field too long. These served as meat for the settlers.

For about four years our nearest railroad towns were El Reno and Kingfisher, both sixty miles away. The grain raised had to be hauled to one of these towns. Often when a man raised a good crop of grain or cotton he would hire teams to haul it to one of these markets, usually to El Reno. Most everyone had a set of wagon bows and cover and usually would take three and four days to make the round trip. Part of the roads were very sandy, and from forty to sixty bushels of wheat would make a good load according to the size of the team. I remember at one time one of my neighbors had a good crop of wheat and hired eight teams to haul it to El Reno at 10 per bushel for hauling, which made the hauler from $4.00 to $6.00 for the round trip. Times were very hard then (due to the "Panic of 1893," a depression which lasted until 1897). Most people came here with very little means, and many hardly had more than a few days' rations ahead, and were very glad and considered themselves fortunate to make a few dollars to keep soul and body together.

At one time two neighbors and myself took a wagon load of one hundred cedar posts each and hauled them a distance of about 80 miles into an older settled part of Oklahoma and sold them for seven dollars, being gone six days. We brought back with us provisions. We bought second grade flour at 75¢ per hundred, and other things in proportion. There were a number of little stores and post offices scattered over the country, but as they had to haul their supplies so far, it made everything very high that they had to sell; and butter and eggs were about all the produce they would buy, and often they would not pay over 5¢ per pound for butter and the same per dozen of eggs.

Source: Abraham B. Miller (1922): 528–29

-≫-≫-≫-≫-≫-≫-≫-≫-

Threshing in North Dakota

DAVID LUTIIY

T*he Amish who settled in North Dakota needed to hire young men to shock and thresh grain during the harvest season. The acres of flax, barley, oats, and wheat were too large for Amish families to undertake. Most families consisted of young married couples with few children. As early as 1896, Amish settlers wrote letters to other Amish communities appealing for help with the harvest.*

The most commonly grown crops were flax, barley, oats, and wheat. It was not unusual for a settler to have eighty or more acres of grain to shock and then thresh in a season. This was impossible for one man to do alone. A settler with a lot of sons could do it, but most of the homesteaders were young married men with small children. They needed a lot of help to harvest their grain.

It became a standard practice for unmarried Amish young men to go to North Dakota for the harvest. . . . As many as sixty were there one season. They came from as far away as Lancaster County, Pennsylvania. Some, however, came not merely for the opportunity to make good wages but to "have a good time." Such were not appreciated by the settlers.

The world-traveling Amishman, Jonathan B. Fisher of Lancaster County, stopped in North Dakota in 1943 and wrote an account of the threshing season in Rolette County in *The Sugarcreek Budget:*

The former straw burning steam engines are practically a thing of the past. Formerly it required a number of hands to accompany a full rigged gang. One such in a certain large grain section I visited was still in existence.

The thresherman furnishes all hands and boards them as well. A cook shack on wheels follows the rig. About 18 men, usually young unmarried men, and two women cooks generally comprise the gang. The grower generally furnishes the team for hauling to the machine. The former larger threshers had cylinders of 40 and 42 inches. Loads of grain were brought to both sides of the machine and four pitchers tossed the sheaves into the fast devouring self feeder. Most of the threshing is done with smaller and more numerous rigs now. . . .

. . . M. C. Schmucker, the veteran thresherman of Mylo-Wolford section, informed me that at his best day he threshed some over 4,000 bushels in a single day with one of the former bigger machines. In his peak year (1915) with two threshing rigs he threshed some more than 140,000 bushels.

Source: Jonathan B. Fisher letter (November 25, 1943), in *The Budget;* also in Luthy (1986): 317–18, with introductory comments by Luthy

⇛⇛⇛⇛⇛⇛⇛⇛

Kansas Prairie Life

DAVID LUTHY

Cheap land prices on soil that had never been broken, and the hope of prosperity, attracted the Amish to move to Kansas, where there was tough and hardy Buffalo-grass country.

The Troyer families lived in the settlement only three months before they had a hair-raising experience. A tornado struck on May 31, 1904, causing a path of destruction four or five miles wide and forty miles long. Both men's barns were "torn to pieces." Their houses were only blown several feet off their foundations and could be repaired. Mrs. Mose Troyer's cupboard tipped over, breaking nearly all the dishes. Thinking back to her first evening at Bucklin when she had sat on the crate of unpacked dishes and cried, she likely thought that had been a minor event compared with the damage done by the tornado.

There were other frustrations of prairie life. Sometimes the men stood by helplessly watching their crops destroyed by millions of grasshoppers. And sometimes the women stood beside their kitchen stoves wondering what the next meal would consist of. Mose Troyer's sons, Neal and Harry, never forgot the family's hardships. Many years later their recollections were captured in poetry [by Lavera Hooley]:

They lived in the state of Indiana till 1901,
Then said, "Reno County, here we come."
Little Ida was born the two years they were there.
But the itching to go to Ford Co. got into their hair.
So they pulled up their stakes,
Their short Journey to make.
The family stayed in Ford County for fifteen years,
Through much happiness and many tears.
In 1906 Dad was ordained minister to the Book,
So the teaching of the Lord he undertook.
Eighteen months later being Bishop was his call;
This was in 1907, of late that fall.
The years got lean through their stay,
So Mom sold butter and a few eggs for pay.
If head cheese and fried mush was their desire,
They used cow chips to stoke up the fire.
Harry and Lydia, with a baby carriage they hauled,
Cow chips to the house before company called.
For Mom would be quite ashamed,
If a stranger found out what she burned in her range.
Seems they had company most all of the time,
When they scarce owned even a dime.
But Mom somehow always put a meal on the table,
For she was always ready, willing, and able.
'Tis quite funny, indeed, how people thought they had the best beef,
When they were really just eating ground-up jack rabbit meat.
Yes, those were hard times way back then,
So they really didn't have much food to can.
The grasshoppers were so thick,
They didn't have any corn to pick.
Hoppers sat along on the track in big gobs.
So that getting the train to move was a bad job.
The wheels slipping and sliding to get traction.

They poured sand on the tracks to get action.
No, you didn't want to leave a coat out in the yard,
Or a few hours later those hoppers had it devoured.

Source: Luthy (1986): 141

->>>->>>->>>->>>->>>->>>->>>->>>

To Texas in the Conestoga Wagon

WILLIAM J. OVERHOLT

Joseph S. Overholt and his family left
*Ford County, Kansas, on November 5, 1909, and traveled four hundred miles
to Plainview, Texas. The caravan consisted of a Conestoga wagon and a supply
wagon followed by ten horses and colts, which were herded by William J.
Overholt (1901–1986), who was astride a pony.*

The sides of the supply wagon were lined with bunk beds for the children,
with another bed fashioned at the top directly underneath the cover of the
wagon.

As the occasion demanded, Mother made a fire in the laundry stove that
was fastened securely inside the supply wagon. We collected buffalo chips
(dried manure) along the way for fuel. Mother cooked the navy beans for
soup while we bounced over the rough trail. The older girls, Fannie and
Mary, had to hold the sliding bean pot on the stove. Besides being a hot job,
it was painful, for once in a while they spilled a few beans and burned their
fingers.

Mother had her hands full with the cooking and the care of the children.
Amanda was thirteen months old, while Catherine was a baby of only six
weeks.

At times we didn't have enough water to drink or to use in cooking. Since
it was November, however, neither we nor the horses suffered as much from
the heat. But the horses would be glad when we came to a stream, so that
they could cool their parched throats.

Dad and Charles helped to keep meat on the table by keeping the gun at hand, as they watched for jack rabbits, cottontails, and other game. Fresh meat was always a welcome supplement to our simple diet.

The rough trail, often with deep ruts, gave evidence that we weren't the first to travel this way, for much of the time the going was so bumpy that the horses could New Testament trot as they pulled the wagons. If our Conestoga wagon was a "ship of the prairie," it most certainly did not have smooth sailing.

Source: Overholt (n.d.): 23

-))>-))>-))>-))>-))>-))>-))>-))>

Kansas Dust

ALVIN J. KAUFFMAN

*N*ative grasses in the prairie states *were plowed under by the homesteaders, including the Amish, who wanted to grow crops on native soils, which was their practice in the East. The result was often disastrous, as described by Alvin J. Kauffman, a young homesteader in the spring of 1920.*

Some time in April on a Saturday night a wind storm from the northwest started drying off the topsoil, and as it dried it sucked it up in the air and carried it away. There was an 80 acre field joining us on the west side. It had been plowed as soon as the 1919 wheat crop was harvested. Lots of the wheat had not yet sprouted. Part of the field started blowing away, and of course our buildings were in its path.

When we got up Sunday morning everything was covered with dust. Mom Hochstetler couldn't find her cap that she had laid down when retiring the evening before. While Dad and I did the chores, Mom made breakfast which turned out to be quite a big problem. By the time she had the table set, the dust had settled so thick on our plates that she realized it wouldn't be fit to eat in the kitchen. She had already given up trying to cook any breakfast until we came in from choring. Meanwhile she cleaned up the pantry and hung a quilt over the door to the pantry. She managed to fry eggs and cook oatmeal on the oil stove which we had carried into the pantry.

How did we see to get to the barn? We did not see because we couldn't see the fingers of our outstretched hands an arm's length away. And we couldn't breathe without choking. Well, Dad had a thin rope in the wash house which he tied one end to the garden fence and headed for the barn. He missed the board fence that was in front of the barn but felt that the wind wasn't as strong, so he headed against the wind and in a few steps touched the fence, followed it around to the gate at the corner of the barn, and tied his rope to the gate post. He came back to the house and got me. We both had a cloth tied over our faces.

As we were finished with our chores and meal at some past 9 a.m., Dad decided to go see if anybody did come to church as it was only 40 rods north of us at Aaron A. Yoder's. We had a barbwire fence running due north to Aaron's barn. He followed the fence to their barn. When he got within 10 or 15 rods of their barn he got out of the dust storm and he saw there were wagons and open buggies there and heard them singing.

Source: Alvin J. Kauffman letter (July 25, 1978), to David Luthy, in Luthy (1986): 149

⇉⇉⇉-⇉⇉⇉-⇉⇉⇉-⇉⇉⇉-⇉⇉⇉-⇉⇉⇉-⇉⇉⇉-⇉⇉⇉

North Dakota Blizzard

IDA SHETLER

Several Amish families formed a settlement in North Dakota in 1894. A nationwide depression and a governmental promise to give away several million acres to homesteaders in that state attracted fifty families from other states. The severity of the winter storms was unanticipated. Ida Shetler describes her experience in the storm of 1920.

It was one of those mornings when you thought you smelled spring in the air and could hear sounds for miles. It was in the spring of 1920 around March 13th. We went to school in the morning. It was about a three and a half mile trip, and in winter we used to drive through the fields as there were no fences around the fields in those days in North Dakota.

We had a covered sleigh we called a cutter. It had little windows on the sides and back as a top buggy, and a big window in front. In later years we took a big sled and got it covered. It had seats along the sides and a stove in the middle which kept us nice and warm. The sled did not upset as easy as the little sleigh did.

Dad took us to school that morning and little did we realize what the day may bring forth. By noon it was snowing and blowing. A real blizzard was coming. So the teacher let the children go home who had rigs there. But we and a few others stayed as we couldn't go until somebody came after us.

This was a two-room schoolhouse in the country with upstairs and basement. The teachers lived upstairs. One was a girl. The other was a motherly woman. Her husband had died. She had a daughter and son that went to school, too.

When Dad came after us it was storming real bad. But we got ready to go with him. There were four of us, me and three of my sisters. As we got out of the school yard our sleigh upset so that two of the girls fell out through the door. They found their way back to the school house. And Dad with the two of us set our sleigh up again. Then we girls also went to the schoolhouse.

The teachers persuaded us to stay with them overnight and wanted Dad to stay, too, but he thought he should get home so Mother wouldn't worry so much. He finally started for home again, after the teacher had given him her stocking cap as he had lost his hat. But he didn't get home that night.

The horses always wanted to go the opposite direction from what Dad wanted them to go. He thought they did not want to go against the wind. But if he would have let them go, they would have taken him home, as he was so mixed up he didn't know which direction he was going.

Dad's sleigh upset so often and he set it up again that he finally unhitched the horses and rode them. The wind was so strong, but he finally came to the railroad tracks and he knew one way went east into Mylo, the other west to Rolette. But which way would he go?

He rode along the tracks, but the wind was so strong he could not stay on the horses, so he left them stand and started to walk. But it kept on blowing, so he finally crawled on hands and knees till he got to Mylo. There was an old hotel there in those days, and he found it and went inside. They swept the snow off him with the broom as it was frozen on. When they had him thawed out, they put him to bed.

Next morning when Mother could see out the window, and the storm had died down, she could see Dad's sleigh lying about ten yards out in the field away from the house. And her first thoughts were that we were all scattered along the way and frozen. (There were some people and children frozen that night.) She got herself ready, left the little children alone in the house, and walked a mile to the neighbor's through deep snow sometimes going down to her knees.

The neighbor's hired man came after us in the big open sleigh. We could see God's wonders piled up everyplace. When we got home, we met Dad coming out of the house with the stocking cap still on. He had walked home from Mylo, found his horses by a straw stack. He rode the horses home about three miles.

I was around eleven years old then. I can't remember thanking God for bringing us all safe home again. But I know Mother did.

Source: Ida Shetler letter (undated), to David Luthy, in Luthy (1986): 314

⇉⇉-⇉⇉-⇉⇉-⇉⇉-⇉⇉-⇉⇉-⇉⇉-⇉⇉

Pests in New Mexico

DAVID LUTHY

Several Amish families in Kansas moved to Colfax County, New Mexico, in 1921. They encountered lean years, drought, and a variety of pests before their departure in 1929.

The settlers' lives were quite simple in their pioneer homes. In the evening after a hard day's work in the fields, they would stand in the doorways of their flat-roofed houses and look out across the gently rolling prairie. They could watch the sun sink in the west behind the Rocky Mountains. And sometimes they would see a herd of antelope passing by. Every evening they would hear the howling of coyotes in the distance.

Naturally the children were frightened by the evening serenade of the coyotes. One of Jacob T. Borntrager's sons, Ira, told many years later how scared he was of this:

One Sunday evening when we came home, it was dark and we had to do the chores yet. Of course it was my duty to get the cows home, which were back in the corn stalks $1/2$ mile from the barn. I was so scared to go because every evening we would hear the coyotes howl back there, and they sounded fierce. But Dad said go, so I went. I hurried back there and just ran back and forth to get the

RACHEL *(undated)*
Anonymous artist. *Drawing.*
Mifflin County, Pennsylvania. 8 × 8¹/₈.

Private collection.

TWO BIRDS, 1856
Barbara Zook (1839–1920). *Drawing.*
Mifflin County, Pennsylvania. 8 × 12¼.

Private collection.

BOOKMARK, 1795
Attributed to Heinrich Augsburger.
Berks County, Pennsylvania. 2 × 4¹/₄.

Courtesy Muddy Creek Farm Library.

POT OF FLOWERS, 1822
Christian King (1802–1865). *Drawing.*
Lancaster County, Pennsylvania. 7¹/₂ × 10¹/₂.

Dear little picture, should someone come and want to take you away, tell them, let me lie in good hands because I belong to Rebecca Stoltzfus. God grant great fortune, many blessings and in the hereafter bring me to everlasting bliss. Written on the second day of February 1822.

[Given to an eight-year-old girl.]

Courtesy Muddy Creek Farm Library.

SINGLE BIRD, 1869
Attributed to Barbara Ebersol (1846–1922). *Drawing.*
Lancaster County, Pennsylvania. 7 × 8¹/₂.

Sarah Ebersol. 1869.

Courtesy Rare Book Department, Free Library of Philadelphia.

FLOWERS WITH TWO BIRDS, 1856
Barbara Zook (1839–1920). *Drawing*.
Mifflin County, Pennsylvania. $7^3/4 \times 12^1/2$.

Private collection.

DECORATIVE TOWELL, 1855
Barbara Zook (1839–1920). *Embroidery on woven cloth.*
Miffin County, Pennsylvania. $12^{1/2} \times 12^{1/2}$.

This work of mine
My friends may have
When I am in my silent grave.

This work of mine
My friends may see
When I am in eternity.

[Contained in the wreath, the initials J Z and S Z are those
of the artist's father and mother.]

Private collection.

MERIT AWARD, c. 1760
Attributed to Christopher Dock. *Drawing.*
Montgomery County, Pennsylvania. 3 × 3⁷/₈.

Courtesy Schwenkfelder Library.

cows started, as I was afraid to call them to come. I had them all started for the barn nicely, when suddenly the coyotes started their evening jubilee. My hair stood straight on end and I froze stiff. The cows started running and kicking their heels and bellowing. By that time I had come to life again, and those cows just couldn't outrun me because I was in the middle of the herd all the way home!

Coyotes were plentiful in the area and so were rattlesnakes. The Amish boys liked to collect rattles from the dead snakes' tails. One time Jacob C. Borntrager was out in a field with his team and three rattlesnakes started jumping at the horses' heads. He had quite a time until he got the snakes killed. More of a nuisance, however, were the jack rabbits and wild donkeys which ate the settlers' crops. Another unwelcome creature were bedbugs. When Jacob T. Borntrager built an addition to his house, he discovered that the lumber was full of bedbugs. He and his family tried washing the lumber with kerosene and put jar lids filled with kerosene under the legs of all the beds. But the bedbugs soon learned to crawl up the walls and along the joists and drop down on the sleeping people. Other pests were bobcats which liked to steal the men's dinners when they went to the mountains for wood. Wild donkeys there also stole the horses' feed.

Source: Luthy (1986): 281–82

➤➤➤-➤➤➤-➤➤➤-➤➤➤-➤➤➤-➤➤➤-➤➤➤-➤➤➤

Memories of Missouri

EZRA E. MILLER

Ezra E. Miller *moved from Michigan to Sikeston, Missouri, in 1927. Nearly fifty years later, he recalled many of the hardships faced by his family.*

In 1927 my wife and I with four small children started for Sikeston, Missouri. We went through Illinois where she stayed for a week or so to visit her sisters. I went ahead and was there before they came. Our furniture and things arrived, so friends and I had all in order when she came. It was a very small house and full of chiggers or small bugs. We could not sleep at night.

So after fighting them for a week, I got the gasoline engine in and ran it until everything was black from smoke. After that there were no more bugs and we could sleep.

Early in the spring it started to rain. We planted oats and corn between showers. When the corn was knee high, the wash worms came through and ate the heart of the corn out, causing a lot to die. In June we had a very heavy rain, overflowing the Mississippi River. In some places it was sixty-five miles wide. My folks came to see us and they had to get a boat to cross the fields for many miles. After the water went down we had a cyclone. We did not have much when we went, but now nearly everything was gone. We had one cow, but she went dry as there was no pasture. The horses were very thin and poor. At last we had nothing to eat but mush three times a day. There were a lot of wild blackberries, so we canned some of those.

In the fall I husked my corn—what was left—and got about half a load. We had to do something. In November I wrote to my brother-in-law, Ed Yoder of Illinois, asking him if I could get work there. He wrote and said there is plenty of work. Come when you can.

I went to the bank for money but the banker said he couldn't give me any and that I should ask Manasses Bontrager for some. I went to Manasses. He gave me a check of fifteen dollars. I took this to the Tanner store. I bought $5.00 worth of groceries for the family. The rest of the money he gave me in change: 5¢, 10¢, and 25¢. I had a pocketful of money. This paid my trip to Arthur, Illinois.

I arrived at Ed Yoder's at one o'clock at night, the evening before Thanksgiving. Friday and Saturday I husked corn. Then it snowed and I could not husk any more. I then went to Dan Otto's shop. His wife was my wife's cousin. From Thanksgiving until Christmas there were only four days I could husk. But I worked at Dan Otto's. The money I got I sent to my wife and children. I left for home the day after Christmas.

I had three thin horses. I thought if I could sell them, the money will take the family to Illinois. But I could not sell them. No one had any money. Eli Schrock and Ed Yoder said they would pay our transportation when we arrived. I left the horses with Dan Borntrager to sell, which he never could. We had one cow which I traded on a pony, so I had something alive to put in our freight car. That way I could ride free if I had to tend to an animal. Our cow was too thin; I was afraid she'd never make it alive.

We also had one sow with pigs and eight goats. I sold these for thirty dollars which I took to pay some of our debts. Just as I had loaded the freight car, I saw the lumber man coming toward me. "Oh," I thought, "he won't let me go." For I owed him thirty dollars; I had bought lumber in the spring to build a chicken house.

"I see you are leaving, Mr. Miller," he said.

"Yes, and I owe you some money. As soon as I get it, I will send it to you."

"That is okay. I hope you will soon get there and can find a job. It was nice to have you folks here a while."

Source: Mrs. Joe Schmucker, Goshen, Indiana, letter (October 30, 1976), to David Luthy, in Luthy (1986): 256–57

➤➤➤-➤➤➤-➤➤➤-➤➤➤-➤➤➤-➤➤➤-➤➤➤-➤➤➤

A Hair-raising Journey

NOAH B. TROYER

Benjamin H. Troyer of Reno County, Kansas, bought a farm in 1920 when prices were high. He and his family worked hard to pay off their debts. By 1933 they had paid all but $2,000. The bank foreclosed and they lost the farm. A son, Noah, describes their decision to move and their trip to a new home in Oklahoma.

Dads had an auction sale. We loaded one boxcar with household goods and some implements. A big question was where are we going to move. One morning at the breakfast table, Mom said we will have to decide pretty quick—not many days until we are loading. By this time it was between Mississippi or Oklahoma. We children said Oklahoma as sister Beatrice (Mrs. Joe Mast) and brother Henry were there. So the decision was soon made to move to Oklahoma.

We had 13 head of horses to take there; we always said it was 300 miles at that time. Since they built new roads, it is now closer. So on a Thursday morning Dads with two daughters Clara and Amanda left early in a car to try to find a place to move to when we got there with the horse teams and wagons. The same morning five brothers—Al, 21 years old; Levi, 18; Noah, 16; Demas, 13; and William, 11—hooked up the wagons. This is the way we traveled: first wagon was a hay wagon on low steel wheels. We hadn't driven far until we saw that it pulled too hard for two horses, so we arranged four horses to pull it. Behind it we trailed a two-wheeled cart for a suckling colt to ride in. On each side of the cart we tied a horse to the wagon to lead. Next wagon was a high-wheeled box wagon towing a buggy; next a spring wagon with two horses also towing a buggy; next two small horses in a single top buggy to run out ahead to see where we can find a place to park for the night where there was water, and if the people allowed us there overnight— sometimes this was a problem. So our procession was sort of a parade, or some town people thought so.

The first night it rained a lot. Next morning the creeks were flooded over. The farmer where we had stayed had dairy cattle which were on the other side of the flooded creek. The man couldn't swim and was worried about his cattle. Al said he would ride a horse through and run the cattle through the creek, but maybe some might drown. The man told him to get the cattle as the water might stay for several days and their bags would be ruined by then. So Al went and brought them all safely through. The farmer was very thankful we had spent the night there.

Our front wagon was loaded with good alfalfa hay. At night and noon we would tie the horses around the wagon. We didn't have any grain to feed them, but they did real well with the hay. We just walked the horses at a good walk.

Traveling on Saturday we had a hard time to find a place to park for the night. We begged a young couple to let us camp on their farm. He was scared of us, so by Sunday noon we thought he might shoot at us, and we moved on. That evening we had a nice place to be. The farmer had heard of Amish but never seen any, so he was glad to have us there. He had a watermelon stand out at the road. He made us sleep in there so no one would molest his melons. Next morning he loaded the lower portion of the box wagon pretty well full of melons, all for one dollar; so we were happy.

Monday evening we were nearing a bigger town. Saw a sign saying how far it was. We wanted to stop before we entered the town but people that would let us park didn't have water for the horses. So we had to go through the town. It was dark by now, and we had no flashlight or lanterns. It was pitch dark, and we worried about keeping on the road. We made it through the town and kept on going, looking for a place to park. By 10:30 the moon came out, only a quarter moon, but we were thankful for the light. We noticed that the moon reflected out to one side of us. We climbed down and examined it and found a wide-open prairie pond.

We unhooked the horses and let them have a drink. Then we led them to the hay wagon. Around 1:30 our dog which slept with us barked, and we heard trampling of feet coming running full force. We soon saw it was a big herd of cattle. They pushed in between the horses to eat our hay! We knew we couldn't let them do that, so Al took the dog down with him to heel some cattle. But as the dog barked, the back cattle just pushed on up nearly getting Al and the dog. So we put the dog on the wagon.

Al got his light denim coat. He put it on with the front corners over his head. He then began to kick at the cattle's noses, hoping to scare them away. He told us all to do the same thing and spread us around the wagon. There were some boys who hesitated but cooperated. It worked well. They left on high as fast as they had come!

We climbed back onto the wagon and slept one hour when our dog began to bark again. We heard the cattle coming again in high gear, but saw right away it was no cattle. This time it was horses. It was a herd of 150 horses and mules. This was a hair-raising experience. They went right in between our horses with all but one tearing loose. We didn't realize it until we got off the wagon and were laughing at how our dog was making all the horses run. Then someone said, "Where are our horses?" Our laughter turned to sadness real quick, for the reply was, "With the other horses." We could hear them running and the dog barking about one mile away from us already.

We stood there and stared. Then one of the boys said, "There is one horse yet tied to the wagon. Let's put a bridle on it and get the others back." But this horse was a branded bronco and the only one we couldn't ride!

As we stood staring into the direction the horses had run, we saw something walking toward us. As it came closer we could see it was one of our horses. Just then we saw another coming. One by one all our horses came back to the wagon. We managed to tie all of them some way or other with broken halters or ropes. Here we boys realized the power of God's hand was with us. It couldn't have been otherwise.

In the morning we felt we had had a tough night. At night we had just pulled the harness for the horses and put them on the ground. Oh, the tangled harness—the cattle and horses had mixed it all up. Finally we had the horses harnessed and the wheels greased. We had watermelons for breakfast, noon, and supper. On Wednesday evening when it was nearly dark we arrived at Joe Mast's at Chouteau, Oklahoma. All the watermelons were eaten up.

Source: Noah B. Troyer, Paris, Tennessee, letter (January 31, 1978), to David Luthy, in Luthy (1986): 159–60

⇛⇛⇛⇛⇛⇛⇛⇛

Moving the Cemetery

WILLIE WAGLER

Moving a cemetery is frequently *done to make room for a major highway or to build a dam. In 1939 the Amish moved the cemetery of an abandoned community for other reasons: to properly care for the cemetery grounds and to bring the coffins of the deceased infants and children closer to their living parents.*

It may be of interest to some *Budget* readers, especially to those who are former Ford County, Kansas, residents, to hear a report from someone who was an eye-witness to the moving of the remains from the Amish cemetery near Bucklin to the Amish cemetery near Partridge, Kansas.

From the year 1905 to the year 1917, when there was a fair-sized congregation near Bucklin, seventeen children died and were buried there. These ranged in age from infant to one who was thirteen years of age.

The last family moved away from there in 1922, and since then the cemetery has been poorly cared for, so that it was an eyesore to the surrounding residents, being so overgrown with weeds and sunflowers. And furthermore it did not look respectful to our departed loved ones to leave it in such a condition. Dr. Bandy, our old family doctor, said, "I could not help but have a creepy feeling come over me every time I passed your cemetery to see that it was neglected so."

So feeling duty bound to alter this situation, it was agreed to take up the remains and move them to the cemetery near Partridge. On April 26th a group of sixteen men, some of them former Ford County residents and others neighbors and friends who cooperated heartily, went out to the cemetery near Bucklin, armed with disinterment permits from the State Board of Health at Topeka, and brought back the remains of the seventeen children. Transportation was furnished by car and pick-up truck.

It was surprising to find so many of the coffins in such good condition. One of the best preserved had never taken water, as the earth for several feet above the rough box was dry and cloddy just like it was the day it was put there. Others weren't preserved quite as good but were still in good condition. Seven coffins were brought back intact. The other ten were too far decayed to be handled, so their contents were put in white sacks and these placed in a large rough box that was taken along for that purpose.

While we were there, negotiations were made for the sale of the land, which will bring enough to defray the expenses involved.

Reinterment was made the following day at the Amish cemetery near Partridge where sixteen remains were put in one broad grave. Jerry Miller, the thirteen-year-old son of Bishop J. H. Miller, was buried beside the grave of his mother. Here is a list of the children and the year of their death.

Infant daughter of Isaiah Schrocks, 1905
Benjamin and Elizabeth, children of Crist D. Bontragers, 1907 and 1910, respectively
Infant son of Dave C. Bontragers, 1907
Infant son of Jonas Troyers, date unknown
Infant daughter of Joni J. Millers, 1909
Sovilla, daughter of Dave Planks, 1910
Infant son of Abe Coblentzs, 1911
Infant of D. A. Millers, 1911
Moses, son of Mose J. Troyer, 1912
Infant daughter of Perry Troyers, 1914
Henry, son of Joe Stutzmans, 1914
Samuel, son of Edward J. Hochstetlers, 1914
Perry Alvin, son of Mona (Emmanuel) Yoders, 1914
Mary and Martha, twin daughters of Peter Waglers, 1916
Jerry, son of J. H. Millers, 1917

Source: Willie Wagler, *The Budget* (May 4, 1939), in Luthy (1986): 145

4

AGRICULTURE AND
EVERYDAY LIFE

In Europe, the Amish acquired the knowledge to manage farms and to transform unproductive lands into fertile farms. They excelled as farmers in Switzerland, Alsace, and Germany. As early as the seventeenth century, they practiced indoor feeding of livestock, rotation of crops, and meadow irrigation, they used animal fertilizer, and they raised new varieties of clover as a means of restoring soil fertility. These productive practices have been effectively transmitted for generations.

The account of Creation and the parables in the Bible inform the Amish that they must be stewards of the soil. They are to till and care for the soil with their labor and oversight. The Amish believe that with good management the land will not only yield a livelihood, but, as in the Garden of Eden, their farms should reflect pleasantness and orderliness.

Lancaster County, in southeastern Pennsylvania, has long been acclaimed "The Garden Spot" of the nation, not only because its soil is the most productive in the world but also because of the sound management of the land. No other Amish community surpasses this area in outward appearance—in well-kept farm dwellings and fields, abundant gardens, and tidy children.

Like most Christians, the Amish believe in the authority of the Bible. Their understanding of the Bible requires them to live in a redemptive community where each adult lives in unity and harmony with all others.

Amish communities are not communes or monastic orders in which all property is held in common. They are scattered throughout the countryside, around small rural towns, and interspersed among "English," or non-Amish, families. These religious communities constitute a subculture in American life, and all members strive to maintain "one mind" and one discipline. The communities have no central headquarters and no public relations department. Each settlement is made up of local congregations, or "church districts." Each has its own elected leaders and constitutes a face-to-face association and a self-governing unit.

The community is not simply a ceremonial unit but also a community of work, consumption, sharing of resources, and mutual aid. To remain viable, the Amish must have a strong economic base, and this base must attract and hold their offspring. Family members are the labor force. The young work on the parental farm until they are trained. Once trained and responsible, they may hire out to relatives or other Amish families who need help.

The following selections describe the deeper religious roots of community life, as well as some practical details of daily life.

-->>>-->>>-->>>-->>>-->>>-->>>-->>>-->>>

The Amish Farmer

WALTER M. KOLLMORGEN

In 1940 the U.S. Department of Agriculture selected six rural communities for intensive study. The objective was to learn more about stability and instability in American community life. The Lancaster County area was chosen for its highly stable characteristics. A "dust bowl" community (Sublette, Kansas) was chosen for its instability. The four other communities represented positions between these two extremes. The following selections are from the departmental report by Walter M. Kollmorgen.

The Amish farmer is wedded to the land not only by a deep and long tradition of good agricultural practices, but farming has also become one of the tenets of the Amish religion. A rural way of life is essential to these people so that their nonconformist practices may be perpetuated. Their desire to live on the land, and to live together as well as separate from the world, has been an ever-present stimulus to good farming practices. When the Amish began to invade this plain in the middle of the eighteenth century, it was already occupied by communities of Pennsylvania-German Lutherans and German Reformed, as well as communities of English Quakers, English and Welsh Episcopalians, and Scots-Irish Presbyterians. Today the churches of these people stand as monuments to former communities that have disappeared. . . .

The Lancaster Limestone Plain, which is in part occupied by the Old Order Amish, has an east-west axis, comprises about half the area of Lancaster County, and is located largely in the southern part of the county. The soils in the plain have weathered largely from limestone and are among the better upland soils in the eastern part of the United States. Originally they were blanketed with a heavy forest. They are acid in nature and their supply of organic matter and native fertility was not so great as that of the grasslands of the Middle West. Their high productivity today is the result of continued constructive farming programs, some of which were introduced during the late colonial period. . . .

Agriculturally this plain is part of the famous Pennsylvania-Germanland which includes most of the better farming sections in southeastern Pennsylvania as well as much of the good limestone land of central Maryland and the upper part of the Shenandoah Valley [in Virginia]. In fact, the Amish, Mennonites, and other nonresistant people who now prevail on this plain may be said to epitomize the good farming practices for which the Pennsylvania-Germans have long been famous. As early as the period of the American Revolution, Lancaster County (really the Limestone Plain) was known as the garden spot of Pennsylvania, and the state in turn claimed this distinction in the emerging nation. After a few more decades the county was heralded as the garden spot of America, and now its thrifty farmers are not quite clear whether the county is the garden spot of America only or of the world. . . .

There is a close tie between religion and agriculture among the Amish. It is doubtful that any other socio-religious body has so consistently distinguished itself in agriculture enterprise as the Mennonites, of which larger religious body the Amish are a part. A popular history of Lancaster says of these people: "They are the most patient farmers on the face of the earth and as a community are the best." Similar references to these people appear again and again in literature that refers to or describes their agricultural activities in this and other countries. These Mennonites from the Rhineland of Europe (German, German-Swiss, and Dutch) have created and maintained garden spots in other parts of Germany, in Russia, in Mexico, and in several states of this country. These garden spots persisted so long as group solidarity and community integrity prevailed and so long as the old order was not modified too drastically. Herein lies an extremely interesting field of study.

Source: Kollmorgen (1942): 3, 4, 16, 17

-->>>-->>>-->>>-->>>-->>>-->>>-->>>-->>>-

The Rule of Love in Everyday Life

WALTER M. KOLLMORGEN

The aged farmers in the Amish and Mennonite communities in Lancaster County are a rich depository of the lore of agricultural experience which reaches back to early colonial days. Many of them, particularly in the Mennonite community, occupy farms that have been in the family for more than 200 years, and were acquired directly from William Penn or his land agents. Buildings may have been built, at least partly, shortly before or after the Revolutionary War. As the farm place was handed down from father to son, so were many experiences handed down from generation to generation and with them a good deal of wisdom. Many an old-timer remembers the recurrent depressions in the latter half of the nineteenth century which were occasioned by financial instability and the severe competition with the emerging granary of the Middle West. Moreover, the old-timer remembers hearing his father tell about the hard times during the days of Andrew Jackson and before. The family farm place and many of the family heirlooms focus attention on the activities and experiences of the forefathers. These experiences were not all speculative. As early as 1809, land in the beautiful valley of the Pequea in Lancaster County, which is now in part the heart of the Amish settlement, was selling for $100 an acre. By 1814, 40 banks were chartered in the state, 5 of them in Lancaster County. Money became cheap, and soon land was selling for $200 per acre. In a few more years many of the banks went broke, many of the farmers were bankrupt, and land dropped to $50 an acre. This adventure with cheap money and high land prices more than 100 year ago left its imprint on the farms and farmers of the county. The farmers learned long ago that, if they wanted to have money, it had to be made in constructive farming and not in skimming off unearned increment. . . .

Biblical injunctions concerning love and mutual aid were given practical application, and this gave them strength and integrity. The poor were helped as a matter of course, but the help that was extended enabled the poor to become productive and to help themselves. Begging was not tolerated. Members who met with reverses, but were not poor, were given work aid and even financial aid to rehabilitate them, or to help them over difficult periods of adjustments. Moreover, the Brethren created what may be termed one of the first credit unions for farmers in Europe. This aid movement grew out of a feeling of responsibility in the brotherhood and was for some time free of commercial motives. Investments in outside organizations were forbidden, and for a long time money was loaned without interest. Other religious groups were not so closely tied together and it is doubtful that most peasants enjoyed similar credit opportunities.

The rule of love, which was translated into everyday life, prohibited unnecessary competition and rivalry. The congregation prohibited the over-bidding of a tenant when the lease on his land expired. The congregation was closely welded together in advice relationships. No big or ambitious undertaking in agriculture or related activities was begun without the approval of fellow members. Rash undertakings were usually precluded and individual members and the entire congregation were saved from failures. Even debts could not be contracted without approval by the group. In these advice relations the leaders enjoyed unusual prestige, based on both secular and religious grounds. Apparently most of them were successful and so were in a position to give practical advice.

Source: Kollmorgen (1942): 26, 19

->>>->>>->>>->>>->>>->>>->>>->>>-

The Family: Building Block of the Agricultural Enterprise

JEAN SÉGUY

Jean Séguy, a French sociologist, has systematically researched European archives and has written extensively on the origins, religion, and community life of the Amish in France. In this passage he describes how the agricultural practices are congruous with family life.

The familial character of the Mennonite agricultural enterprise [in Europe] is well attested. In the 1780 investigation, one notices that each family occupied a farm. The father, the mother, sometimes a grandparent, the single children, all worked on location. In some cases, the married children lived with their parents and participated with them in the work of the farm. They may have been waiting for the opportunity to rent a farm of their own.

As in all rural societies, occupational initiation and participation by the children in farming began very early, and took place on the farm itself. Louis Ordinaire mentioned this characteristic in 1812. During the same period, his friend, Jacques Klopfenstein, symbolized this fact by placing on the cover of his agricultural almanac a drawing of two children working by the side of the Anabaptist "farmer by experience." According to the sub-delegate of Belfort, since Mennonites married young, the parents "divided up their savings early in life." Thus, "the parents resort to retiring to their children's (farm) where they spend their old age at work." In this way all the generations of a given farming family were integrated by their agricultural work. They provided a type of labor which was always available and which cost only the price of room and board. Since these families were quite large, the amount of work over large tracts of land was at a maximum, with labor costs at a minimum.

The family also played an important part in the transmission of leases which allowed the improvement of the land to continue for long periods of time in the same tradition. This was, as well, a guarantee of quality and of efficiency. In most cases, the children replaced their parents when the latter died, or well-to-do Anabaptists sub-let some of their lands to more distant relatives or to co-religionists who were not yet in a position to pay a first installment. In some cases where old age or sickness prevented one of the Brethren from continuing his work he would ask the landlord—and in general the request was granted—to be replaced by a relative to fulfill his lease; sometimes the contract with its original stipulations was then extended for the relative after the expiration of the first lease. Cooperation between parents and in-laws could also occur, as in the case of Pierre Graber and Jean Rich and their dairy farm at Clemont. Of course, these practices tended to establish a de facto Anabaptist monopoly on the lease-farming of lands owned by the higher nobility, with the consequence that the indigenous population protested against what they called a seizure. In reality, however, the majority of the plaintiffs would have been incapable, as we have noted, of fulfilling the lease stipulations, because, among other things, they lacked the necessary familial labor force.

Mennonite tenant farming was characterized by methodical, intensive, and varied cultivation and by an inclination toward innovation.

One of the foremost agricultural abilities of the Brethren was their skill in clearing of the land. From their days in Switzerland the need to survive forced them to make use of it. In Sainte-Marie-aux-Mines they cultivated land that had never been farmed before, and were highly praised for it. Similarly, in Salm, in the Vosges, the archives report that in 1730 Christian Schlaster "cleared a considerable amount of land." The village of Hang, also in the principality of Salm, was entirely Mennonite and had been created by Brethren who had cleared the land surrounding it.

Source: Séguy, trans. Shank (1973): 186–89

⫸⫸⫸-⫸⫸⫸-⫸⫸⫸-⫸⫸⫸-⫸⫸⫸-⫸⫸⫸-⫸⫸⫸-⫸⫸⫸

Butchering

GIDEON L. FISHER

After a career as farmer and machine-shop operator, Gideon L. Fisher wrote a book containing thoughtful observations and homespun wisdom on a wide range of farm life. In these selections he describes butchering, the limekiln, hat-making, corner ball, and a pair of mules.

In my childhood days, a special custom for Amish farmers during the winter months was butchering as many hogs as there were members of the family. Often a few neighbors or relatives would go together to help out in the event. The women could help as well as the men. Usually they chose a cold crisp day in December or January. The day before was spent in preparing and cutting wood to heat the water, sharpening knives, and getting the butcher tools together. A set of butcher tools consisted of a scalding trough, meat grinder, sausage stuffer, meat cutting bench, a saw, and knives. The tools were often owned by a group of neighbors, and transported from one to another. Everything was ready for an early start the next morning.

Every member of the family that could help was up bright and early. The women got the fire going under the large iron kettle which was filled with water. This was brought to a boiling point by the time the men had killed the hogs. Often the first hogs were cleaned and ready to be dressed by the break of day. After they were cleaned and hung up at some convenient place in the barn to be dressed, they were cut in half and carried to the wash house.

On a four-legged butcher bench, two feet wide, eight feet long, the fat hogs were cut up into hams, shoulders, sirloins, and porkchops, and bacon, while the other meat was used for sausage or puddings. The women's work was to clean the pig stomach and the small intestines, which were to be filled with sausage meats. When evening came the lard was rendered, put in cans, and set out in the cold air to cool off. The hams were trimmed and sugar-cured. In about a week they were ready for the smokehouse. The butcher tools were spotlessly cleaned and ready for the next neighbor to use.

The old-timers seasoned the hams with a good old hickory smoke flavor. The smokehouse was a small building used only for smoking meats. Quite often a number of neighbors would share one smoke house, which was at some convenient place. It was a building of stone or brick structure, eight feet square, and about twelve feet high with no chimney, but a double floor. The lower portion kept the wood fire and was separated with a floor not too tight. The smouldering fire gave off smoke which penetrated the meat. It took about a week to smoke the large juicy hams which were then hung in the attic of the main farmhouse, to be further cured and dried, then used the next summer.

The home-cured hams and bologna were considered a special dish by the Amish folks.

Source: Gideon L. Fisher (1978): 286–87

꧁꧁꧁꧁꧁꧁꧁꧁

The Limekiln

GIDEON L. FISHER

Wh*hen the soil became depleted, it was discovered that burnt limestone and manure would restore the original fertility in a few years.*

The limekiln was usually built along a steep hill, where the top was ground level as well as the bottom. Situated close by was a stone quarry with blue limestone. The kiln was usually about eight feet in diameter and sixteen feet deep, walled up with flint stones. Flint is a kind of stone that will not burn to lime. The bottom had an archway to get the lime out after it had gone through the procedure.

To fill the kiln, limestone was quarried in rocks of up to about five pounds, and hauled with a one horse dumpcart. The bottom of the kiln was a layer of dry wood, alternated with pea coal and stone, and was filled to the top. A fire was started with the wood, which ignited the coal, and burned its way to the top. In about a week the fire would burn out, and the stone that was sky blue was now turned to milkwhite.

The lime was now ready for use. The lump lime was taken out of the bottom of the kiln, loaded on two horse wagons and hauled to the field, placing heaps about twenty feet square over the field. Then they waited for a heavy rain. Water dissolved the lumps into fine granulated pebbles. The pebbles were then scattered out with a shovel.

An old-time story goes, that when a farmer asked his neighbor how much lime was too much to put on his land, the answer was: "Up to the first rail of your fence is too much." They had no soil-testing equipment to indicate how much lime was needed. All they knew was that lime helps to grow crops. This man probably had the idea that the more lime, the better the crop. But his neighbor gave him a reminder that there is a limit.

In operating a limekiln a number of farmers usually worked together, quarrying the stones, filling the kiln, and hauling it to the field. In that way one kiln could provide the neighboring farmers with lime, as only labor was involved.

Pulverizers came into the picture about 1920. The lump lime was ground into powder, handled in bags, and spread with a drill. A few farmers made a business of quarrying and selling agricultural lime.

By 1950, limestone quarry owners installed equipment to pulverize limestone rock into powder for agricultural purposes. This had almost the efficiency of burnt lime, and was not as expensive. By 1970 quarrying, processing, and pulverizing limestone was a big business.

Source: Gideon L. Fisher (1978): 254–56

-⟫⟫-⟫⟫-⟫⟫-⟫⟫-⟫⟫-⟫⟫-⟫⟫-⟫⟫

Hat-making

GIDEON L. FISHER

In Lancaster County there are a number of women who have a practice of making men's and boy's straw hats. This is a tradition that has kept up from our early immigrants, or perhaps it could be traced back to the old country. No one seems to know how or where it started. Making straw hats is quite an art of its own, and is a year-round job for those who practice it as a business.

They are made from rye straw. Rye is sowed in the early fall about the same time as the farmers sow winter wheat. Rye is a vigorous growing crop, dormant through the winter, and the first to show signs of new growth in the early spring. It grows faster than any other foliage crop. By early May it is already four or five feet tall. When it is about to show the grain heads it is cut by hand with a scythe and carefully tied in bundle, so as not to break the tender stems. The leaves are stripped off and the knots cut out of each stem. A stalk of rye is coarse close to the ground and the top part is of fine quality straw. Each stalk is separated into three different grades: coarse, medium and fine.

The straw is then laid out on a clean surface to dry and bleach by direct sunlight. After the straw is bleached it is ready to be braided, using a three straw braid. Long strings of this braided straw are made up and separated when the hat is started and finished. The sides of the braids are sewn together to make any size hat. The finer type of hats are worn for Sunday dress and the coarser type as an everyday hat.

Felt hats are manufactured from rabbit fur plaited together in circle-like mats, then shipped to the hat-maker. With machinery they are shaped and trimmed to any size. After they are dyed and ribboned to style they are ready for the customer. About 1972 an Amish retired farmer bought equipment from a firm who discontinued the hat business. Felt hats that are worn by Amish men and boys are now being manufactured in this home shop in large quantities.

Customarily the everyday work clothes are made by the mother, or girls who are old enough to make their own dresses from yard goods. But the Sunday dress suits for both men and boys are made by a seamstress who specializes in making suits, buying large rolls of suiting from the factories, then cutting and shaping to each special size. Very few men need exactly the same size and pattern, but all have the same design. An experienced seamstress is required to make perfect fits for the dress suits. These are finished out with hooks and eyes on coats and vests, while buttons are worn on pants.

Source: Gideon L. Fisher (1978): 82–83

-≫≫-≫≫-≫≫-≫≫-≫≫-≫≫-≫≫-≫≫

Corner Ball

GIDEON L. FISHER

There was a large number of farm dispersal sales from 1925 to 1955. They were usually held between February fifteenth and March fifteenth. It was a custom for farmers to attend these public sales. It was a season when most farmers were relieved from being real busy, tobacco stripping was well underway, and spring work had not yet started. Besides doing their morning and evening chores, they found time to buy machinery or livestock, but mostly for social gatherings, and curiosity, and as the saying goes: "To see and be seen." Late news and social problems were discussed at these afternoon farm sales.

One event which drew a large crowd and much attention was the ball game. Quite often the ball game had more spectators than the sale itself. People traveled from far and wide to see a special game. In those days most homesteads still had the Swiss type barnyard, where the manure was covered with a good layer of clean straw. It made an ideal place to have a four cornered ball game. Where the game originated is unknown.

Six players were chosen for each side, quite often boys on one side, and young married men on the other. After playing the best out of three games, the losers were relieved, and another six players were chosen to play the winners. Occasionally old-timers from forty to fifty years of age were pushed into the game to loosen up stiff muscles. These old-timers often showed the young men some cunning stunts and old tricks in playing ball.

Occasionally players came to the sale from other areas. There were Mennonite boys from Chester County, and the Team Mennonites from Weaverland, who had practiced corner ball playing since the cradle. Quite often these boys left for home with the honor of winning most of the games. If it happened that they had farm sales in their area they would notify the Amish, and invite them to their sales. At times the Amish also went home with the same reward. These ball games always drew large crowds. It is not unusual for two or three hundred men and boys to take an afternoon off to watch a well-matched ball game. The spectators often gave the players a boost by cheering for their respective sides.

Corner ball games have special rules, the same as all other games. These were handed down by our forefathers, and no basic rules are published. At these farm sales no one received a special reward except perhaps a ten cent hot dog, or an oyster stew from a friend.

After the men and boys watched and cheered for three or four hours out in the fresh air, battling a brisk wind, it stirred up a good appetite. To solve this problem, some people had a business of providing a lunch counter at the sale. They served their customers a variety of food. To quote a few prices: in the early thirties oyster stews sold for 15 cents, hot dogs 10 cents, large chocolate bars 5 cents, small bars 2 for 5 cents, ice cream sandwiches 10 cents, and peanuts 5 cents a bag.

In 1950, a man who came home from attending a farm sale was asked by his wife about prices of the items being sold at the auction. After hesitating a bit, he finally said: "Oh, well, hot dogs still sell for 15 cents." This proved that he was not interested in the livestock and machinery, but had watched the ball game.

Source: Gideon L. Fisher (1978): 74–76

Breaking in a Pair of Mules, Dick and Jewel

GIDEON L. FISHER

hen tractor power overtook horse-power in American agriculture, the Amish retained their horse-drawn implements. They argued that "tractors don't make manure" and that "they ruin the land." The Amish insist that tractors also compact the land. An Amish farmer usually has six draft horses and one or two light horses for road transportation. Men attend auction sales to trade, buy, or sell horses and cattle. Some Lancaster County Amish farmers prefer mules for field work. They maintain that mules eat less and have greater endurance in hot weather, though mules are acknowledged to be more obstinate than horses.

In our second year of farming, I was interested in buying a pair of young mules for my farm operation. Upon hearing that a dealer had just received a carload of western mules, I made it my business to see them. They were mostly black, with a light colored nose. There were a few sorrels, as well as dapple grays. Most of them were a nice size, ranging from two to five years old. While the dealer and I were in an enclosed pen checking out a pair of mules from a choice of forty head, I noticed a pair that were always in the far corner of the pen. If we walked to the other end, again they managed to be in the far corner. So I inquired of the dealer about them, they seemed to have very sharp eyes and were up-headed. "Well," he said, "you are probably not interested in those." They had just come off the ranch, had never been haltered and were man shy, and just turning three years old. The way they performed, they had seldom seen human beings.

Then we discussed prices, the average price was from $550 to $650 a pair. After comparing quality and prices, it was hard for me to make my decision. Finally I asked how much he wanted for the pair back in the corner. The dealer replied "$450." "Well," I said, "let's get a better look at them." We finally got them cornered in a separate pen. They tried to jump a six foot partition to get away from us. After lassoing and tying them up, we got halters on them for the first time. We came together on the price, with a trade-in on a horse. After the dealer delivered them to my barn, I tied them in a double stall. I led them out for water twice a day, and spent a lot of time that winter petting them, and trying to teach them that if they would respond, I would be a kind master.

In a few days they had their halter ropes chewed off and both were loose, but penned up. It was a great change for them to be stabled. I fed them well, their sparkling eyes seemed to be watching everything that went on in the barn. When a stranger entered they were restless. I was anxious to see how they would perform in harness. I named them Jewel and Dick.

When the spring plowing started, with the help of a hired boy we decided to give Jewel a try. She cooperated better than we expected. The next day we tried Dick, and that was different. When the harness touched his back he snorted and carried on, and did most anything to get out from under. After about an hour he gave in and responded fairly well. He was sweating hard before we ever got to the field. After we had a team of three hitched to a walking plow with Dick on the off side tied back with two hitching straps, neck rope, jockey stick, and a long line on the outside for the hired boy to hold him back, it went fairly well until we came to the end of the field. I turned the plow over to turn around and go back along the next furrow. When I said "Whoa, Dick," he would not stop. My pair of old stand-bys stopped in their tracks, but Dick kept on going, he did not know what whoa meant. It seemed nothing would stop him. The hired boy was hanging on the outside line for dear life. Dick turned the team in a short circle and got them all tangled up. In about an hour we got started up again. I decided when I came to the end of the field I would turn in such a way that I would not need to stop, set the plow up while in motion and keep it going. After Dick was tired out somewhat it didn't go too bad. He did his full share of pulling until later in the afternoon. By evening he appeared to be so stiff he could hardly walk. He had injured his shoulders and the vet said to let him stand for six weeks. At that time we tried again with the same results. With a lot of patience we got him to cooperate. I always worked him on the off side.

The first time we hitched Jewel and Dick together was to a wagon out in the open field. They soon started running, so I let them run, even encouraged them to run and gallop as fast as they could go. After they found out I didn't care, they slowed to a walk. When I said "Whoa," they stopped. After starting and stopping for about an hour, they did real well. Jewel seemed to be natured with good intelligence, even if she did not like strangers, she was very sharp and keen. Her alert eyes proved to me that she would mind her business. The first year I spent a lot of time trying to prove my kindness. I never punished her by striking her with some object, if I had she would have lost confidence in me. But I had to let her know who was boss.

Because Dick was not able to work for awhile, we gave Jewel more attention. By mid-summer I worked her as a lead mule. By August I decided to see how she would do in the single line for plowing wheat stubble. I couldn't believe my eyes how well she could be driven with a single line, and only three years old. One day I decided Jewel had a lesson to learn yet, that was, to be ridden. After she was in the plow for a few days in the warm August weather she seemed a little tired. At noon I thought I would give it a try. I led her up in the plowed field with her harness on. I stopped and petted her a little, then I grabbed the hames and swung myself up and landed square on her back. Off she went, she jumped and kicked, the harder she tried to get rid of me, the tighter I wrapped my legs around her body. I was not worried, as long as I could keep her on the plowed field she could not do much. But when I pulled on the reins to turn her, she would turn the opposite way. So we soon left the plowed section of the field, and away she went. I never rode so fast, I tried to keep her from heading toward the barn, but that was where she wanted to go. Back of the barn she turned toward the meadow gate, and jumped, clearing a four foot gate. After making a few circles in the meadow, she headed for a wire fence. I felt I had enough, and slid off to the side just as she came to the fence. She jumped, but did not make it this time. She stayed hanging with her hind legs in the fence. I ran to the barn to get wire cutters to free her. Neither of us was hurt. On the way to the barn I kept petting her as if nothing had happened. That first year I worked her any place a horse or mule could be hitched.

Another time when hauling manure the hired boy made the turn at the end of the field with the spreader still in gear. A noisy motorcycle passed on the road, the mules started out on a dead gallop as if a spark hit them on the back side. They ran until they reached the other end of the field. I discovered that was a good method to clean a manure spreader, if everything stayed together.

Source: Gideon L. Fisher (1978): 233–37

➵➵➵➵➵➵➵➵

The Adaptable Whitetail Deer

DAVID KLINE

Animals, especially wild ones, are a
serious interest of David Kline, an Amish farmer in central Ohio. In seeking
natural ways to grow and protect his crops, he has befriended barn and cliff
swallows, killdeer, and other birds and animals on his 125-acre farm. In the
following selections he describes whitetail deer and bluebirds.

I can't exactly explain it, but the sighting of a splendid whitetail never
fails to fascinate me. It is only during the last ten years that we regularly see
deer on our farm after an absence of probably over a hundred years. Twenty-
five or thirty years ago if somebody saw one of the shy creatures, people soon
heard about it. . . .

It is remarkable how well the whitetail, when afforded some protection,
has adapted to man and civilization, so much so that they're fairly common
in the suburbs of some cities. Some wildlife biologists even claim that there
are more deer now than there were at the time the first white settlers arrived.

However, there must have been quite a few deer in Ohio in the early 1800s
as Henry Howe recorded in his "Historical Collections of Ohio." A gang
hunt in 1818 that covered one township in Medina County produced 300
deer, plus 17 wolves, 21 bear and other game. . . .

John James Audubon, on a trip through New England in 1833, saw so
many whitetail deer that he wrote, "In that wild and secluded part of the
country, the common deer were without number, and it was with great
difficulty that we kept our dogs with us." Nonetheless, with the settlers' taste
for year-round venison, and relentless hunting with dogs, snares, and guns,
by the late 1800s the deer in Ohio and throughout parts of the eastern U.S.
were virtually extinct. Finally, under public pressure, laws were passed ban-
ning market hunting, and in Ohio, deer hunting was prohibited for over forty
years.

The game management people like to point to the whitetail deer herd as
one of their truly successful efforts. Of course, their limited stocking of deer

in the 1920s and 1930s, along with strict game law enforcement helped the deer but a natural occurrence likely did more than their efforts for the whitetail's comeback.

Because of topsoil lost due to poor farming practices and the economic crunch of the Great Depression, thousands of hill farms in southeastern Ohio and in the midwest were abandoned. As these farms reverted to forest, excellent deer range was provided. Another factor that should be considered is that, since deer are ruminants, they are subject to the same diseases that cattle are. It was about this time that brucellosis (Bang's disease), through testing, and later, vaccination, was all but eradicated in dairy and beef herds. Leptospirosis is another disease that deer are susceptible to and this too is fairly well under control. As the cattle on pasture were protected from these two devastating diseases which cause reproductive failure and often sterility, so, indirectly, were the deer. At the same time, with the large predators such as wolves and mountain lions gone, the conditions were excellent for deer, and with the astonishing fertility of the whitetail, the herd began to recover. . . .

In 1943 Ohio opened three counties to deer hunting and 8,500 hunters bagged 168 deer for a success ratio of one deer for every 50 hunters. By 1973 hunting was allowed in 59 counties where 108,000 hunters harvested 7,500 for a success ratio of 1 in 14. Last year, 1983, all 88 counties were open for hunting and 265,000 hunters bagged 59,000 whitetails for a hunter success ratio of 1 in 4.4.

Now, it seems, the Division of Wildlife desires to undo what has been accomplished as this year the season is open to both sexes, including fawns in most of Ohio's counties. Their claim is that it's almost impossible to overhunt whitetail deer.

Maybe I'm overly pessimistic concerning the state's permissive season, but now that we frequently see deer about the farm we'd regret to see their numbers decline. The crafty animal's ability to survive is amazing, particularly an older buck that has survived several hunting seasons.

I'd like to give one example of the whitetail's survivability. Two years ago, on the last day of the gun season, we were at the supper table when I happened to see my neighbor walking down the road on his way home from hunting. I went out on the porch and asked him if he had any success.

"No," he replied, "I haven't seen a live deer since Tuesday." But then he added, "Look at that!" Here a doe had jumped into our pig lot and following her was a nice buck. The buck stopped hardly over 150 feet away and looked at us. In the growing dusk I thought I detected a grin on the buck's face. Levi quickly checked his watch—5:10. The season closed at 5. With a wave of his tail the buck jumped across the fence, passed the pond and the last we saw of him he was headed down the valley. Safe for another year. Levi ruefully remarked, "Where was he all week?"

Source: Kline (1984b): 13–14

›››‑›››‑›››‑›››‑›››‑›››‑›››‑›››

Bluebirds

DAVID KLINE

The primary problem plaguing bluebirds is competition for nesting sites. With the removal of many fence rows and replacing wooden fence posts with steel posts, along with the aggressive aliens—the house sparrow and the starling—the bluebirds are often hard put to find suitable nesting holes.

This is where we can help them.

Around twelve years ago we constructed and put up six wooden bluebird houses. Blackbirds nested in several of them the first year. But house sparrows posed a constant problem. The pesky sparrows would usurp the nesting box in early spring and were extremely difficult to evict. But evict them we did. We now have bluebirds nesting close by the house.

Anyone with an aptitude for carpentry can build bluebird houses. Don't worry if they aren't perfect. These enchanting birds aren't hard to please. Many of our houses are made from scrap lumber, but we also constructed a few out of new cedar. Both work equally well. Some of the houses have their roofs slanted towards the back and the others to the front. For reasons I cannot explain, the most successful houses are the ones with the roofs slanted towards the front.

Mount your box, preferably on a pipe or steel tubing, at least 5 feet off the ground facing east or southeast. The steel pipe prevents house cats and raccoons from raiding the nests and, during the wintertime, the white-footed mice can't gain entry. Cute as these little critters are, they're a nuisance in bluebird houses.

The ideal time to erect the houses is in late March or early April. But anytime through early summer is also okay, as the bluebirds upon fledging their first brood usually seek a new location for their second and sometimes third brood. We have put up houses in mid-summer that were still used that season.

You are now ready to sit back and reap the benefits. Not only will bluebirds nest but also tree swallows, chickadees, and of course, house wrens. Should one of these other species make a nest in your box, simply provide more houses.

I feel sorry, indeed, for the farmer who on coming to the end of his field, stops the team, turns and rests against the plow handles and doesn't hear the soft, sweet warbling song of the bluebird.

With more people putting out nesting boxes, the voice of the bluebird will again be heard throughout the land.

Source: Kline (1984a): 10–11

A Chase in the Night

URIA R. BYLER

Some of the excitement on Amish *farms may serve the function of recreation, but in this case excitement brought moments of danger.*

One September night, "Mom" and I had a good scare. Two years ago we bought a bull calf from a dairy farm in Wisconsin. By now Ferdinand weighed about 1,400 lbs., but he was gentle to handle, and had never shown any signs of evil.

On this particular night, the dog started barking. Something was wrong, so I got up and out there by the load of corn ensilage was Ferdinand, messing around, diving into that load of corn. I went back in and told "Mom" about it, and gave her orders to stay inside.

I pulled my boots on, grabbed a stick, and went out and opened the barn door, figuring to chase him in there. Then I heard "Mom" let out an unearthly scream. I started running. Up there near the house, the bull was chasing "Mom," right on her heels. I took off as fast as possible to save her, for by now she had fallen down and just managed to crawl inside the woodshed door.

I gave him all I had over his rump with my stick. In a second he had switched ends, and let out an angry bellow. I also reversed directions and took off, thinking I could escape into the milkhouse about 30 feet away. But Ferdinand was right behind me, and I had no chance to make the turn into the door.

There was only one way to go, and that was the barn, 40 yards away. I believe that bull was surprised. No doubt his intentions were to catch me and gore me to death, but he had to catch me first. He never had a chance. Can an old beagle catch a speeding rabbit? Down that path we went, the bull roaring, which only speeded me up. According to "Mom," I gained the door a safe distance ahead of the bull.

I doubt if very few people, 35 years old and with boots on, ever ran a 40 yard dash any faster than I did that night. In a matter of life and death, the human body can do marvelous things.

Source: Byler (1985): 246–47

The Stress of Debts

NAME WITHHELD

The high cost of farms, high interest rates, and the thought of foreclosure remain deep concerns of young Amish couples who start farming. Here is advice from a person who seems to have had first-hand experience.

To the young family with too many debts, I would say, "The relatives mean well, but there comes a time in life when you have to stand on your own two feet and face facts that borrowing more money will only prolong your problems."

We, too, did with less at times than some members of our family thought was prudent. But in general we just kept quiet about it, and didn't mention it. Now years later some more of the family are having hard times financially, and are doing some of the things we did that they hadn't thought very highly of at the time.

As for worrying about your children, it is something we can always do in one way or another. Do not neglect to talk with them and to them *as* you work. If you must sacrifice somewhere, let it be in simpler meals, clothes, and yes, even in frequency of cleaning, if you must, but don't neglect their souls and minds and habits. Commit them into God's care and keeping.

To the tired and tense young farmers, I would say you are not alone in your struggles. Many others have gone through the same in their young years. A verse comes to mind, "He will keep him in perfect peace, whose mind is stayed on thee." Translate that into living, and you will probably find that it means you are trying too hard in your own strength.

Let your problems of finding and buying and paying for a farm be a little more a matter of prayer. Do what you can, of course, but trust God for leading and guidance in this matter. The same way with your work on a daily basis. My guess is you make your plans and set your goals for the day, or perhaps even for several days or the week. Then there are constant interruptions and frustrations. This breaks down what needs fixing. While trying to fix it in a hurry, the bolt breaks, or you don't have the right tool. Or a neighbor or a salesman stops by, or Mom needs some help with the children, or she needs something at the store, or needs something fixed. Or else the cows get out, or the pigs break a water pipe, or it starts to rain before you are done.

One thing that might help you is to think of these words, "The world won't come to an end if this *isn't* done today." Or else, "Tomorrow is another day. If it isn't, we won't have to do this." Or else think of this saying, "Too many people during the first half of their life, spend health to gain wealth. During the second half, they spend wealth trying to regain their health!"

Spending a little time after each meal playing with your children (and forget the work for a few minutes) can be a wonderful relaxer.

I know a husband who many a night dragged himself into the house so tired he could hardly get one foot in front of the other. A lot of this was tension, and if he'd sit and talk with his wife a while, he'd forget his problems and even most of his tiredness. And afterwards he could sleep better, too, instead of troubled dreaming and jerking muscles. If you can learn to let go, and dwell more on spiritual things, you will discover the meaning of the words "My peace I give unto you; not as the world giveth."

Source: Name withheld, *Family Life* (June 1984): 4

⇝⇝-⇝⇝-⇝⇝-⇝⇝-⇝⇝-⇝⇝-⇝⇝-⇝⇝

Sheriff's Sale

GIDEON L. FISHER

Some Amish farmers today are keenly aware of the Depression and its consequences, when grain and livestock were worth very little on the market. Gideon L. Fisher recalls that in 1931 he attended a farm auction in which a tenant farmer was forced into a sheriff's sale.

In the winter of 1931 I witnessed a farm sale at which the tenant farmer (non Amish) was forced to let the sheriff manage the sale. Upon arrival at the sale there were no preparations made whatsoever for the sale. So the sheriff appointed a few of the bystanders to bring the farm machinery out of the barn, where it had been stored for the winter. Everything was sold as it was, and no one seemed to know if it was in working condition or not. Each one had to use his own judgment.

When the sale was well under way the tenant farmer came out from the house and witnessed the sale like a total stranger. The owner of the machinery was now among the spectators, and still the tenant farmer wouldn't give any information on the condition of the equipment, so the items of the sale sold rather cheaply.

When the time came to sell horses and mules, no one had anything to say regarding their age or working ability. It appeared that the livestock had received very little attention all winter. It also appeared that the sheriff was not too well acquainted with livestock and the purchase price was very low. Mules sold for 25 to 50 dollars each, compared to $100 to $200 for good mules. The harnesses and bridles that were stored in the stable were taken off the hooks and brought out to the auctioneer to be sold. They brought from 3 to 5 dollars per set, while good used harnesses brought from $20 to $30.

The last item offered was the manure pile, which looked as if it were a year's supply. The sheriff read the conditions of the sale, that the manure on the property should be sold in order to meet the debts. After the condition of the sale was read, the auctioneer asked for bids. Upon this the landlord raised his voice and made it known that the manure on the farm was not the property of the tenant farmer, but belonged to the farm itself. But the auctioneer did not pay much attention to what was being said, and kept on asking for bids. The landlord raised his voice again, and made it known that if anyone attempted to remove any manure off the farm, he himself intended to be there with a shotgun. So the auctioneer called it off at $10 for all the manure on the farm.

There is no doubt that this poor tenant farmer had good intentions when he started farming. He probably wished to enjoy life on the farm, and hoped to make a good living and save some money for the future. Instead he lost all that he made in the years he was farming, and perhaps what he had saved before he went into farming.

Source: Gideon L. Fisher (1978): 9–11

→》》-→》》-→》》-→》》-→》》-→》》-→》》-→》》

The Barn Raising

GENE LOGSDON

Barn raisings are a form of mutual aid, still preserved by the Amish people. A neighbor of the Amish, Gene Logsdon comments on the efficiency and low cost of rebuilding a barn.

I was invited to a barn raising near Wooster, Ohio. A tornado had leveled four barns and acres of prime Amish timber. In just three weeks the downed trees were sawn into girders, posts, and beams and the four barns rebuilt and filled with livestock donated by neighbors to replace those killed by the storm. Three weeks. Nor were the barns the usual modern, one-story metal boxes hung on poles. They were huge buildings, three and four stories high, post-and-beam framed, and held together with hand-hewn mortises and tenons. I watched the raising of the last barn in open-mouthed awe. Some 400 Amish men and boys, acting and reacting like a hive of bees in absolute harmony of cooperation, started at sunrise with only a foundation and floor and by noon, *by noon,* had the huge edifice far enough along that you could put hay in it.

A contractor who was watching said it would have taken him and a beefed-up crew all summer to build the barn if, indeed, he could find anyone skilled enough at mortising to do it. He estimated the cost at $100,000. I asked the Amish farmer how much cash he would have in the barn. "About $30,000," he said. And some of that would be paid out by the Amish church's own insurance arrangements. "We give each other our labor," he explained. "We look forward to raisings. There are so many helping, no one has to work too hard. We get in a good visit." Not the biggest piece of the Rock imaginable carries that kind of insurance.

Source: Logsdon (1986): 74–75

5

CHURCH AND COMMUNITY GOVERNMENT

Despite some variation, the Old Order Amish have maintained a remarkably uniform life in all the places they have lived. The process of social ordering is embodied in what the Amish call the *Ordnung*. The *Ordnung* specifies the rules of order recognized as essential for the welfare of the church community. Before the semiannual communion service, the leaders propose and the members endorse the regulations for their own congregation.

Two biblical passages are central to the practice of separation from the world. One is Romans 12:2: "Be not conformed to this world, but be ye transformed by the renewing of your mind that ye may prove what is that good and acceptable and perfect will of God." To be separate from the world is not only to be different from it but also to be different in specific community-approved ways. The communal rules help individuals to remain "unspotted from the world," in dress and grooming, in conduct, and in seeking life goals. Another weighty passage supporting separation is 2 Corinthians 6:14: "Be not unequally yoked together with unbelievers; for what fellowship hath righteousness with unrighteousness? What communion

80

hath light with darkness?" This teaching admonishes individuals from having close associations with non-Amish. Marriage to nonmembers, or joint ownership of businesses, are examples.

The Amish today are very aware of the danger of technology, which would undermine family labor and communal dependence. The *Ordnung* covers a wide range of human activity. The most universally shared prohibitions among all Old Order Amish are highline electricity, telephones in homes, central heating systems, automobiles, and tractors with pneumatic tires. All married men wear beards but not mustaches. Also required are long hair (covering part of the ear for men, uncut for women), hooks and eyes on dress coats. Horses must be used for farming. No formal education beyond the elementary grades is the rule of life, but there are rare exceptions. Radio and television are prohibited. Divorce is forbidden.

The Amish recognize two kinds of regulations—those growing out of special intercongregational meetings, which have existed since the sixteenth century, and the contemporary (unwritten) *Ordnung* of their church district. The former have been transmitted by handwritten or printed copies, and the latter have been transmitted orally. The older rules clarify the basic principles of the faith—separation, nonresistance, and exclusion. The contemporary *Ordnung* guides the member in the application and practice of the principles.

The basic theological statements that influenced the nature of Amish community life are the Schleitheim Statement of Brotherly Union (1527) and the Dordrecht Confession (1632). The following selections are directly concerned with the application of the basic beliefs—that is, behavior patterns that are required and those that are forbidden.

⇛⇛⇛⇛⇛⇛⇛⇛

The Redemptive Process in Old Order Communities

SANDRA L. CRONK

For many years the "old orders" among Mennonites and Amish communities were viewed by the public as backward if not static. Recent scholarship has reversed this interpretation. Sandra L. Cronk, *a Quaker scholar, has contributed new understandings of the spiritual significance of these so-called conservative groups.*

The Old Order communities are not static remnants from an earlier age. The Old Order movement is a conscious attempt to maintain a style of Christian living based on principles different from those of the surrounding society. The goal of all the distinctive patterns of living in the Old Order communities is to create a loving brotherhood. The Old Order way of life is structured by a series of rules and regulations called the *Ordnung*. These rules and regulations define how members live together. Although the *Ordnung* deals with ethics, it encompasses much more than the word ethics usually implies. The *Ordnung* orders all facets of life, from the furnishings of the house to the manner of earning a living. These regulations are the Old Order religious ritual. They are not ritual in the sense of some sacred, set-apart activity which takes place at a special time and place. However, they are ritual in the sense of an activity which brings the participant into contact with the power of God. They provide the concrete ways in which members embody the goal of loving community. Amish and Mennonite ritual takes place in the ordinary spheres of everyday life. The *Ordnung* is the divine social order which the Old Order people believe God ordained for human beings.

Old Order members understand the nature of this divine order by looking at the life, teachings, and death of Jesus Christ as recorded in the New Testament. They believe Christ is the revelation of God's will to the world. When the Old Order people look at Christ they see something startling both about God's relationship to people and about the relationship people should have toward one another. Christ, the son of God, was born in a stable in lowly Bethlehem, not in a palace in Jerusalem. Christ was a King who washed the feet of his disciples. Throughout his life he taught humility, meekness, and suffering love. Although Christ was all-powerful, he never used his power to manipulate or coerce others to achieve his will. He would not even allow Peter to use his sword to prevent his capture when Judas betrayed him. He yielded so completely to God's will that he allowed himself to suffer and die on the cross.

This picture of Jesus is not an image of a savior who conquers through might. Instead it is the image of the suffering servant whose power to save came through his yielding and submission. Through this image of Christ the Old Order people see God working in the world with the power of powerlessness. This understanding of power is paradoxical. On one hand, the use of love instead of coercion means the rejection of the usual forms of power. On the other hand, Christ's love had a power to bring about radical change.

Although his love was characterized by yielding and submission, it was certainly not weak. The Old Order movement tries to incarnate this paradoxical power of powerlessness in its communities.

The understanding of powerlessness affects much more than the overt exercise of physical force in the armed services or in the judicial system. The Old Order practice of building community through yielding self-will has ritual embodiment in the economic sphere of life as well. Unlike the outside world, which depends on an impersonal distribution system for its goods and services, the Old Order world functions largely through personal gifts of work. By working hard a member shows he is more concerned with others than with his own comfort. If a daughter does not make a rug from fabric scraps, the family may have no rug on the floor. If a son does not cut the lumber from family land and make the kitchen cabinet, his mother may have no place to put her dishes. In light of these immediate consequences of laziness, only a self-centered person would shirk work. Work is thus transformed into a service of love for others. It is not primarily a way of gaining personal wealth, power, and prestige.

Work as a ritual means of expressing love and creating community has many embodiments. A man helps his neighbor when his barn burns even if it means taking time from his own work. Instead of encouraging a daughter to get a higher paying job in town, a family lets her work for very low wages at the home of a church member to help a new mother with the housework while she recovers from the birth of a baby. An Amish or Mennonite mother will not go to the store to buy ready-made food or clothes for her family. She makes the meals and clothes as her self-sacrificing gift to them. She fears that the work-saving conveniences will reduce the sharing, caring relationships of family life to a system of impersonal living.

Source: Cronk (1981): 5–9

->>>- ->>>- ->>>- ->>>- ->>>- ->>>- ->>>- ->>>

On the Meaning of Ordnung

JOSEPH F. BEILER

An Amish historian, Joseph F. Beiler *comments on the meaning of church discipline. He prepared the statement in 1974, at the request of a Christian renewal group calling itself Gemeinschaft II. The statement was discussed in a meeting (which Beiler did not attend) at the Salford Mennonite Church, in Harleysville, Pennsylvania.*

The most common definition of *Ordnung* in today's way of thinking is "discipline." That is a surface description, for the true meaning is more than pen and ink can yield. It cannot be defined by any word in any language because church *Ordnung* cannot be lived by the letter. It must be lived in the spirit.

During the nineteenth and twentieth centuries great changes came into our land. Factory-made dress materials, machinery, and many other things came upon the American way of living. Our church fathers had a strong desire to hold on to the old way of life, and although much has changed over the years, they have been successful in "holding the line" to the point that we have been separated from the world. This did not come overnight, nor did it come through rash or harsh commands from our bishops but by making wise church decisions to hold firm the old faith. The bishops and ministers do not make the *Ordnung*. They only attempt to hold the line.

A respected *Ordnung* generates peace, love, contentment, equality, and unity. The latter is the key effect of church *Ordnung*. It will focus the individual to one body, one flesh, one mind, and one spirit. It creates a desire for togetherness and fellowship. It binds marriages, it strengthens family ties; to live together, to work together, to worship together, and to commune secluded from the world.

But a church of *Ordnung* is not without problems. We will always have members that, when they fall prey to sin, will blame the *Ordnung*. A rebelling member will label it a man-made law with "no scriptural base," causing "discord," and a "church-wrecker." We have those who resist *Ord-*

nung, and they are of two classes. One is prone to look for "greener grass," and the other is made up of those who are unconcerned. They want to live for today, forgetting the lessons of the past.

Obedience is a close associate of *Ordnung.* It signals whether you love the church or if you do not. You are either in the church or you are outside. There is no happy medium.

Only a person who has learned to love and live a respectful church *Ordnung* can fully appreciate its values. Based on the Word of God and the Spirit of Christ, it gives freedom of heart, peace of mind, and a clear conscience. A person within the *Ordnung* actually has more freedom, more liberty, and more privilege than those who are bound to the outside.

We do know of examples where church ordinances were over-enforced. When self-opinion rules it will go as with the house built upon the sand. A time-proven *Ordnung* over generations and centuries, directed by the Almighty Powers and led by the Holy Spirit, will stand unto the end.

Source: Beiler (1974)

⋙ ⋙ ⋙ ⋙ ⋙ ⋙ ⋙ ⋙

Some Early Rules of Conduct

The following rules, selected from early Amish leaders' meetings, illustrate the diverse social circumstances that the Amish faced in their attempt to maintain a redemptive community. Most are still observed in some manner. (Each item contains the date and place of the rule.)

No brother shall engage in any large buying, building, or other large business or give himself to any unnecessary profiteering and usury without the counsel, foreknowledge, and consent of the brethren and elders (1779, Essingen, item 4).

Tobacco, smoking or snuff-taking and such-like evil practices shall be stopped (1799, Essingen, item 12).

All the young men who take off the beard with the razor shall be warned and admonished that if they do not stop, they shall be punished with the ban, as likewise those who cut the hair off the head according to worldly style (1779, Essingen, item 13).

All those members who leave us and join other churches, shall be recognized as apostate according to the Lord's Word and his ordinance, and shall be separated and recognized as deserving the ban (1809, Pa., item 3).

Whoever transgresses the rule of shunning out of weakness or ignorance, can be reconciled by confession before the congregation that he has erred; anyone who transgresses intentionally but who is not stubborn about it when admonished, must make a full confession; but whoever stubbornly refuses to hearken to admonition must be excommunicated too (1809, Pa., item 5).

Immoderate sleigh driving or excessive driving of other vehicles shall not be allowed, and neither those decorated with showy or two-tone colors, as too often has happened (1837, Pa., item 5).

Concerning the excesses practiced among youth, namely those youth taking liberties to sleep or lie together without any fear or shame—such things shall in no way be tolerated. If such things take place without the knowledge of the parents . . . the parents themselves shall not go unpunished (1837, Pa., item 9).

Decided not to allow attendance at worldly conventions, fairs, or annual fairs, or to take part in them, or to enroll in worldly insurance companies or to erect lightning rods on our buildings (1837, Pa., item 2).

Source: McGrath (1966): 10–37

-->>->>->>->>->>->>->>->>-

A Pennsylvania Discipline

SADIE C. NEWMAN

Sadie C. Newman (1880–1960) *worked for an Amish family and joined the Amish church. She made notations of the church rules in Mifflin County, Pennsylvania, in 1897 at the time of her baptism at age seventeen.*

FOR THE MEN:

Do not cut the hair too short, trim the beard, or shave too low.

Only one suspender, plain black, is allowed.

No zipper clothing.

Blouses or shirts bought in the store may not be worn unless the pockets and collars are first removed.

No [decorative] rings on the harnesses of the horses.

No bicycles, telephones, or electricity.

Buggy seats with a fully closed lazy back may not be used.

Do not use so much English talk, but it may be used when English folks are still around. No English singing is to be used at the youth singings.

No lightning rods on the farm dwellings.

Do not have your picture taken.

Do not use sleeve holders, and do not comb your hair parted.

FOR THE WOMEN:

Do not make the caps so small, but keep them large enough to cover the ears. And do not make bonnets so small.

Do not make such broad pleats in the dresses or such broad hems

Do not comb your hair high on the head.

Do not wear jewelry for pride. Do not use lace around the skirts.

Do not hang framed pictures.

Do not have your picture taken.

Keep plain carpets on the floor, no stripes through them.

There shall be no flowered oil cloths. Do not wear short dresses and light stockings [which] show bare legs.

Source: Newman (1897)

-->>>->>>->>>->>>->>>->>>->>>->>>-

Discipline of an Indiana Congregation

NAME WITHHELD

*C*hurch rules of today differ in certain ways from those of the past. New rules are made in response to those changes in the outside world which the Amish regard as erosive to the life of *the community. The following 1978 discipline of an Indiana congregation expresses the common understanding of what constitutes the rules of conduct.*

No worldly insurance or Social Security benefits.

Farm with horses, not with power machinery in the field.

No rubber tires on implements or buggies.

No unnecessary lights on buggies except what is for safety.

No bulk tanks or milkers.

No registered cows or horses.

No one shall operate cars or trucks.

Clothing on men shall be plain and humble; no small rim or band on the hat. No cowboy style or creased hat. Hook-and-eye coats are required. No outside pockets on coat or shirt. No hip pockets or slit pants or double-crease pants. No belt loops and no suspender clamps.

No members shall go without suspenders or without shoelaces. After marriage no oxfords shall be worn.

No bright colors on shirts like pink, yellow, orange, or bright cloth. No quilted coats or jackets. No zippers. Dark plain stockings must be worn.

No form-fitting clothing in respect to the sisters. Shawls shall be worn when going from home.

The dresses shall be plain and not striped or made of luxury material, or with bright colors like pink, yellow, orange or bright red. No large collars or large openings at the neck.

The shoes shall have strings, be black and have no high heels.

Aprons shall always be white as also the cape for the church service. No wide bands on the apron. Hair shall not be combed over the ears.

The young people shall not run after pleasure places, have radio or TV, or watch movies. No wrist watches, bicycles, no drinking or tobacco. No ball playing on Sunday.

No bed courtship or other shameful behavior. Couples are not to see each other excessively and shall be home by midnight. Foul speech and unnecessary language and bywords are not to be found among us.

No electrical generators except for welding. No lightning rods. No white rings or overchecks on the harness of the horse. No Sunday milk is sold.

Houses shall be plain with no large picture windows or push windows, nor two-toned trimming.

Kitchen worktables are to be plain with no trimming.

No sinks, worktables or colored stool or colored tub in the bathroom.

No decorative colors on bathroom floor.

Laundry shall be washed at home, not at the laundromats.

Source: Name withheld (1978, unpublished)

-≫>-≫>-≫>-≫>-≫>-≫>-≫>-≫>

Excommunication

JOHN S. UMBLE

I*n describing life in Union County, Pennsylvania, John S. Umble explains, in his unique way, the procedure leading up to excommunication.*

Discipline had a twofold object: to keep the church pure and to reclaim the erring. Three methods were employed: requiring confession of a fault, setting back from communion, and excommunication.

Minor offenses were punished by requiring the transgressor to make a public confession, to "confess a fault." Such minor offenses consisted in disobeying some church rule, like sitting for a photograph, for instance, or wearing some forbidden article of dress, or cutting or combing one's hair different from the prescribed mode.

On one occasion two of the deacon's daughters let down their hair, combed out the heavy, rippling tresses, bound them with a ribbon, and sat for a photograph. Certain members were shocked, especially since it was falsely reported that they had borrowed fashionable clothing for the occasion. The unhappy young women were obliged to submit to the ordeal of a public confession. When the incident was closed, the elder sister remained somewhat unreconciled, but the younger, grieved and repented at having caused her good old father pain, brought the photographs to him and said: "Here, Dad, are the photographs. You may have them. You may put them in the stove if you wish."

The aged deacon looked at the photographs for a moment, then handed them back and said earnestly, "That looks too lifelike; I can't put that into the stove."

Unfortunately disciplinary problems were often left until near the time for the fall or spring communion service. Since the congregation practiced close communion, it was considered necessary that every one coming to the communion table be properly prepared. Communion was possible only in a pure and united church, the body of Christ. Accordingly two weeks before this service the congregation held a preparatory service. At this time every one was asked, individually, three questions. "Do you have peace with God? With your fellow-men, so far as possible? Do you desire to participate in the communion service?" One of the methods of discipline was to deny such participation to offenders against the church rules or to those who refused to confess a fault for such infraction.

The third and most drastic method of discipline was excommunication. This was mandatory for open violation of the moral law. No attempt was made to shield offenders or to whitewash their offense. On one occasion two young men and two young women were convicted of immorality and publicly excommunicated at once. On such occasions excommunication took place in the presence of the entire congregation. Offenders were always tried in a secret session of the congregation, however, to avoid unnecessary publicity.

The excommunication of the members was an awful and a solemn procedure. The members to be expelled had been notified in advance and were absent. An air of tenseness filled the house. Sad-faced women wept quietly; stern men sat with faces drawn. The bishop arose; with trembling voice and with tears on his cheek he announced that the guilty parties had confessed their sin, that they were cast off from the fellowship of the church and committed to the devil and his angels ("dem Teufel und allen seinen Engeln übergeben"). He cautioned all the members to exercise "shunning" rigorously.

Excommunication had for one of its objects, however, the reclamation of the erring member by showing him his real condition and thus leading him to repentance and reformation ("Busz and Besserung"). As soon as the transgressing member was expelled, no faithful member would eat with him. To impress the excommunicated member with the seriousness of his condition, members were forbidden under pain of excommunication to receive any help from him. They were required to show him every possible kindness but could receive no favors in return. In a very real sense he was an outcast, rejected of God and man. His only hope was not to die before he should be reinstated, lest he should be an outcast also in the world to come. Such extreme punishment was meted out only for infractions of the moral law, or for stubborn and continued refusal to submit to milder forms of correction for minor offenses.

Source: Umble (1933a): 89–92

➢➢➢-➢➢➢-➢➢➢-➢➢➢-➢➢➢-➢➢➢-➢➢➢-➢➢➢

Suffering under the Ban

ROY L. SCHLABACH

Just as children and young people must be corrected and conform to the discipline of their parents, so must members of the church community suffer the consequences of their disobedience.

Back in the year 1890 an issue came up in the Amish church here in Holmes County, Ohio, that caused quite a controversy. Like it usually goes, truth and gossip were mixed together. The overall issue caused a deep concern. The problem was there and had to be dealt with. So with a prayerful attitude and taking into consideration the welfare and the future of the church and also the souls of those involved, some older leaders worked on it.

It came to a point that Jacob Schrock was expelled and placed under the "Bann." He was an elderly man who had the reputation of having a strong will and of being easily hurt. Therefore, it was very hard for him to accept this verdict, and he allowed himself to get very worked up about it.

Jacob was retired and lived in the "Daudy Haus." His son Emanuel (often known as Monie) lived at home and did the farming. He was a young man about twenty-two years old at the time.

One Sunday evening while doing the chores Monie was in the feed aisle, feeding the horses, when his father came to him, burst into tears and said, "What has been done to me today is far too much. I cannot bear it. I know there are others that feel the same way. If you stand by us, we can make a big thing out of this."

After a pause, Monie said to his father, "Ach, Daudy, mir welle net so denke. Mir welle des uf uns nehme. Es kann uns zum Guten dienen. Denk mol an Jesu, was er gelitten hat und huts alles gedulitch angenommen, und war doch ganz unschuldig." (Oh, Grandpa, don't think like that. We want to take this upon ourselves. It can work for our own good. Think of Jesus, how he suffered, and took it patiently upon himself, even though he was completely innocent.)

Jacob seemed reluctant to accept this advice, and expressed a "let down" mood. However, after some time had elapsed, he changed his views and was taken back in full fellowship with the church.

Years passed by. Monie moved about eight miles away. Old Jacob's health began to fail, and Monie often went to visit and help care for his ailing father. One of the last times he was there before Jacob's death, the old man said, "I do not think my time on earth will be long anymore. I want to thank you for that advice you gave me that Sunday evening in the feed aisle. It has helped me more than anything else I can think of. I have a good feeling toward the ministers and the church, and have no ill feelings toward anyone. I have hopes that God has forgiven me, and that I can die in peace."

Jacob died soon afterwards. How this story would have ended, had his son supported him in his rebellion, we do not know.

Source: Schlabach (1984): 40

⋙-⋙-⋙-⋙-⋙-⋙-⋙-⋙

Restoring a Fallen Member

JOSEPH UNZICKER

The procedure for readmitting excommunicated members following their penitence is described in a ministers' manual by Bishop Joseph Unzicker. The date of origin is unknown. The basic procedure is still followed by the Amish.

The chapters suitable to the occasion are read, namely that of the Prodigal Son and a part of II Corinthians 2, and then the matter is explained with suitable remarks. Also one brings in especially Matthew 18. Then the passage concerning the faithful Shepherd and the lost sheep and also several Penitential Psalms. And at the end I find it fitting to discourse on the last two verses of the 119th Psalm with the words, "Oh Lord, let my soul live so that I may bless thee, for I am like a wayward and lost sheep. Seek thou thy servant for I do not forget thy commandments." And Psalm 118, verses 18 and 19, "The Lord chastises me indeed but he hath not given me over unto death." Then the erring one is addressed by name with words. If you believe that you have sought the All-Highest God with a penitent heart, then you may come forward and kneel in the name of God. Then one says:

This kneeling is not to be before me, but before the All-Highest God and his church.

Do you believe and acknowledge that you have deserved this punishment on account of your sins and that for your repentance this punishment was laid upon you justly by God and the church? (Answer, "Yes!")

Do you hope and believe then that you may be able to guard yourself better henceforth against sin and all unrighteousness, better than has happened previously, and do you promise to adjust your daily walk to the Holy Gospels and the teaching of the apostles insofar as the dear God gives you grace and power thereto? (Answer, "Yes!")

Do you hope and also believe that you have called prevailingly and sufficiently on the All-Highest God, with tears and a penitent heart and earnest prayer, that he would through his grace forgive you your past sins? (Answer, "Yes!")

Then one gives him the hand and says:

So I also forgive you in the name of the All-Highest and in the name of his church through Jesus Christ, Amen.

He raises him up and gives him the kiss of peace and tells him to depart in the name of God.

Then one may bring in several comforting verses, accompanied by fitting words.

As in the 118th Psalm, verses 20 and 21, "This is the gate of the Lord; the just will go in there at. I thank thee, Lord, that thou hast humbled me and hast helped me again."

And Psalm 116, "Now be satisfied again, my soul, for the Lord does you good. The Lord has delivered my soul from death and mine eyes from tears and my foot from slipping. Therefore I will walk before the Lord in the land of the living so long as I am here." One may also bring in Isaiah 38, how King Hezekiah thanked the Lord that he had extended his life.

Source: Joseph Unzicker, in Umble (1941): 111

6

HOME
AND FAMILY

In the Amish community every person has a designated place at the family table. When a husband, wife, or child is absent, the rest of the family is keenly aware of the empty place. People deprived of a home, parents, and relatives are pitied. Vacancies due to marriage, travel, runaways, illness, or death have appropriate symbolic meaning. Home is the center of Amish family life. A place of security, it is a center for decision-making with respect to work, play, and exposure to the local community and to the outside world.

The place of each person in the family and home is clearly defined by custom, by religious teaching, and by practical considerations. Usually the husband and father has overall authority, in keeping with biblical teaching (1 Cor. 11:3). Cooperation between husband and wife prevails in many ways, depending upon their personalities. In practice, much authority is shared. The wife's domain is the home and its management, including cooking, cleaning, sewing, and gardening. The most important activity for both husband and wife is child-rearing and -training. The farm is the husband's kingdom, for he plants, harvests, cares for the animals, and buys and sells livestock and farm products. In Amish life there is no provision for divorce.

Parents try to be effective examples for their children, who must accept important work and responsibility. Boys learn to care for farm animals, gather eggs, feed the calves, and drive the horses. Girls learn by helping their mother with cooking and housekeeping. In adolescence, boys and girls are usually given a pet or farm animal. The fate of the animal is linked to the care and attention given to it by the owner. The child learns the consequences of routine feeding, growth, birth, as well as those of neglect, sterility, disease, and death.

Many Amish farms have two domestic dwellings, one of which is the "grandfather house." At retirement the older couple moves into this house and a newly married son or daughter takes over the farm operations. The retired couple not only has a separate house but also their own horse and buggy. They entertain many guests, and they enjoy a continuous association with people of all ages in the community. Because of their belief in the biblical teaching of separation from the world, the Amish do not accept governmental assistance for the elderly or pensions. Neither do they have life insurance. With retirement, respect and consideration from the younger generation continues. For as long as they are able, both grandparents continue involvement in some kind of activities, often quilting or woodworking, and visiting their relatives and friends. They are not faced with the choice of having to be employed full-time or not at all.

⇛-⇛-⇛-⇛-⇛-⇛-⇛-⇛

Log Cabin Days

BARBARA SCHMITT

*B*arbara Schmitt, the wife of a minister of the Adams County, Indiana, Amish church, recalls some of the pleasant experiences of frontier days.

When this century was young, around 1908, my father bought a farm in what used to be the swampland of Adams County, Indiana, around Monroe, Indiana. It was very rich dark loam, after the land was drained by open ditches and tile drains. The tiles of clay were made by three tile mills, one in each of three towns, Decatur, Berne and Monroe, Indiana. The one in Decatur is still going strong, but the other two have been closed for years.

Because the land needed a lot of tiles for drainage, the Amish church permitted their men to work in the tile factories to help build up good farming ground which otherwise would have been useless.

At the time the county seat or Adams County Court House was built, Monroe was not much more than a swamp hole. It would have been in the exact center of Adams County, but the court house was built in Decatur on higher ground.

The Monroe Territory was mostly woods and swamp. When the white settlers came it was Indian Country. The Algonquin Indians mostly roamed the woods in this vicinity. There also were some mixed marriages.

When Father (Christian J. Schwartz) bought this place, all the buildings were out of log. I can well remember the old barn, a log house, and a log woodshed.

My grandparents (the Jacob C. Schwartzes) lived on this place about four years. Before we moved there Dad built a living and bedroom, two stories high, to the log part, as we were a large family. We lived there for eleven years and during this time the log buildings were all replaced with frame buildings, except the house. The log part served as our kitchen; it had a cellar, also an upstairs, but the logs framed the walls with nothing over them. The kitchen was kept whitewashed with the lime, instead of paint; it cost so much less.

At that time there were many log cabins and houses around this part of the country. Now they are all gone, except some were preserved by covering them over inside and outside with other material. There are more of these old log houses around than one realizes. One of our neighbors to the north of us about one-fourth mile has a nice modern farm home and about one half of the house is still log. It is repaired so nice and neat inside and outside, no logs showing.

When my grandparents (the Jacob C. Schwartzes) moved off of our place in about 1912, they moved on a farm with two houses. One was built of logs with a frame kitchen to it, the other was a frame house, much newer. In this house, they lived in, and had the log house for a summerhouse. The big log room was so nice and cool to eat in in summertime. I often was there to visit Grandma after my aunts were married.

On October 18, 1917, my aunt Mary was married to Jacob J. Schwartz. Their wedding table was set up in this big room in the old log house. This was the last wedding, to my knowledge, that lasted two days. The first day was the church service in the morning, when the marriage was performed, then dinner and supper, like is customary in the Amish church. The second day everyone was supposed to go back for dinner. After dinner everyone was called into the house and when all was quiet the bishop told everyone to kneel in prayer. This is the way they closed the wedding. (For reasons unknown to the writer this custom was dropped after the wedding of October 18, 1917.) Then the people went home, all except the helpers who stayed to help wash dishes, take down the tables, and help clean up and put things in order again. It was a nice Christian way to end a wedding.

Source: Schmitt (1970): 19–20

-->>>--->>>--->>>--->>>--->>>--->>>--->>>--->>>

On Living Peacefully with Grandparents

A WIDOW IN KANSAS

R*espect for elders, obviously inculcated in children, is also pronounced with regard to mature adults. Regardless of age or sex, respect is due parents, grandparents, and great-grandparents. This writer describes how the young Amish couple should not intrude on the life of the grandparents.*

When we moved in at one end of the house with his parents, my husband and I already had a few children, and we made guidelines for ourselves.

Rule Number 1: Not to expect them to care for our children while we did the chores. My husband always said that they took care of their own children, so why bother them with ours. I made many a trip to the house during chores to check on them.

Rule Number 2: Don't expect Grandpa to come out and help with the field work.

Rule Number 3: If Grandpa and Grandma wanted a few chores to do as long as they were able, cooperate with them. So we had the chickens and hogs on a 50–50 basis. Each of us did a share of the work, with the cleaning of the houses always being our job. My husband and I always tried to do the heaviest part of the work.

Rule Number 4: Never get aggravated at Grandpas if they advise us how to be more saving. (Even though we felt we were already trying.) They started up farming in the early 1900s and we in the early 1940s.

Rule Number 5: Always pay our rent when due. We knew that's what they depended on for their living, especially after Grandpa's health failed, so he had no share in doing chores anymore.

Rule Number 6: Never interfere with their plans if they want to go somewhere. Always be willing to hitch up a horse for them when they need one, even though they could have done it themselves.

Rule Number 7: Never expect them to care for your children so that you can go to the field, but we'd fix a special place at the end of the field for the little ones if the weather was nice.

Rule Number 8: Always be very appreciative if Grandma comes over to help with the work.

Rule Number 9: If the Grandparents ask you to do something for them, small tasks which they can't do anymore, always be sure to say "You're welcome—I was glad to do it for you." This means so much to the Grandparents.

Rule Number 10: Never go to your brothers or sisters and complain about Grandma and Grandpa, especially after one is left alone. Try to work these things out between you in a nice way.

Rule Number 11: Realize that it costs the Grandparents something to live, and if Grandma has taken in quilting or quilt piecing to supplement their income, take an interest in her work and respect her for it. Even though you don't have time to help (she doesn't expect it). Just let her know you care and love her.

Source: A Widow in Kansas (1985): 4–5

The Influence of Our Hired Man

ELI J. BONTRAGER

An Amish bishop, Eli J. Bontrager *recalls the farmhand who worked for his father. Bontrager also discusses some of the negative influences that the farmhand had on him.*

Father taught us children to work when we were quite young. I learned to work and to do my work well. Digging yellowdock and burdock, etc., around the yards and fence rows was a continuous job in the season, although I detested it. We always "raised cane" for molasses and stripping cane was my job in season in those days. I also spent many a day alone digging potatoes with the old dunghook. I did not like to work as I was naturally lazy. However, I did not want anyone to see or know that I was lazy. I kept at work quite steadily. When only eight years old, I was out daily in the cornfield in the husking season with the hired man husking the corn.

This particular man was of a low class as far as morals were concerned. The smutty stories that he told and the dirty songs that he sang for me still linger in my mind after nearly seventy years. My memory recalls much of the early teaching of my parents and, as I was always an eager reader of anything that came into my hands, I can still recall many moral stories, and many good health rules, and much advice in secular and moral and spiritual matters. However, those smutty stories and songs that immoral hired man implanted in my mind have crowded out what otherwise could have had good effects upon me.

I believe now that those dirty words and deeds were a factor in filling my mind with carnal thoughts that aroused my carnal nature. It was a continuous struggle ever after to keep my carnality from getting the best of me. "Continued struggle" is the right expression.

Others may also have the same struggle, but with me this carnal nature was aroused at the age of eight years in that cornfield with that immoral young hired man. He married later. All his life, I knew him. When I became a minister I had to deal with him. I saw him when he lived on the west coast, and during his later years when he lived near the east coast, and he never seemed to be a moral or conscientious man. He had trouble and made trouble wherever he was. His large family, with a few exceptions, are not of the desirable class of church members.

I often thought that if father had known at that time the type of young man this hired man was, and what his influences were on his young son, he never would have tolerated him on the place. It is our sacred duty to try to safeguard our children in their tender years so that their baser nature may not be aroused while still in their childhood. I have learned this lesson, but I have paid dearly for it.

Source: Eli J. Bontrager (1953): 5

⇛·⇛·⇛·⇛·⇛·⇛·⇛·⇛

Confessions of a Hired Girl

NAME WITHHELD

There is a constant need for maids and hired men in an Amish community. By hiring out, young people discover their capabilities and independence. Personal growth and maturity are acquired outside the family but within the Amish culture.

Once more I'm on the job. I have a new baby to care for. And that's not all—I have the rest of the family to care for, too! What a challenge for an inexperienced teen-age girl. Who can tell what work, what mistakes, laughters and tears will make up my life for the next few weeks.

I wonder whether the poor mother could rest if she knew what a trembling greenhorn was invading her kitchen. I doubt it, but hope that by the time she realizes how inexperienced I am, she will be stronger. Poor mother, stuck with a clumsy girl who doesn't know where things are, and who doesn't get the diapers washed out clean. She has a hired girl whose tears drip into the wash water because she's lonely for mom and home. She has a hired girl who sometimes scolds, nags, and threatens her poor darlings when their mom is sleeping.

Poor woman. She has a hired girl who mixes cornstarch with water for the children's lunches when she packed them in the morning, thinking it is the lemonade mix. She has a girl who prays half-tearful prayers that the father of the family will eat anything—burned, over-salted, unsalted, and every other way it might be served!

And those are only some of the mistakes I made while working as a hired girl. However grand my ideals, I'm always humbled, homesick, and dejected when I leave. (Is that good for my pride?)

However, there is a bright side to everything—even to a hired girl's life. Nothing is sweeter than a child asking for a "night-night kiss," and then a whispered, "Aunt Beth, I love you." That blots out all the miseries of the day, fills my heart with happiness and sends me on my way with a song.

The baby is another source of joy. Bathing the baby is a bright side, providing baby's mother isn't watching. If she is, I am too worried I'm not doing it right to enjoy the privilege. I think all mothers should be encouraged to let their hired girls bathe the baby at least once, all by herself, just for the challenge of it, and the fun of it.

I've only one more thing to confess. If I ever need a hired girl, I hope I can be as nice to her as some mothers have been to me. Thank you, patient moms.

Source: "Confessions of a Hired Girl" (1984): 32

﹥﹥﹥-﹥﹥﹥-﹥﹥﹥-﹥﹥﹥-﹥﹥﹥-﹥﹥﹥-﹥﹥﹥-﹥﹥﹥

Amish Women and Their Kitchens

BILL RANDLE

B*ill Randle, an "outsider" who became interested in religious communities that offered a more satisfying life, became interested in the Amish. He paid extensive visits to their Ohio communities and was struck by their simplicity, their food preparation, and their cooking. He writes sensitively about the work of women in their homes.*

Amish women are hard workers. They start when they are small children and by the time they get married they have picked up all of the essential housekeeping and farming skills that make them such a valuable economic asset in the Amish community. . . .

The kitchen is the center for Amish family life. The kitchen table is where everybody eats. Sometimes there is oilcloth on the table, most often it is bare. There is no table linen although cupboards sometimes have inside shelves draped with folded paper napkins. Regular dishes are plain heavy china, sometimes picked up at an auction. Utensils are usually stainless steel, never silver. Some families have brightly-colored dishes and other pretty things displayed even though "pride and vanity" are outlawed. Painted tomato cans and clay pots are placed on window sills, a riot of flowering plants inside brighten up the kitchen. Occasional embroidered pieces are also colorful and charming.

101

Plain single blind draped curtains, blue or green, are found in many windows, but a large number of the older families have no curtains at all.

The stricter families have historically used coal stoves and kerosene or oil lamps. Propane and natural gas, some of it produced on Amish farmland, is now used by more liberal Amish districts. Thousands of mantels burn in gas lit homes along the main and back country roads. Gas stoves and ovens abound, and there are even homes with central heating systems here and there. But fine quilts filled with wool and heavy blankets and comforters are depended on more than heating plants.

There are plenty of outhouses as part of the country landscape, although many families have added more sophisticated plumbing in recent years. Tub baths, once common and sometimes communal, have been in many cases replaced by fixed bathtubs and showers as water systems have been developed that are acceptable to the various groups. Clothing is hand-washed and sun- and wind-dried summer and winter.

There is little time for back fence gossiping and coffee-klatching in the Amish woman's day. She makes her own clothes (except for shoes and simple underwear) and also makes work clothes for the men in the family as well as all the children's clothing. She is a sometime barber and doctor, bandaging up the cuts and abrasions that are everyday problems on the working farm. She is constantly mending and fixing the house; there is always something to be done.

It would be a serious mistake, however, to think that there is not a lot of joy and happiness in an Amish home because of the constant work and never-ending responsibilities built into raising such large families in severe surroundings. Most Amish women love flowers and there are always patches of colorful geraniums and marigolds, mixed with nasturtiums at times, decorating Amish lawns. There are apple-paring parties and auctions, town trips and visits, church Sundays and family reunions, barn raisings to cook for, and weddings galore. There are Amish women who play baseball and Frisbee with enthusiasm and great style. At the other extreme, Amish mothers read Bible stories in German to their little children with great reverence and feeling. . . .

Amish women do not use cosmetics. They usually don't have to. The rosy cheeks of the Amish and their fine clear skin, often freckled, needs no enhancing. They are naturally good-looking people, vigorous and healthy women playing roles prescribed for them by tradition, maintained by perseverance, and apparently more than satisfying their needs for a complete and dedicated life.

Source: Randle (1974): 13, 16–17

﹥﹥﹥-﹥﹥﹥-﹥﹥﹥-﹥﹥﹥-﹥﹥﹥-﹥﹥﹥-﹥﹥﹥-﹥﹥﹥

Staying Healthy

GIDEON L. FISHER

G*ideon L. Fisher writes about health from experience. His first wife, Mary (1914–1978), had severe arthritis for thirty-four years. Due to the calcium deposits in her joints, she required almost the same attention as that of a small child during the last ten years of her life.*

When our forefathers set foot on American soil they not only faced problems of clearing land, erecting buildings, and providing food and clothing for the family. They also had the problem of keeping their bodies in good physical health. Their living conditions were by no means an easy life. They accomplished their physical labor the hard way, from early morning to late at night, withstanding the summer heat and winter cold, even though they ate their food with high nutrition value, drank water not contaminated from sewage systems, breathed the air at its purest, well filtered by the thousands of acres of woodland surrounding the countryside. They became a vigorous type of people; with their own body resistance they could fight off the common colds and minor diseases.

Due to the heavy growth of underbrush, there were large areas of swampland with poor drainage. There were areas where it was impossible for the sun's rays to reach the earth's surface. This caused a very high humidity, which made an ideal harbor for mosquitoes, houseflies, and other insects. These pests were known to spread contagious diseases from one colony to another, causing high mortality rates. Sometimes whole families were wiped out by malaria, typhoid fever, yellow fever, smallpox, and tuberculosis. Because sanitation was not really practiced by our early immigrants, common colds, and what we call children's diseases—measles, whooping cough, chicken pox, etc.—seemed to make their rounds every few years.

The early settlers were primarily self-supporting, making their own living off the soil. The housewife not only supplied the table with an abundance of food, and made the clothing, but also kept watch to see if any member of the family did not have a keen appetite, or could not sleep well at night. She had her medicine cabinet filled with home remedies for chest colds, upset stomach, sore throat, earache, and also a blood tonic that would even give the old man a boost. Her remedies were made from the receipts that trace back many generations. With special care, these formulas were preserved and kept with property records, and others were passed by word of mouth from one generation to another.

Every housewife kept an herb garden which consisted of a variety of teas; catnip, peppermint, spearmint, sassafras, sage, hops, pokeberry, garlic, etc. Sometimes the roots of different plants or bark of certain trees were boiled to obtain the ingredients to make blood tonic, poultices, salves, liniment, antiseptic, etc. It was claimed by people who studied herbs that every plant, tree, or weed has some value for human consumption, if made in the right proportions. Quite often these old-time formulas were blended with strong spirits, and often proved their value as good medications.

Medicine men had a thriving business, going from house to house on foot or horseback, visiting the sick, twenty or thirty miles around, rain or shine, heat or cold, making regular trips peddling medicine. There were no telephones and mail was slow, and sometimes it took him three or four days to answer a message that a sick person needed certain medicine. The majority of these medicines proved to be of some value, others were practically worthless. This medicine business turned into a money racket. With some smooth talking, the housewife was convinced that she was getting a cure-all medicine for all members of the family. If a sick person used the medicine and got good results the medicine man felt he deserved the credit. If the results were the opposite, he would say the person did not accept his rules, or the case was too far advanced.

Most of these medicine men, or quack doctors, had little professional training, they doctored mostly from hearsay experience. By 1900 the government passed laws that medicines must be labeled, stating the ingredients, and what portion was alcohol, and if it was to be used for human consumption. Some of the potent medicines were less effective than the housewife's own remedies.

During the Depression people did almost anything to earn some money, and this was oftentimes not the easy way. It was nothing unusual to see an elderly man walking the road carrying a large basket loaded with needles, pins, thread, thimbles, combs, pocketknives, cough syrup, liniment, shaving cream, corn cure, worm syrup, pain and indigestion pills, etc. He had a leather strap over his shoulder and around the handle of his basket to make it more easy to carry. Occasionally along his way he asked the housewife for a bite to eat, or if he could stay awhile under the shade tree to rest his weary legs, or if he might sleep in the barn at night.

Source: Gideon L. Fisher (1978): 292–94

➤➤➤-➤➤➤-➤➤➤-➤➤➤-➤➤➤-➤➤➤-➤➤➤-➤➤➤

Old-time Remedies

FAMILY LIFE

As *in most societies, Amish adults vary greatly in their attitudes toward home remedies. Here are several anonymous recommendations for remedies by those Amish who testify to their value.*

Red Beet Poultice

I have used red beets a number of times and feel we have saved doctor bills. When I was a small girl I had a very sore hand with red streaks to my elbow. An old neighbor lady said to put on a red beet poultice. Cut beets in half and scrape out the inside and put on a cloth. Tie on sore. It healed right away. When my daughter went to school the nurse brought her home one evening at 3:30, saying she has a fever, a lump under her arm and streaks from a scratch on her finger. I knew I could hardly make it to town for the doctor, for I had chores to do. I put her to bed, gave her a laxative, and put poultices of the beets on the sore, changing them a few times during the night. By morning she was much better and soon was all right again.

A few years ago I went to visit my parents. The first evening there, Dad stepped on a tack. He soaked his foot and put something on it right away, for he is diabetic. This was Tuesday evening. By Thursday morning he couldn't put his shoe on anymore. We applied a poultice of red beets at noon. By evening he was much better and by Friday morning he could wear his shoe again. I don't think I have ever used this remedy that it failed to help.

Source: Family Life (January 1974): 35

For Colic in Babies

Take 1 glass of water and add 1 teaspoon sweet fennel seed. Bring to a boil. Boil for 5 minutes. Let cool to lukewarm, then strain. Honey may be added before giving the tea to the baby.

Source: Family Life (April 1974): 35

To Remove Dandruff

Boil an ample amount of stinging nettle (which has to be gathered with gloves) in vinegar diluted with water for 30 minutes. Cool and strain. Use this tea for the last rinse when shampooing. Repeat as necessary.

Source: Family Life (August/September 1974): 39

For Hay Fever

Here is a health hint for those who will be suffering from hay fever this year. Don't drink raw milk. Heat milk to the boiling point, then cool before using. This seems to kill the pollen in the milk. Although this isn't a cure-all for hay fever, it certainly has been a big help to me. I would like to hear what remedies others have for hay fever.

Source: Family Life (August/September 1974): 39

-->>>-->>>-->>>-->>>-->>>-->>>-->>>-->>>

Healing Charms

Most Amish people, and certainly *not the young, know nothing of the powwowing or sympathy cures, which were longstanding in their past. Jacob J. Hershberger, a minister in the Beachy Amish church, wrote a column in* The Budget *and touched off a debate when he struck down powwowing as the work of evil spirits. Not all readers were convinced of this, as two responses to Jacob J. Hershberger's column indicate.*

JACOB J. HERSHBERGER

We do not deny that cures, even miracles, are often worked by those who use enchantment, powwow, etc. After all, there are many evil spirits in the world, and like Pharaoh's magicians who turned water into blood and dust into lice with their witchcraft and sorcery, the same evil spirits can work wonders today. It is even quite possible that there are those today who practice these "curious arts" and don't realize that the source of their power is the devil rather than God.

God has given instructions in His Word for curing and healing the sick—according to His will. He has instructed to "lay on hands, anoint with oil, call the elders of the church and pray," etc., but nowhere has God commanded to perform some of the "shenanigans" some "powwowers" have thought up. Who ever read of God commanding to pass a child around a table leg or laying it on a sewing machine and measuring it, or putting a piece of string around an eggshell and burning it, etc.? Are these things of faith—as outlined in the Word of God—or are they some superstitious beliefs handed down by godless heathen?

Source: Jacob J. Hershberger (1961)

EFFIE TROYER

To those who object to "brauch" when all doctor's medicine has failed to help, would you refrain from taking your sick child to a medical doctor just because a neighbor or friend or relative was opposed to an M.D., believing only in divine healing? I have heard of parents refusing to take their children to a chiropractor even after a medical doctor was unable to give relief. To my way of thinking we need both the M.D.s and chiropractors and yes, those who "brauch" too. How could anyone give themselves so completely to the devil's power as to be able to "brauch" only through his power but otherwise live a Christian life? No, I do not believe in witchcraft, nor do I believe there is any connection between witchcraft and "brauching." Are you absolutely sure that powwowing and "brauching" are one and the same? Some years ago one of our little boys could not sleep nights, being so restless that neither he nor parents could get their needed rest. After taking him to be "brauched" for worms he began to sleep all night long.

Source: Effie Troyer (1961)

WILLIAM ZEHR

Some of these old ideas I will let as they are, but as for actual "brauching" which is done by repeating a paragraph or two out of the Bible, it is hard for me to believe that those words will put the evil spirits to work. In Mark 8 and John 9, you can read what was done there when Jesus rubbed clay on the blind man. I don't think it was the clay that opened his eyes, but because he believed if he did as he was told, he would be helped. I don't think the evil spirits were a part of it.

Source: Zehr (1961)

ANONYMOUS

Some feel that "powwowing" is about the same as "hypocrisy," but I feel it is far from it. I looked up the two words in the dictionary, and still I feel none of them is "braucha." As I understand "braucha," it is a certain gift of God which He does not give to all people, but to certain ones. God heals people through the "works" of the ones He has chosen. And the "secret words" are prayers to God. And about using an egg to "brauch," could not Jesus have made the man to see with an egg and string as well as he could with "clay"? Read St. John 9th Chapter; people could hardly believe what the man Jesus had done with clay.

Source: The Budget (October 12, 1961)

SARAH YODER

Some don't believe in doing silly things like putting a child through an arch of raspberry plants to keep them from getting whooping cough or wrapping a thread around an egg and putting it in hot coals for stomach distress. Well, I saw them both work.

I'd like to ask a few questions. How could that brass serpent in the time of Moses have anything to do with the healing of the children of Israel? How could that dirty water of the Jordan clean Naaman of his leprosy? What about the pool of Bethesda? Jesus could heal the people without going into the pool. I know it, because He did it. It's Faith with works and obedience. Faith without works is dead. We can find many instances where Jesus healed people but they had to meet conditions.

Source: Sarah Yoder (1961)

LEVI BONTRAGER

Forty years ago a certain braucher (a minister) told me that I could also learn to brauch. I did not see anything wrong about it, until he told me a man must learn the trade from a woman, and a woman from a man. That was sufficient for me. I never learned the trade.

Source: Levi Bontrager (1961)

MRS. S. M. MILLER

I guess I am too old-fashioned but I do have to wonder if some of those old remedies wouldn't be better for babies and small children than those many shots they get.

Source: Mrs. S. M. Miller (1961)

7

PHASES
OF LIFE

All societies have rites associated with significant life changes. In Amish society, baptism, marriage, ordination, and death are observed by important community rites. Not all changes in life are celebrated equally. Birth, for example, is accepted without religious or secular ceremonies. Baptism, which may be an awesome experience for the individual, confers on the person the highest expectations of spiritual and moral status. In baptism an individual formally rejects carnal life for eternal life. Marriage is an elaborate celebration of both religious and social significance. The whole community has a stake in marriage. It is a rite of passage from youth to adulthood. The selection of male leaders and their installation is marked by important rites—the use of the lot and ordination. Excommunication of members, both male and female, is preceded by a formalized procedure.

From birth to death, individuals pass through a series of distinct age stages: babies, little children, scholars, young folks, adults, and old folks. There are models of appropriate behavior and discipline for each age group.

When expectations are clearly defined, there is a high degree of security and personal trust among members. Far from having only negative connotations, discipline is accepted as a positive ingredient essential for community and personal life. Formal commitment signifies self-sacrifice, submission, obedience, right living, and caring, without lofty words and language.

Stability of family life is achieved by how well parents demonstrate in life what they teach. Parents do not stress individual rights, but responsibilities and obligations for the correct training of their children. In establishing a home, every couple knows that they must teach, train, admonish, chasten, love, and guide their offspring, and do so with patience and wisdom.

➤➤-➤➤-➤➤-➤➤-➤➤-➤➤-➤➤-➤➤

Disobedient Children

ANONYMOUS

*A*lthough children are believed to *have an inherited sinful nature through no fault of their own, they are perceived as loving and teachable. Parents are responsible for training their children and are morally accountable to God for teaching them right from wrong. During their age of innocence, children are regarded as pure and not in need of ceremonial baptism. Some principles of discipline are discussed in these three selections.*

Why are children disobedient? This question, we know, is one that many troubled parents have wondered about. Part of the answer lies in the Adamic nature of the child, but part of it, also, is the fault of the parents, who have failed to train the child as they should. This failure in training may stem from ignorance, as well as from an unconcerned attitude. The following are some reasons why children are disobedient:

1. Instructions are not always stated in the way they should be. The child does not feel that the parents mean what they say, or that the command is to be obeyed to the word.

2. Promises are frequently made to the children, but they are not kept. This encourages disobedience.

3. A threat of punishment is made, but is not carried out. The child loses respect for the parents.

4. The parent forbids something, yet later allows the child to have it, because the child has cried. Many a child is master of his parents through his crying.

5. Immediate obedience is not insisted upon as it should be. Putting things off till later has brought great trouble, and will bring trouble in this instance.

6. The parents neglect to explain to the child that disobedience to father or mother is also disobedience to God, and that it is a sin before God to disobey.

7. Too much is expected from the child. The parent gives the command, but fails to explain how it should be carried out. The child loses heart.

8. The child sees that his disobedience makes his parents angry, whereas it should make them sorrowful. Let your child know that his misdeeds sadden your heart, but never anger you.

9. Prayer is too often neglected. The best rules fail if God does not give His blessing. And His Spirit is the only thing that can bring true obedience. A good rule for training children, as for anything else, is—"Pray and Labor."

Source: Anonymous, *Herold der Wahrheit* (January 15, 1882) (trans. from German), in Stoll (1967): 35

How Not to Spank

JOSEPH STOLL

Do Not Spank When Angry. Anger begets anger; respect begets respect. Immediately preceding the well-known words in Ephesians 6, "Bring them up in the nurture and admonition of the Lord," are the words "Ye fathers, provoke not your children to wrath."

Do Not Spank with Words Only. Have you the common weakness to keep repeating, "If you don't behave right now, I'm going to spank you?" The child rarely behaves right now, simply because the spanking rarely materializes.

Do Not Do Bodily Harm. Be careful that you do not injure your child.

FLOWERS AND BIRDS *(undated)*
Anonymous artist. *Drawing.*
Mifflin County, Pennsylvania.

Private collection.

BOOKPLATE, 1863
Barbara Ebersol (1846–1922).
Lancaster County, Pennsylvania. $3^{1}/_{4} \times 5^{7}/_{8}$.

This small book belongs to me Barbara Ebersol.
Written on the 29th of April, 1863.

[In script, Catherine Ebersol 1922.]

Courtesy of the collection of Hiram and Mary Jane Lederach Hershey.

ESCH BIRTH FRAKTUR, 1849
Anonymous artist. *Drawing.*
Lancaster County, Pennsylvania. $4^1/_2 \times 6^1/_4$

In the year of our Lord on the 12th of July, 1835, Maria Esch was born in
Union Township, Mifflin County, Pennsylvania.

Private collection.

FLOWERS, c. 1874
Henry Lapp (1852–1904). *Drawing.*
Lancaster County, Pennsylvania. $3^{15}/_{16} \times 5^{5}/_{16}$.

Courtesy Historical Society of the Cocalico Valley.

STRAWBERRIES IN OVAL, c. 1874
Henry Lapp (1862–1904). *Drawing.*
Lancaster County, Pennsylvania. $4^7/_8 \times 4^5/_{16}$.

Courtesy Historical Society of the Cocalico Valley.

SQUIRREL EATING ACORNS, c. 1874
Henry Lapp (1862–1904). *Drawing.*
Lancaster County, Pennsylvania. $8^1/4 \times 6^1/2$.

Courtesy Historical Society of the Cocalico Valley.

TURKEY, c. 1874
Henry Lapp (1862–1904). *Drawing.*
Lancaster County, Pennsylvania. $4^{1}/_{2} \times 6^{1}/_{8}$.

Courtesy Historical Society of the Cocalico Valley.

FARM HOME, 1961
Anonymous. *Oil on canvas.*
Mifflin County, Pennsylvania. 20 × 18.

Private collection.

Your palm may be heavier than you think. If a strap or switch is used, make sure it is not too light to be effective, nor too heavy to be safe.

Do Not Use the Strap Unnecessarily. It definitely is not true that if one spanking will make a good boy, two will make him a better one. Used too frequently, the rod becomes a part of routine.

Do Not Spank a Baby before he is old enough to understand what it is all about. If an older child really needs a spanking, he will know what it is all about without being told.

Do Not Forget to Respect the Child. The child is an individual. A child should feel respect for his parents, not fear. There have been cases where children have cringed at the slightest word of command from their parents. This is neither desirable nor Christian.

Finally, the spanking is for the child's benefit, not your own. Discharge any excess steam elsewhere, where it will do no one any harm.

Source: Stoll (1967): 36

➤➤➤-➤➤➤-➤➤➤-➤➤➤-➤➤➤-➤➤➤-➤➤➤-➤➤➤

What about Corporal Punishment?

URIA R. BYLER

As one who helped to raise a family, I have found one of life's most tasteless tasks is to spank your child. However hard that may be, it is much more so if you punish someone else's child, and I don't believe the teacher lives who does not dread that thankless task. It should be used only as a last resort, after all other methods have been tried and have failed.

The teachers in the Amish schools are very fortunate that they have the right to apply the rod if necessary. The parents usually do not resent this, and the great majority will cooperate with the teacher. The few that do not, and who look unkindly on such practices if their children are involved, are only doing harm to themselves, and to their children, besides making it miserable for the teacher.

We have heard it said quite often by teachers that a child's home life, or environment, is mirrored by his actions at school. Very true. A teacher does not have to be a wizard or a magician to figure it out. Here is a never-failing test to decide whether little Johnny is under proper discipline at home, . . . watch his reactions when he gets punished, however lightly, for breaking school rules.

We'll say Johnny decides to do his spelling the easy way, and cheats. Due punishment is administered. If he is the friendly little chap as before, then it is a good guess that he is used to behaving at home, and to being punished if he is not. But if he pouts for a few days, then you may be quite sure that he does not like to be under any authority, simply because it's something new to him, and that he probably has his own way at home.

It is conceded by many noted educators in public schools that a great thing was lost when they took the rod away from the teachers.

Source: Byler (1963b)

-->>>-->>>-->>>-->>>-->>>-->>>-->>>-->>>-

Hot Rod Buggy Races

THE GOSHEN NEWS

Decades ago, as in modern times, there were occasional newspaper reports of rebellious and rowdy behavior among Amish young people. That there are more incidents now than there were fifty years ago seems doubtful. However, one thing is certain. There are more Amish people today than ever in their history and their communities are larger than in years past. Although outbursts of defiant behavior are an embarrassment to leaders and parents, they respect the right of the young to accept voluntarily the vow of baptism.

A group of Amish youths defied the rules of their strict religious sect today with plans to stage a "hot rod" buggy race.

From 15 to 20 teen-agers clad in the somber buttonless suits of their denomination will race stripped-down buggies at the Elkhart County Fair Saturday for a $350 purse.

To the 500 local members of the stern German sect, that $350 purse means gambling—a thing forbidden to church members.

But the youths said they thought it was time someone broke away from the strict code of the Amish.

"We'll cope with the consequences later," one said.

Goshen residents were surprised at the announcement. Several, however, said they had been expecting something like this to happen.

"These kids are breaking away more and more from the old ways," one said. "We call them 'pinkies' or 'yanked-over Amish.'"

Amish boys living on farms around Goshen have been racing their stripped-down, high-wheeled buggies on back roads for a long time. But this is the first time they have ever raced in public—much less for money.

Harness races have been held at the county fair for 30 years, but officials thought they would have to be discontinued this year because of lack of attendance.

Source: The Goshen News (August 24, 1951)

-->>>-->>>-->>>-->>>-->>>-->>>-->>>-->>>

Courtship: The Bartmann

CLYDE SMITH

A*mish young people meet one another not only at Sunday evening hymn singings but also at weddings, work bees, and frolics. They may intermarry among church communities of the same faith. Clyde Smith wrote this essay during the early part of this century.*

Sol Yoder, junior, when he attained to full manhood, was confronted with the rule of this Church which forbade the shaving of the chin. He had been shaving his upper lip for a time, but this was in conformity with the rules. He had almost unconsciously become a "Bartmann," a name won for his people by reason of the practice of permitting the beard to grow. He, too, came to be filled with the thought that it was time for him to be casting about for a mate. He had contracted some affinities at school. He was in duty bound to seek among his own people.

The trouble was that he had always more than one, so that his chief difficulty was in contriving how best to get rid of "t'other dear charmer."

115

There were two even in the meeting house, where the separation of the sexes was visibly carried out. The women set on one side, and the men on the other. . . .

Where there are several wills there may be several ways, and some confusion may follow. Young Sol had his heartstrings played upon by different players. He seemed, too, to have a new devil in the form of a green-eyed monster to fight within, when he saw his rival flirting with one of his girls. Such things made him conclude that he ought to have one whom he could call his own, and one who would not flirt with others. Here he was faced by a serious problem, for he himself must make a choice. This was the puzzle. One had good looks, a good disposition, but little dowry. The other had dowry but few other attractions. . . .

He was invited to a taffy-pull and sugaring off at Herr Rupp's maple bush. He anticipated that only the young people would be there, and this proved to be correct. Sol arrived in the early evening at the camp, and Katrina was among the number, nor was any rival there to excite his jealousy. Everything was propitious. Two big black iron kettles swung by a chain from a cross pole stretched between two trees, and contained the material of the coming sweets. The fire which blazed and crackled was built between two protecting logs, while the sap within the kettles boiled and blubbered. . . .

There was a novelty in it all, a change in the monotony of their lives, which lent a charm to the campfire and made for animation and sociability as they watched the sparks fly upwards and expire among the still leafless treetops. Nature was awakening from the slumbers of the long winter. The vivifying sap was now coursing through the fiber of the tree trunks, as did the blood through these young people. The flickering light added a charm to the faces around the campfire. "Soft eyes met eyes which spake again."

Work alternated with play. Sol would swing his axe and cut up some of the heap of brushwood with which a moderate fire was now kept burning under the kettles. Then sportively he would snatch a brand from the fire and run into the darkness brandishing it fantastically, or perhaps he would write in the air with this pen of fire the letters "Katy," and then come back to see how she enjoyed it. She stood by the kettle with a beech twig, the tip of which was twisted into a circular loop in order to make the following test. She quickly plunged the twig into the boiling fluid, then raised it to her mouth and blew through the loop; if it blew a bubble, it was ready for sugaring off. Another test was to take out some of the contents with a ladle and pour the same on a cake of ice, when the most delicious taffy was formed, and of which all would partake. This was indeed the nectar and ambrosia of the sugar camp. Perhaps Katrina would mischievously touch Sol's cheek with the hot beech twig, thereby giving Sol an excuse for catching her by the wrists and having a playful scuffle with her. Someone had to keep it from burning.

Presently the twig test revealed the fact that it was now sugar. The kettle was hurriedly taken off the fire and set on the ground, but the stirring process was kept up till it was ladled out into dishes and molds as the finished product. The task ended, Sol accompanied Katrina to her home. As they reached the clearing, the stars never before seemed so bright and sparkling. The great handle of the dipper had swung away up in the northern sky in its circling flight around Polaris. The other familiar constellations had also changed places, for it was now far on towards morning. The old world had swung itself round to the eastward while they were in the sugar bush. The distant sound of rushing waters broke the stillness of the night, for in the breaking up of winter the creeks were full to overflowing, and their waters were hurrying to the great lakes. A slight frost had formed a kindly yielding blanket over the muddy places. The swish of Katrina's gown, the kindly pressure of her arm on his, and the pleasant converse made them both feel that "two is company." All too soon the house was reached, and after an affecting parting Sol began his lonely walk to his home. Even the stars seemed to have come down nearer to him. The glow of the campfire and of Katy's face haunted him in his dreams.

Source: Clyde Smith (1912): 79 82

-≫>-≫>-≫>-≫>-≫>-≫>-≫>-≫>

Marriage

JOHN NAFZIGER

T*his 1781 description of the marriage ceremony is from a bishop's manual written by John (known as Hans) Nafziger (b. 1706). Amish marriage ceremonies still follow this basic pattern, which includes the retelling of the marriage of Tobias and Sara in the Apocrypha.*

As to the procedure of marriage, first, no one is permitted to marry an unbeliever, but is required to marry a member of the church who has accepted the Christian faith and been baptized. Nor may it be one who is guilty of sin or has been set back or expelled from the church.

A person who desires to marry is first to call on the Lord for wisdom, then to take counsel with his parents, and when possible also with the ministers or elders. Then a deacon is to conduct his suit for him. If, however, no deacon is to be had, another minister may act in his capacity and bring the reply according to the example of Eliezer, the servant of Abraham. If a ceremony is finally to be performed, a bishop inquires of the deacon whether the matter has been conducted in proper order and whether there are any objections.

Then both persons are asked by the bishop in council whether it is their desire with the help of the Lord to enter into the state of matrimony, whether there is any hindrance of any sort, or whether they have fallen into sin, and whether they have diligently sought the will of the Lord. If there are no obstacles and they continue to desire marriage then our articles of faith are read to them briefly. If they confess the same and continue in their intention, they are told that we allow no divorce except for adultery, and that they should well consider while they still have the freedom of choice.

When they appear for the ceremony, Matthew 19 is read as far as it deals with marriage. Then I Corinthians 7 and Ephesians 5 from the 9th verse to the end are read and expounded. Then the minister says: Since as concerns the matter of marriage we find little more in the New Testament, we shall turn to the Old Testament.

So we read of Abraham, the father of the faithful, how he said to the oldest servant in his household: Thou shalt not take for my son a wife from among the daughters of the Canaanites, in whose land ye live, but shaltst go to my native land to my relatives and take a wife for him there. How his master took his oath, and how he prayed, and how the Lord brought it to pass that Rebecca became the wife of his son.

Then we tell how the old and pious Tobias of the tribe and city of Naphtali taught his son from youth up to fear God and give alms. He did not go to the golden calves but to the temple of the Lord in Jerusalem, and prayed there to the God of Israel. He also did not defile himself with the meat of the heathen. His father sent him to seek a faithful man, and he found a good young man and brought him to his father, who greeted him and comforted him in his blindness. Raphael the angel accompanied the young man and told him to clean the fish but retain the heart, the gall, and the liver. Tobias asked his companion the value of these things, and also asked him where they should stay, and he answered: There is a man here by the name of Raguel, dear friend, who has a daughter Sara and no other child, to whom all his property belongs, and his daughter is to be your wife, so court her.

Now Tobias was fearful because her seven prior suitors had all died. They had been strangled by the devil Asmodi. Whereupon the angel said: Listen to what I tell you and I will show you over whom the devil has power, namely over those who enter upon marriage without respecting God in their hearts, but rather follow the desire of the body like the mule and the horse, who know nothing else—over such the devil has power. When you take her to wife, withhold yourself for three days. But on the first night broil the fish over a fire and you will drive the devil away. On the second night you will be admitted into the company of the patriarchs. On the third night you will receive the blessing of God to be enabled to have healthy children. So they stopped with Raguel and he received them with great joy.

After these words the two applicants for marriage are asked to come forward. Then the minister says: Here are two persons who desire with the help of the Lord to enter upon the state of matrimony. If anyone is present who has anything against the marriage, speak up. Then the minister remains quiet a time. If no one speaks he says: We trust there is no one. Then he says to the man: Can you confess that through prayer it has been revealed to you that this sister is to be given to you in marriage? Answer, yes. And it is your intention to be true to her and not forsake her, and not to separate from her until death separate you? Answer, yes. Then the woman is asked the same.

The story of Tobias is further told, how Raguel [the bride's father] was frightened for he had dug the graves of seven previous suitors of his daughter Sara. He stood hesitating. But an angel assured him that Tobias was a God-fearing man and his daughter shall have no other. Then the story continues, how Sara [the bride] prepares a room where she goes and weeps. She is comforted by her father, who did as the angel said and broiled a piece of fish liver in the fire, for, as promised, the angel now takes the devil captive and binds him in the wilderness of upper Egypt.

For three nights Tobias and Sara called upon God for mercy and reconciliation, thereby rejecting the conduct of a heathen marriage. Tobias prayed for the protection of his bride. Sara responded by saying: Have mercy on us, O Lord, have mercy, that we may both attain a good old age in peace and good health.

Source: Harold S. Bender (1930): 143–45

The Ambrosial Feast

ANN HARK

nn Hark (1891–1971), a Moravian and a native of Lancaster, Pennsylvania, was a reporter and writer on Pennsylvania German themes. This firsthand account of an Amish wedding is one of the best there is.

The bishop's monologue continued for an hour and a half. And then at last a sudden stir swept through the rooms. The bride and groom had risen. They were standing now before the bishop, silent, ill at ease, their heads bowed low, their eyes fixed straight ahead. The bishop put three questions to each one. With lips that barely moved they answered, and the syllables they uttered were inaudible three feet away. He spoke again with slow and solemn emphasis. I couldn't understand the words, but there could be no doubt about their meaning. It was the Amish version of the old, old promise: "For better, for worse, for richer, for poorer," and it had a specially solemn implication here. For with the Amish there is no divorce. Once married, it's quite literally "till death us do part." No wonder, I thought silently, that Rachel's pretty pointed face beneath the crisp, black prayer cap looked so grave and pale.

A prayer came next, with the entire congregation kneeling on the floor and facing toward the back. Still facing thus, they stood up while the bishop said his final words, then turned around and joined in singing a slow-moving hymn. And now at last the wedding service was completed.

Immediately the rooms became a seething hubbub of brisk motion. The younger men streamed toward the open, followed by the vast majority of older ones as well. A few, however, stayed behind to move the benches and prepare for the next part of the festivities—the midday wedding dinner. With rough-and-ready bustle, windows were thrown wide and bearded members of the Yoder Freindschaft started laying tables, with long benches placed on either side. Unceremoniously they pushed aside all stragglers, and it wasn't long before the rooms which just a short time previously resembled a huge meeting house had suddenly become a mammoth dining hall.

120

One long unbroken table ran the full length of the sitting room, then turned abruptly at right angles and continued through the doorway to the room beyond. This, it developed, was the table where the bride and groom and all the single boys and girls would sit—a trifling sixty couples, I discovered later. Still other tables were set up in the remaining rooms, while everywhere the clash of cutlery and china filled the air with a cheerful noise.

Meanwhile, inside the washshed, from which certain nostril-tickling odors had been drifting steadily throughout the wedding service, there was frantic animation. Mrs. Yoder, Mrs. Esch, and various female helpers rushed about in feverish activity, with certain masculine assistants in the role of waiters shuttling back and forth between the tables and the shed. Weddings, it seemed, were one time when the menfolk didn't let the women carry the full burden of the kitchen labors.

I joined the ranks of those inactive guests who lined the kitchen walls, waiting and watching hungrily for the ambrosial feast to come. And what a feast it certainly turned out to be! Just fourteen of us sat down at the table in the kitchen—two Church Amish couples and four Mennonites among the rest—but there was food enough for twenty times that number. A long, silent grace, with every head bowed reverently, came first and then the battle of the knives and forks began!

Roast duck, with separate plates of stuffing, was the central dish, surrounded by a varied and plethoric menu that included mashed potatoes and stewed celery, cabbage slaw and applesauce, pineapple jelly and pear butter, apricot and cherry pie, all sorts of cookies, cakes, and doughnuts in profusion, tapioca pudding, and of course the usual coffee, bread, and butter as the final touch. Main dishes, entrees, and desserts were placed upon the table all together, and each person helped himself according to his individual taste, while busy servers hovered in the offing, filling emptied plates and urging everyone to greater effort. And when at last each valiant trencherman had done his best, and finally reluctantly admitted his defeat, a second silent grace was said, the table was vacated, and another group sat down to take its turn at the replenished board.

Within the sitting room next door, meanwhile, the long, right-angle table where the young folks sat had taken on an air of carefree fun and relaxation. To the Amish, weddings are the one occasion when the young quite frankly occupy the center stage. Their table, with the bride and bridegroom seated at the outer corner of the angle—a location designated simply as The Corner, I discovered—was the focal point of everyone's attention, and the youngsters were enjoying it immensely. Talking, laughing, eating, with hardly a pause for breath, they were living for the moment in a world all theirs, encouraged and approved of by their beaming elders. . . .

I took my turn with others at inspecting Rachel's presents, after spending several minutes getting to the second floor. For the only stairway leading upward was a shifting mass of girls and boys and women and small children rushing up and down without cessation. Time and patience both were needed to make any progress either way. I got there finally, however, and with others grouped about the bed admired the display of gifts. . . . The beds in every room, it seemed, were filled with babies, some asleep and some awake and all attended by young white-capped mothers patting them mechanically as they gossiped with the other girls and women in the room. . . .

Once more the tables were piled high with food and for the second time the guests assembled for a hearty meal. Raw celery, apples, pickled canta-loupe, potato chips, a chocolate cake, and a black walnut cake were added to the menu at our special board, with custard pie replacing the two other kinds that had been served before. But at the young folks' table there were other dishes, too.

First, though, Mrs. Yoder told me, all the boys and girls had gathered in the upstairs rooms, where each young man had picked his special partner for this portion of the celebration. Hand in hand, the couples then streamed down to take their places at the table, where all sorts of extra treats, including several of the masterpieces from the cellar, were set down before them. And when finally young appetites had once again been sated, suddenly the strains of an old German hymn rose slowly on the overheated air. . . .

The solemn-sounding concert went on endlessly. But finally the young folks rose once more and went outside to play their games and have a little rough but harmless fun. . . .

Mrs. Yoder told me, "I guess you ain't seen anything like *this* before!" She turned to me with patent pride and pleasure showing on her round flushed face.

I hadn't, certainly. The scene was one I'll probably remember to my dying day. Outside the early dusk had fallen, but the rooms inside were brilliantly illuminated by the light from heavy lanterns, fed by gasoline, suspended from the ceiling. Underneath them, like a picture taken from another world, the snowy headgear of the smiling girls, the square, rough haircuts of their callow-visaged partners, the flowing beards and richly colored dresses of the men and women gathering now behind them—all combined in an effect of unreality that left me silent and engrossed.

Source: Hark (1952): 124–30

Amish Wills

GRANT M. STOLTZFUS

This account of Amish wills is from Grant M. Stoltzfus's historical study of the first Amish-Mennonite communities in Berks County, Pennsylvania. Amish wills not only specify the disposition of property but also the explicit social obligations of the kinship.

Amish wills reveal a uniform concern for the welfare of the widow. An examination of John Kurtz's will of 1796 reveals a few additional customary practices of the Amish in Berks County during the eighteenth century. After specifying that his widow should receive ten bushels of "good wheat," and three bushels of "good rye," and three bushels of buckwheat, Kurtz ordered that the grain be taken to the mill "from time to time" and that the meal and bran is to be returned to his widow's dwelling. Fifty pounds of beef and as many hens or fowl or eggs as she needs were to be provided and firewood was to be delivered to her dwelling. The twenty pounds of hatched flax and five pounds of "good" wool were doubtless included to provide the widow with what she needed to make her clothing.

The will designated, too, that she receive one gallon of rum, two gallons of whiskey, and if the apple crop was sufficient she was due to receive two barrels "good cyder." Six pounds of tallow were due her for candles. Her own preference for garden space was to be respected and it was understood that this garden plot was to receive dung as it required. The widow's need for transportation was not overlooked, for she was to have a horse with saddle and bridle "when she will ride out." A cow was to be kept in "good provender" during both winter and summer. This Amishman looked forward to the day when his widow could no longer milk the cow and make the butter. In that case she was to be given "so much good milk and butter as she has need of." Finally as the widow grew "infirm or sick" the children were to "give and find her good attendance."

. Bequests to the children were not nearly as detailed. Jacob Beiler's will gave 30 pounds to each of his ten children in 1765. In Christian Beiler's will of 1804 each of his children was to receive a Bible. . . .

Jacob Mast in 1808 in the Conestoga Valley began his will by specifying that "the house in which we dwell shall be kept in order for my dear and beloved wife." John Kurtz in his will of 1796 provided a place in Tulpehocken Valley for his widow, for she was

> to have the liberty to live in the small room and the use of the kitchen which is inside of it in the house I now live in, so much room in the cellar and on the garret to put her things as she has occasion for and where she pleases, the use of the bake oven with free egress, ingress and regress.

In 1804 Christian Beiler in Lancaster County provided a place for his widow Anna by saying,

> it is my will that my son Jacob Beiler shall build a little house for his mother to live in and by so doing I bequeath to him fifty pounds in gold or silver, but if my son Jacob should refuse to keep his mother and build a house for her, then it is my will that one of my other sons may have her upon the same conditions.

But a house for the widow was not enough. She was also provided furniture in many instances. John Kurtz in the will already referred to also ordered that his widow should have two beds with bedsteads and "whatsoever thereunto belonging," and two chests. Jacob Mast of the Conestoga Valley requested that his widow have the right to keep the beds, chest, and kitchen furniture as she wants.

However, a place to live and furniture for that place are not given as much space in Amish wills as are the detailed instructions about what the widow is entitled to for her sustenance and welfare. Jacob Beiler of the Northkill settlement, in 1765, after bequeathing to his widow "the old house and the stable near it," goes on to bequeath her

> the garden before the door and three cherry trees thereby and one piece of meadow . . . behind the old barn and the privilege of water thereto and one piece of land on the lower side of the lane where the hemp patch lies about an acre more or less. She may use it as she pleases . . . she has the right to two rows of trees in the orchard. These she may choose yearly and ten bushels of wheat and five rye and 20 bundles of straw and one quarter of flax the owner or tenant must give her yearly, but the flax must be on the same land where she has flax. Fourthly, she has the right to keep one or two cows in the field of meadow . . . she has also the right to keep one hog.

Source: Grant M. Stoltzfus (1954): 260–61

※→→→→→→→→→→→→→→→→→

A Will of 1771

JACOB BEILER

Jacob Beiler emigrated from Switzerland *in 1737. He lived in Berks County, Pennsylvania, was the father of ten children, and died in 1771.*

I Jacob Beiler dwelling in Bern Township in Berks County today the 19th day of July in the Year of our Lord Christ one thousand seven hundred and sixty five, in the Presence of the Subscribing Witnesses, make my Testament and it is my last Will as follows:

1. I bequeath to my Widow, which I leave behind me, a Widow Seat, to wit: The old House and the Stable near it and the Garden before the Door and three Cherry Trees thereby and one Piece of Meadow it is measured off behind the old Barn, and the Privilege of Water thereto and one Piece of Land on the lower side of the Lane where the Hemp Patch lies about an Acre more or less, she may use it as she pleases.

2. The owner or Tenant shall haul out the Dung for her and plow and harrow the land where she will have it and haul her first and second Crop Hay under Cover as also the Firewood, but she must make all herself.

3. She has the right to two Rows of Trees in the Orchard running upward in the Orchard, these she may choose yearly, and ten Bushels of Wheat and Five Rye and 20 Bundles of Straw and one half Quarter of Flax the Owner or Tenant must give her—but the Flax must be on the same Land where he has Flax.

4. She has the Right to keep one or two Cows in the Field or in the Meadow, to wit, where the Owner or Tenant has his Cows at Pasture, she has also a Right to keep one Hog. All these the above mentioned is bequeathed to my Widow, which I leave behind, Elizabeth Beiler, to enjoy as long as she remains a Widow but if she married again her Widow Seat is forfeited and hath no longer to enjoy or to demand of all these above mentioned.

5. I Jacob Beiler give to my Son Jacob Beiler a Right to clear 10 Acres of my land and to build a Dwelling House thereon and the Meadow where he has begun his Tanyard which he may enjoy with the 10 acres of Land till the

125

31 day of December 1772 and for these he must pay 10 shillings Rent yearly. At the End of the year 1772 his agreement is expired and has no further Right to dwell there or to enjoy ought, except what belongs to the Tanyard he may carry away and the Executors may appraise the Dwelling House at a reasonable price and pay him for it, but if he will not leave it at this Appraisement he may take it away also.

6. I Jacob Beiler choose and set my Friends and Neighbors, Christian Joder and Jacob Kaufman, as also my Wife Elizabeth Beiler to be Executors over all my Estate and give them Right and Power over my Real and Personal Estate to receive and to pay, to buy and to sell, to make over or assign under my Name be it Deed—Notes or Bonds.

7. All my Estate which I leave behind shall be sold or struck off Public Vendue when and as the Executors shall find good except one Cow and her Bed she may first take and the loom and Gears thereto belonging is bequeathed to my Son David Beiler.

8. I bequeath to my Widow which I leave behind the third part of the Personal Estate and then the two other parts of the Personal Estate must be reckoned with the place and Buildings and what is fastened with the Nails and be divided among my 10 children in ten parts without respect of Persons, to one as to the other.

9. The Payments to my Children which I leave behind me shall be made thus—One Year after my Death the Executors shall begin to pay and shall pay my Daughter Barbara the Eldest Child and give her 30 Pounds and then according to age——youngest——personal Estate Extends and if the personal Estate does not reach so far as to the youngest Child for each to receive 30 Pounds, then they must wait 'till the Executors have Money from the Place. When Each has received 30 Pounds, namely, Barbara 30 Pounds.

Afterwards Anny 30 Pounds
And afterwards my Son Christian Beiler 30 Pounds
And afterwards my Daughter Maria 30 Pounds
And afterwards my Daughter Elizabeth 30 Pounds
And afterwards my Son Jacob Beiler 30 Pounds
And afterwards my Son John Beiler 30 Pounds
And afterwards my Daughter Sara 30 Pounds
And afterwards my Son Joseph Beiler 30 Pounds
And afterwards my Son David Beiler 30 Pounds

10. When each has received thirty Pounds as is here mentioned then the Executors begin with the eldest and being guided by the Payments they shall receive from the Place and pay yearly two or three Children which they shall find good, 'till all is paid. But as some of the Children have received

something and some Nothing, the first thirty Pounds Payments shall be paid on their Accounts.

All the above mentioned Articles the Executors shall certainly truly and well administer and pay to my Heirs and if any Controversy shall happen between my Heirs, the Executors shall decide between them in my Home.

And if any Difference shall happen between you Executors, then shall ye choose two Men on each Part and let them decide between you and thereby ye shall abide.

All these above mentioned Articles we acknowledge and declare I Jacob Beiler and Elizabeth Beiler in good Understanding for our Testament and Last Will with our Hands and Seals.

Source: The Diary (April 1974): 94–95

>>>-->>>-->>>-->>>-->>>-->>>-->>>-->>>

Amish Funerals

JAMES L. MORRIS

James L. Morris was a storekeeper in Morgantown, Pennsylvania. His diary contains many observations about the Amish people in his community, including their deaths and funerals.

The burial of Christian Hertzler at 10 a.m. [September 18, 1842] was very numerously attended. As usual with the Germans, more especially a general and pressing invitation was given out for all to stay and done. The number that sat down to dinner is differently estimated from 150 to 200. The preparations for this meal had been immense. Two whole quarters of beef had been provided, some 30-odd fowl and other things in proportion.

The funeral of Mrs. David Mast [February 11, 1845] was fully attended today. Upwards of one hundred sleighs were there. A general invitation was given to the company to take dinner, which it was reported was plentifully provided for. Orders had been given to have a barrel of flour baked up into bread so that there should be no lack. Other eatables were no doubt provided on the same large scale.

Mary Mast's funeral [August 6, 1845] took place today and was numerously attended. The Homish came in great numbers from a distance. She was about 81 or 82 years old and has resided at the same place now occupied by her son Daniel, 56 years.

Source: Grant M. Stoltzfus (1954): 255

-≫≫-≫≫-≫≫-≫≫-≫≫-≫≫-≫≫-≫≫-

The Funeral of Bishop Mast

THE READING EAGLE

More than 1,500 persons attended the funeral of Bishop John P. Mast, June 14, 1888. All roads in lower Berks led to the Mast homestead, near Morgantown. The mourners came from Robeson, Cumru, Brecknock and Caernarvon in Berks County. Hundreds of others came from Lancaster, Lebanon, Chester and Montgomery Counties. More than 350 carriages came to the farm and more than half of these joined the long funeral procession that plodded its way to the grave. A great man had gone to his reward.

The square-rigged buggies began to arrive at daybreak. Young Amishmen served as hostlers. The first act was to chalk a number upon the horse's bridle and to hand the owner of the team a ticket bearing the same number. Horses were all unhitched and fed by these efficient farm lads, and in spite of over-crowded conditions in the barn and adjoining buildings there was not a single instance of neglect or mismanagement. An eyewitness, reporting the funeral, records that these boys "were courteous and gentlemanly, spoke good English and possessed the rare accomplishment of being able to look a man squarely in the face."

The scene in the funeral home resembled a Biblical picture of a gathering of the patriarchs. The women removed their black bonnets and revealed their little white "devotion caps" of swiss cambric. A black kerchief was worn draped over their shoulders and a black apron covered the dress. Quietly they sat in reverence. The appearance of the children differed from the elders only in size and buoyancy. They were dressed as the old folks were, only the boys were beardless. The older men sat on chairs near to the officiating clergy.

Their long snow-white beards covering their "brust-lappen" and their visages cast in the form of the saints of Old Testament Days.

Once the funeral cortege was on its way to the burial plot in Caernarvon hundreds of busy hands began to prepare the meal which always must follow the funeral. All of the first floor rooms of the farmhouse, adjoining porches and summer kitchens and barn floors were converted into dining rooms to accommodate the 2,000 persons who came to partake of the repast.

The custom of feasting at funerals may appear to be barbarous to persons who do not remember the era when that procedure was the accepted order of ceremony. It should be remembered that the mourners came from great distances in carriages which could not travel faster than three or four miles an hour. Refreshments were a vital necessity in those days. The quantities of food consumed at the Mast funeral will serve to show how life was sustained for the weary travelers in those days.

There were 300 pounds of choice beef, 35 large loaves of bread and 900 rusks and buns. There were hundreds of pies and cakes, two boxes of cream cheese, gallons upon gallons of coffee and high heaps of fruit and vegetables.

The diners were seated at the tables in shirts. The number that could be seated at one time at the barn floor table was 40 Young Amish girls hurried from kitchens to the various improvised dining places, keeping hot dishes filled and waiting upon the needs of the many guests. Long before sunset the mourners were on their homeward way. Bishop Mast had had a fine funeral and everyone agreed that he had been a model. "Peace to his ashes."

Source: "Funeral of Bishop John B. Mast" (1941)

8

AMISH
SCHOOLS

A half century ago when one-room schoolhouses still dotted the countryside, all Amish children attended public schools. When wholesale consolidation of schools occurred (from about 1937 to 1954), the Amish built their own small country schools and staffed them with their own teachers. The Amish sensed that, if their children attended large schools, away from an agricultural environment, and were taught by teachers they did not know, their communities would erode.

All Amish children attend elementary school through grade eight. Most pupils walk to school. The Amish are opposed to accepting government subsidies for any type of school support. Each school is administered by a school board, and attendance records are carefully kept for state inspection. The school is funded by the patrons and by the church. School buildings are heated with coal or wood. The schools are built to maximize the use of natural lighting.

Amish elementary schools support the values taught in the family. The school helps the child to become a part of his or her community and to remain within it. The school emphasizes shared knowledge and the dignity of tradition rather than change. The Amish stress accuracy rather than speed, drill rather than variety, and proper sequence rather than freedom of choice. The curriculum as well as the mottoes on the interior walls stress honesty, thrift, purity, love, and cooperation, but without a heavy religious vocabulary. A well-run school has the atmosphere of a well-ordered family. The older children help the younger, and the pupils encourage one another's good performance so that the whole class or school may do well.

Although Amish children do not study religion in the classroom, they learn a great deal about living their religion. Parents teach their own children within the family but do not teach religion to the children of other families. Personal relationships between teacher and pupil, as well as memorization and recitation, are considered necessary preparation for life now and for eternity. True education, according to the Amish, is the cultivation of humility, simple living, and resignation to the will of God. Like their forefathers, they fear "worldly" philosophy, which stresses self-exaltation, pride of position, enjoyment of power, and the arts of war and violence.

Uria R. Byler, a promoter of the Amish school movement in Ohio, explains in the first two selections how Amish schools originated in that state.

→≫-→≫-→≫-→≫-→≫-→≫-→≫-→≫-

The Need for Amish Schools

URIA R. BYLER

Years ago the countryside was studded with one-room schools in which the three R's were emphasized, minus the modern embellishments of TV and radio. The progressive educational theories of John Dewey were still in their infancy.

In a silent way all this was changed. The country schools were closed one by one. Consolidation, under the label of more "efficient" instruction methods, became the rule. Local districts almost fell over each other to join forces under the state officials, who in turn were more or less pushed by the rich and powerful education lobbies.

This consolidation trend brought other problems in its wake: long bus trips to and from school, gym classes, and more homework. Many Amish parents were finding it increasingly hard to go along with these developments. Here, then, was being created the necessity for a change.

Most social changes of this type come slowly, and the change to private schools was no exception. There was more talk about the problem than there was of a solution. The term "our own schools" was heard for years before any solid steps were taken to actually build some.

Plainly, the need for our own schools was there for anyone to see. The trend in education was toward television, evolution, sex teaching, and other modern worldly ideas in child instruction. These changes were certainly not conducive to the Amish way of life. . . . The obstacles seemed too great. Why?

Source: Byler (1969): 9

➤➤➤-➤➤➤-➤➤➤-➤➤➤-➤➤➤-➤➤➤-➤➤➤-➤➤➤

An Idea Is Planted

URIA R. BYLER

On Ascension Day I walked down for a visit with Bishop Dan A. Byler. It was a memorable afternoon, and one might say it gave me the first real incentive to work for our own Amish schools. That day a small seed was planted that years later had a big part in changing my entire life, and perhaps the lives of others also.

For close to thirty years, old Dan had been the bishop and leader of our church district. I had grown up under his sermons, had been baptized by him, and for most of our married life we had lived in his district.

I was shocked at old D.A.'s appearance. Not having seen him for some time, I was unprepared for the pale, sickly-looking man who was sitting on the porch when I got there. He invited me to take a chair beside him. It was quite evident that this revered old pillar of the church was in his last days on earth.

He asked how everything was at our place, and we talked as usual about the weather. "How are you feeling?" I asked him.

"Oh, not too bad. Just a little weak." But he ended that subject by looking at me intently, and saying, "You know, I've been wanting to have a talk with you for a long time, and had no chance. I'm glad you came today."

Now what did he have in mind? Why would Old Dan want to see me? This sounded unusual, for I felt unworthy to even sit there and visit with him. Perhaps he wanted to rebuke me for something or other.

"I hear you've been having some trouble in the Huntsburg school recently. Someone told me they are forcing the Amish children to attend picture shows. Is that right?"

"Yes, we've had quite a bit of trouble with that this last term," I admitted. "But they promised to change their policy on that, and said it wouldn't happen anymore."

Dan looked at me again, and for a moment said nothing. Then in a kind but firm voice, he poured out his thoughts. "Do you think it's right for us to tell them how to run their schools? The world won't stop with their big ideas on education just because of a few Amish. I won't be here to see it, but you might be, when there will be a big change in this public school business."

There was more to our talk that day, which need not be recorded. Old Dan was concerned about the next generation, and the evil influence that public schools might have on them. His idea was expressed that day in his low, rather weak voice.

"Let them have their schools," was his advice. "They have their reasons, with their kind of life, to go for the modern things. We shouldn't hinder them, or be a stumbling block."

Gradually I began to see what he had in mind. Then bluntly he asked me, "Did you ever think about it, that we could build our own schools?"

I admitted I really hadn't. In my mind, up until that moment, I considered such an idea very far-fetched, a near-impossibility. Our own teachers? Our own schools? All those expenses? No, it seemed out of the question, until—until now, coming from old Dan.

He must have read my mind somewhat. Yes, it would cost money and a lot of effort, but money ought to be the least of our worries. He was sure if the people gave in the right spirit, the good Lord would give His blessing and grace, and no one would lose anything that wouldn't be replaced manifold in other ways.

Again, he hinted that he wouldn't be here much longer. "I'll not live to see it, Uria, but I hope some of you younger parents will think this over and get busy, the sooner the better."

I promised the old bishop that we would certainly consider his wishes, and see what could be done. Coming from him, it must be a good idea. Dan had always been known to be a very rational man, and not given to unreasonable ideas. Certainly, this suggestion of his to have our own schools was not something that had come to him overnight. He had thought it over in his mind, and weighed the matter well, long before today. I was sure his advice on this subject must be good.

Source: Byler (1985): 220–23

Children Taken into Custody

DAVID LUTHY

The Bing Act, which was passed by the Ohio General Assembly in 1921, required all children to attend certified schools until the age of eighteen. If granted a work permit, they could be excused at sixteen. The Amish were upset with the new law. They wanted their children to learn reading, writing, and arithmetic and to become Amish farmers. Some parents told their children not to study certain subjects.

The year 1922 had barely begun when five Amishmen were arrested for violating the state's educational laws. They were brought before Judge Charles A. Estill of the Juvenile Court of Holmes County in January. The fathers were Preacher Moses M. Shetler, Bishop Samuel E. Miller, Joseph P. Hershberger, John E. Weaver, and Eli P. Miller.

The court record reveals that an affidavit was issued on January 4th for the arrests and that the men appeared in court on January 9th. Then on the 12th of the same month [their] children were declared wards of the court. Following is the actual transcription from the court record pertaining to one of the children, Mary Weaver:

Juvenile Court, Holmes County, Ohio
In the matter of   No. 65   Jan. 12, 1922
Mary Weaver, Dependent Child
Commitment for Temporary Care

This day Mary Weaver was brought before the court accompanied by Chas. D. Everhart, Attendance Officer for Holmes County, with being a dependent child and the court having instituted an investigation and having heard all the evidence finds that the law has been duly complied with in this case. That the said child was born on or about March 6, 1910 in Saltcreek Township, Holmes County, Ohio. That name, residence, nationality, and occupation of each parent is as follows. Father, John E. Weaver; Residence, Saltcreek Township, Holmes County, 0.; nationality Ohio; occupation farming.

That the said child is dependent in that said parents neglect and refuse to permit her to study in school the subjects of History, Geography, Hygiene as provided by laws of Ohio, and therefore comes into the jurisdiction of its Court, being in all respects within the provisions of the law concerning delinquent, dependent, and neglected children.

The Court further finds that it is for the best interests of said child that its father John E. Weaver be deprived of its care and custody temporarily for the reason that he refuses, neglects, fails, and prohibits said child from said subjects as provided by the laws of Ohio. The Court therefore orders that said child be committed to the temporary care and custody of the Painter Children's Home of Holmes County, Ohio, it appearing that said child is a suitable person to be so committed. The Court finding further that the said John E. Weaver father residing in Salt Creek Township this County is able to contribute toward the support of said child orders that said John E. Weaver pay to the said Painter Children's Home the sum of $ per month forward after the 12 day of January 1922. The first payment to be made Feb. 1, 1922 and 1st of each month thereafter.

It is further ordered that a warrant issue to Robert Henderson, Sheriff, to convey and deliver said Mary Weaver to said Painter Children's Home of Holmes County, Ohio, and due notice thereof be made to this Court

Chas. A. Estill, Judge

So, the Amish children were declared wards of the court, were seized, and taken to the Painter Children's Home. What a terrible feeling that must have given the parents. Their children were actually taken away from them and confined in a children's home. And to make the experience even more painful the authorities at the institution cut the boys' hair short, braided the girls' hair in pigtails, and dressed the children in town clothing, setting aside their Amish garb.

It did not take the parents very long to weigh the situation in their minds. Which was worse, having their children study history, geography, and hygiene at school, or see them confined in the children's home? Obviously the latter. A little more than two weeks went by before the parents were able to obtain their children's freedom. First of all they had to appear before the court and pledge their co-operation in the education of their children. Then they had to pay their fines.

Source: Luthy (1986): 513–14

━━━━━━━━━━━━━━━━━━━━━━━━━━━━━━━━━━━━

->>>->>>->>>->>>->>>->>>->>>->>>-

To Our Men of Authority

D*irected to the state authorities of Pennsylvania, this statement was drafted as a last resort, after a series of unsuccessful attempts to seek exemption from "oppressive" school laws. It identifies the unacceptable conditions associated with schooling. This collective statement by Old Order Mennonites and Old Order Amish served to unite both groups against the encroachment of school consolidation.*

The new Pennsylvania School Act of 1937, No. 478, as we are informed, requires compulsory school attendance to the age of fifteen years, before the children are exempt for farm and domestic work.

And in 1939 a 180-day school term is required, and in 1940 pupils must go to high school if they get through the elementary grades before they are fifteen years of age.

We, the Old Order Amish Mennonites, and the Old Order Mennonites, believe that this is abridging the freedom of religion, and of bringing our children up as we understand the Bible, and will lead our children away from the faith and undermine our churches. We believe it also detrimental to true religion and farm home work.

And we believe according to the amendments of the Constitution, that this act is unconstitutional, and is a severe grievance to us. Therefore we believe we are not obliged to abide by it.

Since we have tried to get redress for our grievances in every way we know, and got no redress at all, therefore it seems the Christian church must do something themselves, if they want to build and maintain their churches.

So, we, the undersigned, a conscientious folk, pertaining to agriculture, Christian churches in the rural districts, do hereby inform our authorities, that we will agree to send our children to the public schools, in an elementary school, not consolidated or transported; a 160-day term, provided they are taught the Truth; and that when they get through the elementary grades, we require the privilege to withdraw our children from the public school, and further to bring them up with the help of the Lord, in the nurture and admonition of the Lord, and to educate them for farm home work.

We therefore petition our authorities, under these conditions, to suffer or endure us to live a Godly and quiet life in our homes in this commonwealth of Pennsylvania.

Source: "To Our Men in Authority" (1938)

≫≫≫≫≫≫≫≫

The Challenge before Us

JOHN M. BONTRAGER

The decision by the Amish to with-draw their children from the public school system and to finance and staff their own schools was not easy. Parents and leaders had to be convinced. John M. Bontrager, an Amish school advocate in Indiana, gives his reasons for the change.

This part of northern Indiana has passed a milestone. The public school corporation is wanting to build a modern school, costing over a million dollars. In their view, they are being forced by state legislation. The state is closing the five remaining one-room schools, and of course will approve nothing short of the most modern in buildings and facilities.

The cost is inconceivable to us, over $2,500 per pupil in building costs alone. We can build a one-room schoolhouse for thirty-five pupils for $3,000, if the labor is donated.

At least 50 percent of the pupils under the Westview School Corporation are Amish. Now, as we understand it, we can have our own schools if we wish. What, then, should be our course of action?

If we don't do something for ourselves, they will do it for us, and in as modern a way as we will tolerate. Are we going to stand idly by and be sucked down the stream of worldliness? Are we going to let our Amish way of life, our simple and Biblical standards, vanish in thin air before our eyes? The faith our forefathers brought across the waters and suffered untold hardships for—don't we want to preserve it for our children?

One of the greatest advantages of our own school system is to have our own qualified Christian teachers. Our children will be learning Christian morals in between lines while getting their secular education. What we see, what we hear, what we read, what we are surrounded by—all these things influence us. It is our duty as parents to see that our children are under a good influence. If we are united in our interests and efforts, we have a wonderful opportunity with our own schools.

Source: John M. Bontrager (1967): 74–75

꘏꘏꘏꘏꘏꘏꘏꘏꘏

What Is Wrong with Public Schools?

JOSEPH STOLL

T*he difference between secular and religious education is described by Joseph Stoll, the author of* Who Shall Educate Our Children?

The public schools present a secular view of life rather than a sacred view. State schools have always prepared the child for his life on earth, and were never intended to prepare him for eternity. For the world, education is training the mind for success in this life. For the Christian, education is training the child to live for others, to use his talents in service to God and man, to live an upright obedient life, and to prepare for the life to come.

Secular education places too high a value on earthly riches and attainments. The Bible says to seek first the kingdom of God and its righteousness. This the public schools understandably do not do.

C. C. Morrison, former editor of the *Christian Century*, said in an editorial, "Public education without religion creates a secular mentality faster than the church can Christianize it."

Public education, in the first place, was acceptable to the masses of this country only because educators promised that morality and religion would be upheld. For this reason, public schools in the past have started the day with a devotional period, and in other ways formally acknowledged God. In the last few years even this has been outlawed, thus removing the only crutch some Christians have long used to support their lame excuses.

It appears that in the future there will be less and less religion in public

138

schools, and if there is any at all, it will be taught as a subject, a method which is infinitely more harmful than no teaching at all.

Rather than loyalty to God, the pupil in our state schools is taught patriotism above all else. The Bible teaches that we should obey, respect, and pray for the "powers that be," but in some instances, we must obey God rather than men. The secular view is to kill the enemy and bomb his cities. The sacred view is "resist not evil," but "do good to them that hate you, and pray for them which despitefully use you, and persecute you." Which view do we want taught to our children?

Source: Stoll (1965): 28–29

-≫-≫-≫-≫-≫-≫-≫-≫

Showdown in Iowa

DONALD A. ERICKSON

hen the conflict over schooling broke out in Iowa, Donald A. Erickson wrote extensively about its various implications. He later served as an expert witness in the Supreme Court case Wisconsin v. Yoder et. al (1972).

The school bus left Oelwein, Iowa, for the Old Order Amish settlement a few miles southwest. Aboard were a superintendent of schools, a school nurse, and a driver, all intent on bringing some forty children to a public school, against the wishes of the Amish leaders. The Plain People had been violating the law, staffing their private schools with uncertified teachers. It was 7:45 a.m. on Friday, November 19, 1965.

With one exception . . . the delegation called at the homes of all the Amish who had been breaking the school code, occasionally stepping inside to talk. At each stop, Truant Officer Snively declared that he had come to take the children to the Hazelton school, under the authority of Iowa's truancy statute. Many of the parents, knowing what was planned, had hid their young in the fields ahead of time. . . . The group moved on from farm to farm, empty-handed. By the time instruction was scheduled to begin, the sheriff, deputy sheriff, and county attorney appeared on the scene, along with numerous fathers and mothers.

Entering the building, Snively explained that it was legally necessary to transport the pupils to the school in the town. He said he was their friend, wanting only to help them, and promised a warm welcome in Hazelton. Now, he said, would they be good children and quietly file into the bus behind Sheriff Fred Beier. The sheriff started slowly toward the bus, the boys and girls following in an orderly single file. Suddenly, when most of the youngsters were outside, either the teacher or one or the mothers shouted in German, "Run!" The pupils bolted for the field at the rear of the schoolyard, scrambled through the barbed-wire fence, and ran through the adjoining cornfield into the woods beyond. Some never stopped running until they reached their homes.

Source: Erickson (1969): 15, 16–17

→≫→≫→≫→≫→≫→≫→≫→≫

An Act of Self-Preservation

WILLIAM C. LINDHOLM

A Lutheran pastor in Michigan, *William C. Lindholm saw the suffering of Amish people, who in case after case lost their claim to religious freedom. He helped to organize the National Committee for Amish Religious Freedom in 1967 and is today its chairman. He explains the deeper significance of the conflict.*

The intransigence of the Old Order Amish toward sending their children to high school or employing non-Amish teachers has repeatedly provoked more dramatic controversy than any other problem in educational enforcement in the last 25 years. However, the United States Supreme Court has hopefully settled the long-standing struggle with its May 15, 1972 ruling that states may not constitutionally force the Amish to send their children to high school. . . .

The Amish resistance to mainstream education was simply an act of self-preservation, to avoid the devastating influence of the state's technology and secular values on their ethnic, religious, and social patterns. In short, the problem of Amish education is a clash between those who advocate the forced assimilation of minority cultures such as the Amish, and those who seek to maintain the identity and integrity of the cultural diversity in a pluralistic America; it is a clash between those who assert that the majority and the state bureaucrats should define approaches and values, and those who hold that progress and truth are best found when freedom and diversity prevail. Tied closely to this is the issue of the theoretical basis and the limits of a state's power to compel its citizens to get an education and conform to its values.

The Bible says, "I will destroy the wisdom of the wise . . . has not God made foolishness the wisdom of this world?" (I Cor. 1:21). From this source comes the Amish rejection of speculative philosophy and sophisticated reasoning, as well as their rejection of technology. The violent persecution of the well-educated authorities, who drowned them in sacks and buried their women alive, confirmed their suspicions of worldly learning and made them more determined to stress strict moral principles. Today they shun modern conveniences such as electricity, television, automobiles, and government subsidies and instead drive horses and buggies and wear plain clothing—ankle-length dresses, bonnets, and broad-brimmed hats. They believe in small, close-knit communities and consider farm-related living a religious command for life.

For at least a hundred years, the Amish remained in the public schools. They finally withdrew, not because they wanted religious instruction but because of rigid educational policies advancing a changing culture that was posing a threat to Amish identity and values. . . .

The prosecuting attorney wanted to choose the values for the Amish: as he told the U.S. Supreme Court, "What is needed is . . . more pride in intellect, not less." The Wisconsin Supreme Court had clearly seen the issue: "Secondary schools not only teach an unacceptable value system, but they seek to integrate ethnic groups into a homogenized society."

This writer has seen the tears of suffering in the eyes of these "plain people" and has been appalled at case after case of losing farms and suffering heavy fines, jailings, and the threatened loss of children, as well as at the unbelievable lack of understanding by good men—when their only crime was trying to raise their children by peaceful values that they have loved and revered.

We would like to think that our society has moved beyond systematic religious persecution. But we have not—we have only changed its form. Instead of assaulting Amishmen physically, we assault their souls. It is more sophisticated, somehow cleaner, than drowning them or burying them alive, but it is persecution nonetheless.

Source: Lindholm (1974): 488–89, 494–95

141

Wisconsin *v.* Yoder et al., *1972*

WARREN E. BURGER

W*arren E. Burger (1907–) was U.S. chief justice when* Wisconsin v. Yoder et al. *came before the Supreme Court. The issue was whether Amish schoolchildren who have completed the elementary grades and who have not reached their sixteenth birthday must attend high school. Chief Justice Burger wrote the opinion of the court. There were no dissenting votes.*

Whatever their idiosyncrasies as seen by the majority, this record strongly shows that the Amish community has been a highly successful social unit within our society even if apart from the conventional "mainstream." Its members are productive and very law-abiding members of society; they reject public welfare in any of its usual modern forms. . . .

We must not forget that in the Middle Ages important values of the civilization of the western world were preserved by members of religious orders who isolated themselves from all worldly influences against great obstacles. There can be no assumption that today's majority is "right" and the Amish and others like them are "wrong." A way of life that is odd or even erratic but interferes with no rights or interests of others is not to be condemned because it is different. . . .

The Amish alternative to formal secondary school education has enabled them to function effectively in their day-to-day life under self-imposed limitations on relations with the world, and to survive and prosper in contemporary society as a separate, sharply identifiable and highly self-sufficient community for more than two hundred years in this country. In itself this is strong evidence that they are capable of fulfilling the social and political responsibilities of citizenship without compelled attendance beyond the eighth grade at the price of jeopardizing their free exercise of religious belief. When Thomas Jefferson emphasized the need for education as a bulwark of a free people against tyranny, there is nothing to indicate he had in mind compulsory education through any fixed age beyond a basic education. . . .

Aided by a history of three centuries as an identifiable religious sect and a long history as a successful and self-sufficient segment of American society, the Amish in this case have convincingly demonstrated the sincerity of their religious beliefs, the interrelationship of belief with their mode of life, the vital role which belief and daily conduct play in the continued survival of Old Order Amish communities. . . .

For the reasons stated we hold, with the Supreme Court of Wisconsin, that the First and Fourteenth Amendments prevent the State from compelling respondents to cause their children to attend formal high school to age sixteen.

Source: Wisconsin vs. *Yoder et al.* (1972)

9

SCHOOL
MANAGEMENT

Amish young people look forward to leaving elementary school. They know that important work is awaiting them in the home and on the farm. A boy works on his father's farm until he is knowledgeable in all aspects of farm work. A girl learns how to manage the household. A boy or girl may work for another Amish family if their services are needed.

From adolescence to marriage, young people choose their own friends and usually find a "crowd" whose company they enjoy. They may sample the world and then must decide whether to join the Amish church and whom to marry. Some testing of the boundaries is expected, for each individual must discover what it means to be Amish.

Joining the Amish church generally takes place in the late teens or early twenties. Instruction in the faith is followed by baptism. Baptism signifies repentance, as well as commitment to the believing community and to its explicit discipline. The Amish stress voluntary commitment but, once an individual vows to become a member, there is no turning back. By breaking the vow of baptism, an individual invites excommunication and shunning.

-≫≫-≫≫-≫≫-≫≫-≫≫-≫≫-≫≫-≫≫

Speech and Silence Must Have Their Time

CHRISTOPHER DOCK

*A*lthough Christopher Dock, *"the pious schoolteacher of Skippack" who immigrated to America in 1714, preceded the Amish, his exemplary character and methods have influenced the Amish to this day. He died in 1771. He is best known for his* School Management *(published in 1770) and for his beautifully illuminated manuscripts* (Fraktur-Schriften), *some of which he gave to pupils as rewards for excellent work. See the plate entitled* Merit Award, c. 1760. *This selection stresses the importance of not only learning language but also exercising verbal restraint.*

It takes children a long time to learn to speak, and, once they do, they are loath to be restrained from it. It is impossible, among the children in school, to teach anything proper unless speech has its time, and silence also has its time. But this rule is very hard for the children to adjust to; and it seems that we adults ourselves have not yet completely learned this lesson—that speech and silence have their proper times. We ought often to regard our speaking and being silent. Nor does the small member, the tongue, let itself be easily tamed. One cannot discipline it with the rod, like other members of the body; and the transgressions that are committed with words are done by the tongue in accord with the state and the inner condition of the heart (Matthew 12:25). Although the speaking that children do among themselves does not arise from any bad intention, still it is impossible to produce fruitful results unless speech and silence have their time. To bring them to this point I have tried many different ways and means. . . .

A child who is slow in learning is harmed rather than helped when he is punished severely, whether with words or with the rod. If such a child is to be corrected, it must be done by other means. Likewise, a child who is dull is more harmed than helped by blows. A child who is treated with too many blows at home, and is used to them, cannot be corrected with blows in school; he becomes still more injured. If such children are to be helped, it must be by other means.

The children who are stubborn, who do not hesitate to commit evil deeds, must be severely punished with the rod. In addition, they must be addressed with earnest admonition from God's Word; his heart may perchance be touched thereby. But the slow and dull in learning must be corrected by other measures, whereby they may possibly be made freer in spirit and the desire to learn may be implanted. Once the children are that far along, neither the children nor the schoolmaster find it hard. . . . For the words "You shall" and "You must" do not have the same tone as "I obey with pleasure."

Source: Studer (1967): 290–94

⇾⇾⇾-⇾⇾⇾-⇾⇾⇾-⇾⇾⇾-⇾⇾⇾-⇾⇾⇾-⇾⇾⇾-⇾⇾⇾

"They Need a Man"

URIA R. BYLER

Maintaining order has high priority
in the management of Amish schools. Are men more capable than women of maintaining disciplined schools? Uria R. Byler thinks not, and he gives his reasons in these two selections.

Many times we have heard this comment when parents were talking about an unruly school: "What they need there is a man for a teacher." How much substance is there to the widespread belief that men are more strict, and run better-disciplined schools, than their lady counterparts? Not much, if any.

This mistaken notion seems to be based on appearance more than anything else. That is exactly the reason why it is wrong to presume that schoolchildren fear a man teacher more than a woman.

Let's hope that no child was ever "afraid" of a teacher. Teachers have too many personal contacts, and are too close to the interests of the child to be considered a feared enemy. If a teacher can prove he is a friend of his pupils, if he can win their confidence, no child is going to be "scared" of him. Furthermore, a teacher who would not feel hurt if he knew some of the pupils were actually afraid of him has the wrong attitude.

Being afraid to break rules is another matter. That fear should be the same as the fear we have in our hearts to sin. Let's make the distinction—school-

146

children need to be afraid to do wrong in school, not because of a personal fear of the teacher, but because of their own consciences. They should have been taught at home that once they are in school, the teacher takes over the parents' responsibility. A child who has the idea implanted in his conscience that the teacher is the "parent" in school, and is to be obeyed at all times, will seldom cause trouble for the teacher, whether a man or a woman.

Look around at the schools with which you are acquainted. Let your mind wander to bygone schools and compare their discipline problems. Then you will probably realize there is very little basis for thinking, "If that unruly school down there had a man, its discipline problems would vanish."

Certainly, you know of rough and rowdy schools where a man was in charge, and also of good schools where a woman was teacher. It's a good guess that in the former case the children were a little skeptical about what they could or could not do at first, until they found out that this man teacher was soft on discipline. Then their fun began.

Many women teachers have been a surprise to troublesome pupils who may have been misled by a benign and calm appearance. Blessed is the teacher, man or woman, who keeps the voice and actions even, and in a quiet and purposeful way maintains law and order in school!

A school's success depends not so much on whether a man or woman is in charge as it does on the individual himself, his or her character, and the courage to enforce the standards.

Source: Byler (1969): 16–17

-≫-≫-≫-≫-≫-≫-≫-≫-

Discipline in School

URIA R. BYLER

Discipline is the first rung of the ladder to successful teaching. The best-educated teacher in the world can be a total failure if he cannot discipline. All the other talents that make a number-one teacher are sadly wasted if he does not have the gumption, or the know-how, or whatever the term may be, to run a well-mannered school.

Children are complex creatures. Basically they are loving, tender-hearted, affectionate, and well-intentioned individuals who will do anything in their power to please the teacher. When our Saviour said, "Suffer the children to come unto me," He gave us a valuable lesson. Those few words alone convey to us a message which is sometimes lost or mislaid when we talk about children. He did not consider them basically mean, mischievous, hard-to-handle, or He would never have spoken those words.

The question now comes up, "Why then do some children misbehave as soon as the teacher's back is turned? Why do they talk back, get into fights, lie and cheat?"

We won't go into this subject of raising children, or try to figure out their moods and behavior. It's too deep and mysterious and difficult to explain in a few words. We do wonder, however, if parents of schoolchildren realize how much aid and comfort they can be to a teacher, or what heartaches and grief they can cause. Also, it has been truly said many times by teachers that the upbringing and home life of a child can be quite well figured out by the child's actions in school. As is Johnny the child at home, so is Johnny the pupil in school.

However, all parents and teachers will agree that, no matter how large or small a family, there is usually a wide difference of characteristics among the children. Some may be easy to teach and will take home good report cards; others may be slow and disinterested in school, or be problems in discipline. The so-called child experts of our modern era have studied this difference in children and have not yet come up with an answer. They probably never will.

Let's go back to our own school days. How did we behave in school? Did it not depend much on the teacher?

Did we whisper if it was forbidden? Cheat? Abuse the smaller pupils? Sass the teacher? Not if we knew we'd be punished for our misdeeds.

And now, years later, which teacher do we respect as a good teacher, the one who was lax in discipline, or the teacher who "ran a tight ship?"

There are teachers who see nothing wrong in letting one pupil help another with lessons without permission. Visiting different schools will show that, of all the different methods of schoolteaching, nowhere else is there so much variation as in what is allowed and what is forbidden. For that reason we will not recommend or condemn any teacher's system or rules. The important thing is successful results.

For example, one veteran teacher allows her pupils to whisper—providing they are helping each other. This teacher trusts her pupils and they seemingly get along quite well. Another teacher allows but one at a time to whisper, and then only if it's about schoolwork. However, the majority of teachers have a definite rule, "No whispering," though they find whispering a hard thing to eliminate entirely.

Because of the wide difference in rules and discipline, one must hesitate before endorsing any certain plan. We have seen too many qualified teachers allow, and take for granted, certain things that others would consider punishable offenses. One thing that can be said without hesitation is that the less noise there is in the schoolroom, the better your pupils can study and concentrate.

Source: Byler (1969): 13–14

→>>-→>>-→>>-→>>-→>>-→>>-→>>-→>>

Teachers Do a Lot of Self-Study

JOSEPH STOLL

Many people, including school *administrators, are surprised to learn that Amish teachers have no college training or formal certification. For the Amish, college degrees do not have a relationship to suitability for teaching. These three selections describe how not only teachers but also parents and school board members prepare themselves to educate children.*

The art of teaching, unknown in Amish circles a generation ago, has really caught fire among us. In no other work do we see the depth of dedication. In the past decade a hard core of experienced "professionals" has developed, and by our various means of communication—circle letters, the *Bulletin,* and our annual meetings—all newcomers can learn the reins. We know that most of our teachers do a lot of self-study, burning gallons of midnight oil to make themselves better teachers. Many have taken subjects by correspondence.

The public has a spotlight on our schools and on our teachers. For this reason, as well as for our own benefit, we must be careful to hire only teachers who are capable and sound of character. Otherwise, our witness to those not of our faith may be dulled.

Having put our hands to the wheel, let us, with God's help, do our best, so that we may all, with Christian of *Pilgrim's Progress,* at journey's end cross the Jordan to a better Land.

Source: Stoll (1962)

-➢➢➢-➢➢➢-➢➢➢-➢➢➢-➢➢➢-➢➢➢-➢➢➢-➢➢➢-

Qualifications of Parents and Board Members

A SYMPOSIUM OF TEACHERS

Wise Parents Are Those Who Will: Go to the teacher and openly and frankly discuss any problems their child may be having in school. They will remember that many so-called problems are only misunderstandings, and when brought to light may really not amount to much. Not ask of the teacher any special privileges for their child that must be denied the rest of the students for the sake of keeping order and fairness in the classroom. Teach their children respect for the properties and feelings of others. Not pass judgment upon the teacher in front of their children about anything, before hearing the teacher's side of the story. Respect the teacher as a specialist in her field, and realize that she may often have an underlying reason for the thing she demands or does. A person who gets a prescription from a doctor does not expect to fully understand the content of the medicine; but he only trusts that the doctor in his profession knows what he is doing, and if the results are favorable he is satisfied.

A Wise School Board Will: Know what is going on at school; not by what they hear but by finding out for themselves. See that the teacher has adequate materials and supplies for her task. Provide for play equipment and space that will keep the children interested and busy at playtime. Seek to keep the channel between teachers and parents open and friendly. Hire teachers in whom they have faith and confidence, and then stand by them and offer encouragement (not flattery) where possible.

The Best Help the Parents Can Give: Is to pray for their teacher. They should not speak against the teacher to the children, or when they are within hearing distance. Teachers are not perfect by far, but what parent would want to try to perfectly discipline and teach forty children?

If you see or hear that your child's teacher has made a mistake, visit the school for just one-half day. Not only will it give the teacher a great deal of encouragement, but it will show you in part what problems the teacher daily faces.

Source: Blackboard Bulletin (April 1963)

-》》-》》-》》-》》-》》-》》-》》-》》

Qualifications of a Christian Teacher

A SYMPOSIUM OF PARENTS AND SCHOOL BOARD MEMBERS

A *Good Teacher Needs:* A. Love, above all else; love of God, love of children and of humanity in general; love of occupation. Love takes care of some of the other characteristics. B. Firmness, or strict discipline. C. Adequate education. D. Willingness to accept advice or constructive criticism. E. Humility and meekness. F. Courage. G. Patience. H. Cheerfulness. I. Impartiality. J. Unselfishness.

All these will make a good character and personality.

A Good Christian Schoolteacher Should: Be modest in dress and actions, setting a good example. Be free of filthy habits such as foul talk, drinking, or smoking. Have sufficient education and understanding of teaching and learning. Accept the task as a challenge to help prepare young souls for a successful life pleasing to God, that they may be an asset to the church and the community in the years to come. Have an interest and liking for children. Be able to administer discipline fairly and successfully.

A Successful Teacher Is: Alert to the needs of the pupils, the wishes of the parents, and the will of God. Concerned that school life be not only a learning of the 3 R's, but also a living of life's 3 R's—faith, hope, love (I Cor. 13:13). Inspired by the challenge of her responsibilities. Kind to her pupils and to herself. Courteous to all visitors, especially those not of our faith, so that they have no just cause to consider us other than we profess to be. Apt in teaching; if native ability is somewhat below the desired level, it can be improved by practice and self-discipline. Educated, for it is indeed difficult for a teacher to teach others what she herself does not clearly understand. Relaxed but on her toes. Forgiving toward pupils and parents, for grudges are a heavy and useless burden to carry, and are a poison to the heart and spirit. Above all, Christian in word and deed and thought, that the children follow the footsteps of their teacher's Saviour.

Source: Blackboard Bulletin (April 1963)

-⫸-⫸-⫸-⫸-⫸-⫸-⫸-⫸

Why We Prefer A Short School Year

ELI E. GINGERICH

An *Amish minister in Indiana, Eli E. Gingerich points out the advantages that a shorter school year has for the Amish agricultural economy.*

1. Although we appreciate having our own schools and teachers of our choice, we feel this still does not quite come up to having children together as a family unit under the influence of the parents. Having one more month of school would mean less family influence.

2. Although we are a rural people in general, we realize there is a greater and greater need for a sound basic education. However, the old adage "We learn to do by doing" still holds true. Learning from books becomes more meaningful as we tie it in with practical experience. During that last month of school our children would miss much of the basic principles of farming, that of preparing for and planting fields and gardens.

3. We feel that our actual hours of classroom study in eight months would compare favorably with the average public school term of nine months. That is, counting such things as recreation during school sessions, basketball games, spring vacation, etc. . . .

4. The nine-month school term is mainly intended for town and city children. We feel the extra month of school for us is not only unnecessary, but creates a burden and hardship to our way of life, in a spiritual as well as a material sense. We support our own schools, and at the same time support the public schools. This means higher taxes for us, and we are deprived of the help of our children at a time of year when we most need them.

5. We feel that farming with tractors is not only impractical financially on most of our small farms, but with tractor farming we also tend to become more independent of each other, and lose much of the community spirit so essential for love and Christian fellowship in everyday life, as well as in the church.

Neither we nor our school system is perfect, but it is our aim to raise and educate our children to be not only good Christian stewards, faithful to God and our church, but also to be useful citizens in our community. For this privilege we are willing to continue supporting the public schools through our taxes, and to assume the financial responsibility ourselves of educating our children.

Source: Gingerich (1966): 19–20

-»»-»»-»»-»»-»»-»»-»»-»»

Getting along with the Public

URIA R. BYLER

The Amish have neither a department of education nor a public relations office. In this selection, Uria R. Byler gives some advice to Amish teachers about how not to deal with news reporters.

Some years ago a big-city newspaper of a midwestern state sent a reporter to a new Amish school for a story. The season was late winter and the schoolyard was rather messy with mud—there had not been time for grass to grow on the lawn.

The teacher was under orders from the school board to turn away any outsider who might come to visit the school. When this reporter introduced himself and asked to be allowed inside, he was met with a curt, "No, get out of here. We do not allow any of your people in this school."

Then the reporter asked who the president of the school board was. "It's none of your business," replied the teacher, and slammed the door in the reporter's face. From the road the newsman took a few pictures of the muddy schoolyard and then he left.

The next day the story made front-page news. The reporter told how he had been rudely ordered to leave and mind his own business, and of "the ramshackle building which was surrounded by a sea of mud."

Sometime later the county superintendent was also turned away from the school when he came to check the attendance records. The teacher was merely following the orders he had been given by the school board, who felt that it was of no concern to anyone else how the school was being run.

153

Was the board right or wrong? Let's see what happened soon afterward.

It takes only a minor incident to start a big fracas. As a result of that newspaper article several county officials called on the school to check on attendance and general conditions. They were also turned away. One thing followed another, all of which was fully reported in the local newspapers. Reports were soon floating around about the "deplorable" conditions among the Amish schools. This was picked up at the state capital, where certain top school officials scheduled a public hearing on what should be done to improve the Amish schools.

The hearings were peaceable enough except for the testimony and statements of the county officials, whose feelings had been hurt by the lack of cooperation. They had been insulted and made no pretense to hide their feelings. In the end an agreement of a sort was reached, and since then relations between the public and the Amish schools of that area have in general been very favorable.

It would be unfair to place the entire blame on the one little incident when the reporter was ordered to leave. It is quite possible that the whole controversy would have blown up anyway. But we cannot escape the fact that it is poor policy to be impolite, whether to reporters, public school officials, or anyone else. . . .

Any teacher who answers the door and finds a news reporter standing outside may well be on the spot. The only way to handle the situation is to remain as cool as possible, be friendly, and use tact. There are many types of news reporters. Some may ask only a few questions and leave. Others may show themselves a nuisance from the start.

Source: Byler (1969): 57–58

10

CONSCIENCE
IN CONFLICT

During their early history, the Anabaptists were called "defenseless" Christians. They had no rationale for defending themselves or their property against invaders. Today, in the same way, the Amish, in the face of a hostile world around them, are admonished by their bishops to follow the example of Isaac (Gen. 26:15–18)—that is, if the warring Philistines stop up the wells for the cattle, move to new lands and dig other wells.

In keeping with their understanding of the teaching of Jesus to return good for evil, the Amish avoid conflict whenever possible, whether it be physical, verbal, legal, or argumentative. Nonresistance means more than conscientious objection to war. It means a way of living. This stance has sometimes cost Amish people their lives. Their conscience has stood firmly against a variety of pressures. Their path is one of quiet suffering rather than aggression and resistance. This stance has sometimes led them to prison, as described in the selections in this chapter.

In his advice to Benjamin Franklin, William Penn said of the Mennonite immigrants who came to Pennsylvania: "Treat them well for they have a tender conscience."

❀❀❀❀❀❀❀❀

Vote for the Friends of Peace

CHRISTIAN ZOOK, JR.

*T*his document of 1812, addressed "To the Mennonites, Dunkards, Amish, and All Other Friends of Peace," makes a strong plea for going to the polls as a means of avoiding the War of 1812 between the British and the French. Although the document is unsigned, circumstances suggest that it was written by an Amish minister, Christian Zook, Jr. (1752–1826), of Chester County, Pennsylvania. The document proposed that suffering the imposition of an embargo, and not having a market for their grain, was far more preferable to the Amish than was war. This passionate plea, in all probability by Zook, makes this document of unusual interest.

I am an old man, and under Divine Providence I have lived many blessed days. I have endeavored to raise my children in the ways of the Lord, through which they may keep the faith in peaceful piety and eternal truth. For all good things come from the Lord, and those who keep his commandments shall enter into his kingdom and be the sheep of his pasture. As for me personally, I could let the vain things of the world transpire. However, I am concerned for our children and grandchildren and "the land which the Lord gave to them."

It is already more that thirty years since any evil has struck our country [the Revolutionary War, 1775–1783], at least no evil to compare with the one we currently must strive against [the War of 1812]. We have to endure material losses—however, we have peace. I am no "party man," but am opposed to war since it brings sadness, want, and death—making the land desolate—takes father from son and son from father—causing widows' and orphans' tears, and is an abomination before God, who alone gives life and alone has the right to take it away. . . .

I fear our rulers have departed from the path of righteousness. We cannot be in the war with them, for our conscience does not allow it: our religious principles forbid it. However, we should be obedient to the laws and "give unto Caesar what is Caesar's." Accordingly, let us obey the statutes, thus having to pay our taxes and having a right to vote for men to make the laws. When we discover that they are not making good laws, we owe ourselves and our families to vote for other men to protect our rights and possessions. . . .

At this time it is our duty to go to the polls and to vote for the friends of peace. When we vote for the friends of peace, we are voting against the war. . . . Oh, my beloved brethren, is it not the duty of every God-fearing man, at such a special occasion, to exercise his political right, while he has the freedom to vote, and while his single vote perhaps can tip the scales? Oh, what a sweet comfort it would be to think back and know that one has contributed to the aversion of this horrible evil.

Think of the thousands of families who will be reduced to misery—the tender wife lamenting the loss of her beloved husband, who was her only comfort and the protector of her children—the poor orphaned children mourning the death of their beloved father—and fathers and grandfathers will go to their graves with broken hearts because of the loss of their children and grandchildren.

Can any of you, my beloved brethren, consider staying home on election day when by casting your vote in these present times so much evil can be prevented? If anyone who favors the present war party reads this address—if he is a religious man—if he declares himself a Mennonite, Dunkard, or Amish, or is any manner conscientiously opposed to bearing arms, so let him weigh in his own conscience whether he can in present time vote for the war party. At both elections there will be a war-ticket and a peace-ticket. Vote for none but the friends of peace.

Remember that this is no political question—it is not merely a question between Federalists and Republicans—it is a question whether we shall have peace or war.

A Preacher, Chester County, September 25, 1812

Source: Luthy (1984): 2–4

❖❖❖❖❖❖❖❖❖❖❖❖❖❖❖❖

Civil War Soldiers

DAVID LUTHY

he fine line between conscience and civil disobedience is illustrated in this account of Bishop Daniel Beachy's confrontation with Confederate soldiers.

Today there are Amish families still living at Oakland, Maryland, but none at Aurora, West Virginia. The reason often given for the Maryland settlement increasing and the West Virginia one decreasing is that the families lived too close to what is now U.S. Highway No. 50. During the Civil War (1861–1865) it was a main road used by army troops—both Union and Confederate. Soldiers frequently stopped at the farms along the road and took whatever they needed: horses, cows, chickens, grain. Union soldiers once camped for several weeks on Bishop Daniel Beachy's farm near Aurora and helped themselves to supplies from his barn. But it was the Confederate soldiers who frightened and bothered the settlers most.

Christian Petersheim, who was a neighbor of the Beachys, was forced to haul supplies with his team and wagon for the graycoats for a week while his family had no idea when and if he would come home. Many anxious moments were spent and prayers sent heavenward. It is said that one Amishman worried so much about the war that he became mentally deranged. He supposedly insisted that his sons restack a pile of logs whose ends faced the house, for he imagined them to be canons about to shoot his family.

The following account is told of Bishop Daniel Beachy's encounter one Sunday morning with rebel soldiers on his way to preach in Maryland:

On April 26, 1863, a beautiful Sunday morning after days of heavy rains, Daniel Beachy mounted his dainty mare, Baldy, and set out for Gortner to preach at the Joseph Slabach farm. Riding along the turnpike he was joined by two of his members, the trusted Crist Petersheim and Peter Schrock. As the three men traveled eastward they met Confederate soldiers straggling along the muddy road. Just west of the Maryland state line they rode squarely into the main force of General Jones's army.

The men drew their horses up on the road bank to let the soldiers pass. But a trooper, evidently in a jovial mood, approached Mr. Beachy, jerked off his hat, and clapped his own officer's cap on him. At the same time he put Beachy's broad-brimmed hat on his own head. After a round of loud guffaws about the joke, he again changed hats as well as his manner, gruffly demanding that Mr. Beachy dismount and give up his horse.

Daniel, no coward, remained calmly seated. His blue eyes were fearless as he replied, "Sir, I cannot give up my horse. I need it for farming."

The trooper stared in disbelief at this man who refused to obey his orders. Clearing his throat, he said roughly, "Sir, if you don't get off that horse I'll put you off." Profanity rattled about like hailstones as he began to unbuckle the saddle girths.

Still Mr. Beachy remained seated and Crist Petersheim spoke up, "Sir, we are on our way to church, and this man is our preacher. How shall he get there if you take his horse?"

Immediately the trooper stopped, glancing about uneasily for the officer in command. "Why didn't you tell me sooner?" Quickly rebuckling the saddle girths, he sent the men on their way.

Sources: Luthy (1986): 491, based on Mary E. Yoder (1971): 26–27

➤➤➤-➤➤➤-➤➤➤-➤➤➤-➤➤➤-➤➤➤-➤➤➤-➤➤➤

Experiences in an Army Camp

MENNO A. DIENER

Young men who sought conscientious *objector status during World War I were advised to report to military camps and take their stand. There was no formal provision for religious objectors. Most young Amish men obeyed orders to report but refused uniforms, and some refused to obey work orders. Some were harassed by guards and others were court-martialed. Menno A. Diener, an Amish man who lived in Illinois, gives a detailed account of his experience.*

On June 1, 1918, I received notice to report to my local board. With three other boys from the Sullivan-Arthur area on board, our train departed on June 28 for Camp Taylor near Louisville, Kentucky.

On arrival they gave us our bed blankets and overalls and then our trials began. I was given some work to do, and when I refused I was sent to the guardhouse. . . .

At first we had been told to put on the uniform and clean up around the premises and playgrounds. When we refused to do this we were asked to help in the kitchen with peeling potatoes, sweeping floors, and carrying in meat from the trucks. In our quarters it took about 125 lbs. every day. The reason we quit was because many of the soldiers said we were conscientious but not objectors. The officers were saying that what they wanted us to do was no worse than what they were doing.

One day we were taken to the room where the bunk beds were set up. We were told to pile them up in a neat stack. When we had finished we were ordered to put them back again like they were. This kept on for quite some time. . . .

One of the guards became angry and struck me across the breast with the bayonet of his gun, nearly knocking me down. I was so short of breath I could hardly stand. The same guard also struck one of the Ohio boys, knocking him down and stabbing him with his bayonet. He made a cut in his pants and a gash in his hips about two inches long.

One of the guards tried to scare us and held his rifle close to my head, repeated it, and pulled the trigger. He had forgotten to take all the shells out of his gun and it went off, shooting a hole through the ceiling and the roof. He was scared more than we were. . . .

On July 11th we were released from the guardhouse and sent back to our company, where we met more trials. We were taken to the latrine and given orders to clean it. We refused to obey the orders. The commander got a broomstick and beat me across the legs till he broke his stick. I had streaks and swellings on my legs. Then he got a 2 × 4 about three feet long that had four spikes in one end and threatened to hit me in the face with it. He put it near to my face and then back again like a ball bat and said, "If it weren't for the law, I would like to see how far I could sink these spikes into your face. . . ."

But our trials started again and July 28th was one of my hardest days. It was on Sunday and they were determined that we must work. They ordered us to pick up all the cigarette stubs that lay on the parking grounds and when we refused we were thrown on the ground. We were kicked and knocked around and finally I was taken to a building where the company commander said he would teach me to fight. He began hitting me in the face with his hands until I began going down, then he would quit for a moment. Another fellow helped him and they kept on till I started to fall, and one of the men would catch me so I would not fall down.

On August 23rd we were called upon to witness in a court-martial against our officers. I was on the witness stand about two hours before dinner and about that long after dinner.

On August 27th we were transferred to the conscientious objectors' detachment while our partner was still in the hospital.

About September 6th we were again called upon to witness at a court-martial and when we refused we were put under guard and marched in to General Austin for a hearing.

The reason the officials were court-martialed was for disobeying military law in striking anyone on the camp grounds. We felt that we could not conscientiously testify against them for it would be helping to punish them, and cause ill feelings and be a poor example of Christianity in our church and background.

After we had talked to the general we were sent back to our tents. . . .

On November 1st we met the special board of inquiry and were passed for farm furloughs. On November 15th I was let out of farm furlough in Howard County, Indiana, among our own people and my partner went to northern Indiana.

Source: Diener (1970): 22–24

↝↝↝↝↝↝↝↝

Behind Prison Walls

NAME WITHHELD

D*uring World War II there was pro-vision in the law for conscientious objection. Ninety-five percent of the Amish who were drafted chose conscientious objector status and were assigned to Civilian Public Service camps to "perform work of national importance." As long as the draft was in effect, the Amish were assigned to Civilian Public Service and worked in psychiatric hospitals or on other approved projects. A minority of the Amish refused to report for civilian work. To accept govern-mental orders to work in "worldly" places away from their family and com-munity was as threatening as military service. To go to prison was better, they reasoned, than forming "worldly" friendships. The prison experience of the* *young men enabled them to identify with the martyrs, as this account by a young Amish man indicates.*

I was arrested for violating the Universal Military Service and Training Act by refusing to accept a job in the hospital. I was sentenced to prison for two years by a federal judge. The charge was that I knowingly and willfully refused to report for military service.

When I was a boy, one bit of advice was branded in my conscience. It was this: "In case of doubt, it is best for a Christian to choose the course that goes hardest against his nature or desires." When I was to report for I-W service it would indeed have been easier to go with the group. But my conscience would not allow it.

On my arrival at the penitentiary, one of my first trials was the barber chair. The barber, who was an inmate, was ordered to give me a shave and a haircut. Four officers stood by in case of trouble. The barber explained to me several different styles of haircuts and asked: "Which do you prefer?"

I said: "I do not want any other kind except the one I have."

He kept insisting that I pick one of the styles, but I steadfastly answered, "I will not choose any of the styles which you have to offer."

He sympathized with me and finally suggested that he could take off just enough to satisfy the officers. When he had finished he put on enough grease so the hair would lay over in the modern style. But the next morning my hair had returned to its normal position.

On the way to the mess hall I was called aside and told to report to the barbershop after breakfast. This time I was given a short crew cut, the style in which my hair was kept until I had served my time.

Once under the prison rules there were many demands, both from authorities and inmates, which I felt I could not obey. Authorities took turns calling me to their office. I was told if I insisted on taking a stand for my faith I would be rejected by my fellow inmates. They thought I would find it unbearable to be locked up with them. Some officers coaxed, while others lost their temper.

After a couple of days at work [in Allenwood, Pa.] I was called aside and locked in a 5 × 7 room with two of the biggest officers. They ordered me to take off my clothes, which I did. They next told me to put on the clean clothes. I refused to put them on. One of the officers hit me with the palm of his hand. Then they put them on me and I went back to my job.

I did not try to go to the mess hall without clothes and they would not clothe me beforehand. One lieutenant said he would starve me if it was in his power. When I refused to put on the clothes a big crowd gathered around my cell. They all had sympathy and tried to persuade me to do as I was told or I would be severely punished. When I still refused, one of the inmates took some of his clothes and changed them to a way he thought I would wear them.

When he brought me these clothes it tried me very hard. I told him as long as I did not have permission from the authorities I could not wear them. They begged me to wear them, but I did not. It was against the rules to wear another inmate's clothing.

It was hard for me to explain to the inmates that I felt it wrong to complain to the warden. They finally accepted it, but unwillingly.

Soon after this the inmates planned a riot if my religious convictions were not recognized. When I heard it I was very much disturbed because the instigator of a riot is usually transferred at once and may be resentenced. I was afraid I would be put in "the hole," a bare room where they punished prisoners.

While I was in the gym one day watching others play a game, an inmate came over and slapped me across the face. It took me by surprise and I didn't know why it was done. At once the prisoner was ashamed of himself. We had always been friends. He told me that some of the men were betting that I would strike back, so they decided to test me. There were other times when they tried out my faith by betting with each other. It made me feel quite small.

Soon after I was at the first honor camp, a homosexual approached me. I had already been given warnings. At times I hardly knew what to do but each time they would leave me alone. From then on I learned to listen them out, and I was more careful. There were some who said they would protect me if I got in trouble. They threatened to beat up anybody who would molest me.

One of my brothers also served his time in prison. He has had a lot of experiences that cannot be valued in money. The experiences are not pleasing to human nature at the time. But if the trials are met in a righteous way, it can be rewarding and help us toward our goal for a heavenly home in eternity.

When my brother was in prison, a professional gambler made friends with him. He wanted to teach him the ways of a gambler, and tried to persuade him to leave his religion and follow him. He said he traveled all over the states with a lot of money for pleasure. He carried a gun all the time. This man was badly in need of a partner who would be strictly honest and loyal to him. He felt my brother would meet the qualifications if he would put his religion aside. The man was released, but he had not persuaded my brother.

Did you ever stop to think that a crook cannot use a partner who is also crooked? They want honest partners. If a crook cannot use a crook, how could God or the church use one?

I have been asked why I chose prison instead of service in I-W. It was a hard decision, but I tried to go according to my understanding of the Scriptures. I have heard the statement, "Oh, you can do a lot of good working in a hospital taking care of sick people, and learn a lot of valuable information that will come handy later in life."

Read Romans 3:8 and 6:1. "Shall we do evil so that good will come from it?" Is God not able to protect or destroy us?

The responsibility is upon us to lay a solid foundation of faith for the future generation. To do that, we will have to lead a life in which God can help us.

Source: Name withheld, condensed from "Behind Prison Walls," part 1: 112–14; part 2: 16–19

⫸⫸-⫸⫸-⫸⫸-⫸⫸-⫸⫸-⫸⫸-⫸⫸-⫸⫸

Henry Hershberger and the Building Permit

GENE LOGSDON

Laws and regulations made for modern industrialized societies often create hardships for self-governing, simple farm communities. Gene Logsdon, a neighbor of the Amish, describes the logic of an Amish man who refused to apply for a building permit.

Henry Hershberger taught me the deeper truth and wisdom of Amish economy. Hershberger is a bishop [minister] in the Schwartzentruber branch of the Amish, the strictest of the many sects. I went to visit Hershberger in 1983 because he had just gotten out of jail, which seemed to me a very curious place for an Amish bishop [minister] to be. Hershberger had been in jail because he would not apply for a building permit for his new house. Actually, he told me (in his new house), it was not the permit or building code regulations that got him in trouble with the law. He groped for the unfamiliar English words that would make the meaning clear. Most Amish can't meet certain requirements of the code because of religious convictions. But there is an understanding. The Amish buy the permit, then proceed to violate its rules on details, of lighting and plumbing or whatever, that their religion disallows. The authorities look the other way.

Hershberger had given that practice considerable thought. Not only did it smack of dishonesty, but he realized that the Amish had survived more than one case of creeping totalitarianism. The code was particularly worrisome because it would mean greatly increased costs of construction, if indeed some way to get around the religious problem were found. But more importantly, it could mean, with the way the permit business is being handled, that authorities might someday stop Amish from building more houses on their farms. So Hershberger refused to play the game. The bureaucracy was ready to accommodate Hershberger's religion, since it is common knowledge that the Amish build excellent houses for themselves—they would be fools not to, of course, but for Hershberger not to offer token obeisance to bureaucracy was unforgivable. That might lead, heaven forbid, to other people questioning the sanctity of the law.

Taken to court, Hershberger was found guilty and given thirty days to pay up and get his permit. He refused. The judge, underestimating the resolve of a Schwartzentruber bishop [minister], fined him $5,000. Hershberger refused to pay. The judge sent him to jail to work off his debt at $20 a day. A great public hue and cry arose. In two weeks Hershberger was set free, still owing the court $4,720. The sheriff was ordered to seize enough property to satisfy the debt. But local auctioneers said they would not cry the sale. No one would haul the livestock. The judge resigned (for other reasons, I was told). Henry Hershberger lives in his new house, at peace, at least for now. . . .

Building codes protect not the buyer but the builders, the suppliers of the approved materials, and an army of career regulators. The Amish understand all this. When a culture gives up the knowledge, ability and legality to build its own houses, the people pay. And pay.

But there are even more practical reasons why the Amish economy wants to retain control over its housing. First of all, the Amish home doubles as an Amish church. How many millions of dollars this saves the Amish would be hard to calculate. Amish belief wisely provides for the appointment of ministers by lot. No hierarchy can evolve in Amishland. A minister works his farm like everyone else. That is mainly why the religion so effectively protects the Amish culture of agriculture. Its bishops do not sit in exceedingly well-insulated houses in far-off cities uttering pious pronouncements about the end of family farming.

Secondly, the Amish home doubles as the Amish retirement village and nursing home, thereby saving incalculably more millions of dollars, not to mention the self-respect of the elderly. The Amish do not pay Social Security, nor do they accept it. They know and practice a much better security that requires neither pension nor lifelong savings.

Source: Logsdon (1986): 74–76

11

INTERACTION
WITH OUTSIDERS

Nonthreatening relationships with outsiders are appreciated by the Amish. They understand the necessity of government and, in the words of Menno Simons (1956: 193), expect government "to punish the evil, to protect the good, and to administer a righteous justice." They seek markets to sell their farm products, including livestock, whole milk, and grain crops. They buy staples such as sugar, salt, flour, as well as other supplies, in village stores. To remain vigorous, the Amish family must have a strong economic base in which its members are a ready labor force. There is a certain amount of "neighboring" with non-Amish rural people. The Amish may assist "English" neighbors with the harvest or offer assistance during an emergency.

The individual in the Amish community enjoys brief excursions into the outer world. A face-to-face encounter with visitors is frequently appreciated. Some of these chance acquaintances may endure for decades. Virtually every Amish farm household has friends in the outside, or non-Amish, world. These encounters are unstructured, elusive moments of reciprocity. Both insider and outsider are in a sense "tourists" temporarily enjoying a liminal territory. The "urban" outsider relishes temporary relief from the complex, competitive struggle in the industrial world. The Amish person may enjoy temporary relaxation from routine when he or she rides in an automobile with a trusted visitor.

The selections in this chapter are by Amish people.

➤➤➤-➤➤➤-➤➤➤-➤➤➤-➤➤➤-➤➤➤-➤➤➤-➤➤➤

My Travels

ELI J. BONTRAGER

As a mediator, Eli J. Bontrager traveled to many Amish communities, and his advice was widely sought in the days of conscription during World War II. This selection is from his unpublished autobiography.

When World War II broke out in September 1939, it was plain to me that our President was sure to bring the United States into the conflict, notwithstanding his claims and statements to the contrary. Even when he pleaded for a third term and got his conscription bill passed, the general public still seemed to believe that he was sincere in his claim that he would keep the U.S. out of the war. Even his Lend-Lease bill failed to open the eyes of the people to see his real aims. However, some Mennonites sensed danger ahead, and planned a trip to Washington, D.C., in January 1940, to see the President and the Attorney General and a few other officials to work out a plan whereby our conscientious objectors would not be obliged to enter the military training camps when conscripted. I was invited to accompany this delegation to Washington. I accepted the call. There were about eighteen of us from different groups of Mennonites, from the Church of the Brethren, and from the Quakers. The outline of the plan for separate camps for the C.O.'s was presented at that time practically the same as worked out later and put in operation. . . .

Conscription was going on for about six months before this country was in a declared war. I was chosen as a member of the Mennonite Central Committee [M.C.C.] and invited to attend a meeting at Ephrata, Pennsylvania, before I knew that I was considered a member of the M.C.C. I was also chosen as a member of the Advisory Committee for the Bluffton, Indiana, C.O. Camp, without being consulted about it. This camp was later moved to Medaryville, Indiana. I attended a number of meetings in Goshen, and in Chicago, and several in Lancaster, Pennsylvania. In October 1942, Ira Nissley and I were appointed by the Mennonite Central Committee to visit all the camps where any of our Amish boys were.

I have traveled considerably in my time, and have for some years thought that my traveling would likely be very little during the rest of my lifetime. However, I was mistaken in this, as I traveled many more miles in the five months from November 1, 1942, to April 1, 1943, than ever before in that length of time—more than 16,000 miles—over 14,500 by rail, and more than 1,500 by automobile and bus—and was in 35 different states. . . .

The Lord so led that I had the privilege of seeing many parts of our fair land and visiting friends and congregations throughout the country, having traveled many more miles than any other of our brethren ever has—up to this time, more than 43,200 miles on railroads. Since it was to be my lot to be a minister of the Gospel, I also consider it a favor from God that I was called when still quite young—twenty-six years old. At just about the age that Jesus was when He sacrificed His life for us—thirty-three—I was ordained a bishop. It has so happened that I have had many co-ministers to work with in my different home districts and others of which I had bishop oversight, and I have always had such that I could very well get along without any trouble. This is another great blessing that I have had.

I have up to this time (May 16, 1944) baptized 366 persons and married 149 couples, have preached 2,428 times, preached the main sermon in church services 1,343 times, 226 of which were communion sermons, preached 118 funeral sermons, opening services in church service and funerals 684 times, and sermonized on the Old Testament Patriarchs at communion services 50 times. I have ordained 30 ministers and 11 bishops and was present and helped at many more ordinations of ministers and bishops.

Source: Eli J. Bontrager (1953): 23, 29

The Country Store

GIDEON L. FISHER

Complete isolation is neither sought after nor desired by the Amish. They enjoy meeting people from other states and countries, but under circumstances that are not intimidating. Gideon L. Fisher explains, in his unique way, the atmosphere of the country store and farmers' market, and Eli Stoltzfus relates his encounters with tourists.

The old-time country store had the reputation of serving a wide area. From far and wide people came with horse and buggy, perhaps every week or ten days, making a business of meeting the friendly storekeeper. They always found an empty space to tie the horse somewhere at a row of hitching posts. The horse had plenty of time to rest while the driver spent some time visiting with the storekeeper or with someone whom he met from the community. Sometimes a good conversation lasted a few hours, especially if the Mrs. was along choosing her favorite dress material.

People depended on the country store to supply most of their home requirements. The store was open six days a week from early morning to late in the evening. There were usually two or three clerks behind the counter. With no adding machine or typewriter in sight, everything was figured out with pencil and paper, and often a quick answer was given from memory. A person of today would say, why couldn't they give the answer by memory, everything was so cheap that there wasn't much figuring to do, and no sales tax to contend with.

The main store was furnished with a row of benches to accommodate the waiting customers. In the evening the farmers as well as the town folk would gather to get the late news on weather, any minor or major accidents, sickness or death from local areas. . . . Many a hot argument on politics was discussed on these benches. At some convenient place was a well-worn spittoon, conveniently catching the tobacco chewers' aim. A potbellied stove was usually standing in the center, convenient to be surrounded by chairs. . . .

At the far end of the counter were a number of checkerboards. After the news session was over, the skill of a few players was tried out. Sometimes two or three games were going at the same time. Occasionally the storekeeper himself would show his customers how to play checkers, probably winning most of the games of the evening. This event being talked about brought along better players for the next evening.

The shelves of a special showcase were filled with one- and five-cent candy bars. Only the nice-sized chocolate bars were more than five cents. Then there were the two- and three-cent cigars, along with some penny stinkers. A few five-cent White Owls were sold, but not many, because they were too high-priced. Also included were several brands of chewing tobacco. . . .

Several practical jokes were pulled during the long evenings of the winter months. The town dwellers as well as the farmers spent many an evening exchanging jokes and wisecracks before returning home. [The following are perhaps typical.]

A certain man decided to play a joke on one of his friends. He took the tail of a pig with an already inserted safety pin along to the store. While a group were standing in a circle telling stories, the pig tail was pinned on a certain man's coat. The sight of this put a grin on everyone's face. On that particular evening he seemed to draw everyone's attention as he walked down the street on his homeward way. Not until he reached home and his wife saw the pig tail waggling on his coat did he realize why he got so much attention. At first his wife was rather upset about it, but then they concluded it was a return joke.

On a Friday evening a local man came to the store for the weeks' supply of groceries. At the end of his list he asked the clerk for a pound of the old-fashioned chocolate drops. The young clerk was taught to give accurate weight at all times. The paper bag was filled with the large drops from the barrel close by. After setting the bag on the scales, the clerk found he had a problem on hand. The last chocolate drop he put in made a little over a pound, and when he removed it he had less than a pound. After passing it back and forth a few times he found a solution. He bit one in half, put one half in the bag, and that made it "just right." Everybody in the store burst out laughing, for the clerk was giving an honest weight. The boss also had a good laugh, and told the customer he could have the chocolate drops free. The incident saved the customer nineteen cents, that being the price for a pound of old-fashioned chocolate drops. This young clerk knew his customer quite well.

Once a farmer came to the store to purchase a new pair of shoes, as his were well-worn and not worth patching. The manager guided him upstairs to the shoe department. After trying a few different sizes and price ranges, he decided on a pair. He told the storekeeper the shoes were comfortable, and he would wear them right away. While the clerk was packing the shoes back into the boxes, the farmer put his old shoes into a box and put the lid on. With a good conversation going on, the clerk put all the boxes back on the shelf. Sometime later another customer came to the store to purchase a pair of nice, shiny shoes. This time another clerk was present to show the wares, the best quality shoes. After opening a few boxes, and showing the shoes, what was more embarrassing than to roll out a pair of old worn-out dirty shoes. Nothing could be done than to accept it as a practical joke. The storekeeper had a good idea who played this embarrassing joke.

Source: Gideon L. Fisher (1978): 116–21

⇶-⇶-⇶-⇶-⇶-⇶-⇶-⇶

The Lancaster Farmers Market

GIDEON L. FISHER

For many years the city of Lancaster was an ideal place to sell fresh vegetables. On special days truck farmers from a distance of ten or twelve miles away were seen headed toward marketplace. Every week, or perhaps more often, the market wagon was loaded to capacity with the vegetables in season, and butter, buttermilk, eggs, and perhaps a few dressed chickens. After hitching the horse to the wagon, the farmer was set to go find the customer for his wares.

In the early days, before the automobile became popular, the produce dealers were allowed to sell their produce on the main streets in Lancaster. When the farmer arrived at the place of his choice, he would unhitch his horse, and tie him to a street hitching post. (These hitching posts are now replaced by parking meters.) The farmer would back the wagon to the curb, probably set out a little table for a display counter, and fill it with his assorted vegetables, eggs, cheese, etc. He was now ready for business, hoping to sell out in a few hours. This was the farmers' payday, after working and struggling for a length of time to prepare the produce so the city housewife would have the best of fresh vegetables. The farmer deserved good wages.

In nice weather it was ideal to have the market along the street; people would buy as they passed along. Many a good conversation was had at these curb markets. But in cold, rainy weather customers were sometimes few and far between. It was not pleasant to stand and wait for the next customer, while the shivering horse needed another blanket.

Other truck farmers would establish a route, passing through the streets and stopping at the customers' doorstep. The horse was trained to stand without being tied, while the housewife would choose from the various items on the market wagon.

At the turn of the century three market houses were established in Lancaster, the Northern, the Central, and Southern, accommodating the city people with fresh farmers' produce. The farmer would rent a counter, and sell his wares in a heated building where probably fifty others also had something to sell.

About 1960, when the supermarkets became popular, two market houses were closed down, the Central being the remaining one. With refrigerated railroad cars and tractor-trailer trucks with cooling systems, fresh fruits and vegetables can be shipped into all areas in the United States. These are stiff competition for our local produce farmers. Due to heavy traffic and competitive markets, the local truck farmer with horse and wagon discontinued about 1960, and is now history.

In Lancaster County it was a general custom for a farmer and his wife who had tilled the soil for a length of time, showing their age from hard work, and had lost that keen spirit, to get up early in the morning and work late at night, then they wished to sell out and leave the responsibilities of farm work to a younger couple. In years past the machinery and livestock was usually offered at public sale.

Source: Gideon L. Fisher (1978): 72–73

⸙⸙⸙⸙⸙⸙⸙⸙

Tourists in Lancaster County

GIDEON L. FISHER

What is the reason that Lancaster County is becoming one of the greatest tourist attractions in our nation? Why are tourists brought into our community? What class of people are responsible for this profiteering? Why are they commercializing on the Amish people? Who will it benefit? What will be the results in future years? Some of these questions are not easy to answer.

There is a certain class of people from the larger cities who wants to get out into the open countryside to see the producing green fields, the ever-flowing streams of water, the many varieties of trees and plants, and appreciate the blessings, the greatness, and the wonderful creations of God. They want to learn more about where and how natural food is produced, the attention that is required to prepare the food for our local market. They must realize that the food in the supermarkets is not just brought from the storerooms and is not grown in fancy cartons.

For those tourists who have a sincere interest in some practical knowledge of our way of life, it is a pleasure to visit and answer the questions in an intelligent way. There is a class of tourists who treats us as fellow human beings. These will sometimes politely ask intelligent questions about our way of life, and credit us with having retained a rich heritage with our simple habits. With tears of nostalgia, they sometimes tell us of their memories of their own forefathers of fairly recent years. . . .

There is also a class of people who, because of their financial means, want to spend a sightseeing trip, mostly for amusement, making Lancaster County the target to satisfy their curiosity, and to enjoy the many luxuries which are found throughout our community. They want to leave their over-crowded cities and suburbs and spend their vacation out in the country.

People feel that when they have held a job, they are entitled to take time off for a vacation. During times of prosperity we find that people's budgets call for a certain amount of time for sports and amusements, because more money is in circulation. In times of depression people do not have their mind set as much on amusements, but have a more spiritual attitude.

We are now living in a sports-craving period, and the world lures people into participating in sports of all kinds.

Upon arriving in our county, many visitors become confused, and realize they have been brainwashed to a certain extent. They find it is partly a money racket. After they arrive and travel over the countryside, they inquire for information as to where they could see an Amish farm, and where the Amish people live. This proves they have been misled by a wide margin. . . .

This publicity is being advertised by people who are more interested in the financial gains than they are in the Amish people themselves. They use the Amish name to commercialize the tourist business. The tourist bureau is not in the best of harmony with the Amish folks. We can well imagine that many a sensible tourist is simply disgusted. The curious tourist should realize that the Amish people are also human beings. They have trials, temptations, and human nature to deal with, the same as any other person.

The Amish people themselves don't cooperate with the tourists, as far as publicity is concerned. So in turn people who are members of the tourist bureau spend thousands of dollars to build and arrange farm homesteads, to show these curious tourists how the Amish people live, by setting up the most ridiculous stories about Amish craftsmanship, Amish dress, Amish cooking, and Amish ways of life. They also try to explain to the tourist about the Amish religion. All this is done from the profit standpoint, and is of no benefit to the Amish people.

The public officials claim that this tourist business brings to our community more prosperity, millions of dollars are being spent on souvenirs, gas, lodging, eats, etc. But on the other hand, it brings on such problems as already over-crowded highways, the need of building more and better roads, bridges, lodging facilities, motels, restaurants, and gas stations, and brings into our community more industries. More people from our larger cities want to live in our section of the country. For that reason more homes need to be built, and more families with children means more schools are needed. Every year thousands of acres of highly productive land is being used in building developments, new roads and factories, making the price of farmland more competitive, to the extent that the Amish people are being pressed to move to other areas where they can enjoy a more peaceful form of life.

This tourist business also brings to our community people from all walks of life. Some will want unionized labor, such as our larger manufacturing areas have. Therefore strikes, riots, violence and everything that goes with them are bound to follow. It is not the tourist business that made Lancaster County popular.

Source: Gideon L. Fisher (1978): 361–65

Tourists Often Ask Me

ELI STOLTZFUS

While serving as a caretaker at the Amish Homestead, a tourist attraction near Lancaster, Pennsylvania, Eli Stoltzfus answered many questions. He describes some of these encounters.

Tourists often ask me how many children we have. I tell them we have seven and my mother had seven and her mother had seven. It is a perfect number, or a symbol of completion. Sometimes they ask me stupid or laughable questions. One time I was driving in a nail with a short piece of pipe, because I didn't have a hammer handy. Then a lady asked me if it was against our religion to use a hammer.

One time I was hitching up three mules and one horse together. Then a man asked me why I hitched up three mules and one horse together. I told him "to make four." I didn't know what else to say. I guess he was dumbfounded. My landlord said the man came into the shop laughing so much that he asked what it was all about. The man replied, "If you ask a stupid question you get a funny answer."

Somebody asked me whether our goat was a baby horse. I am surprised sometimes to hear gray-haired city people tell me they were never on a farm in their life, and I pity them. They missed half their life.

A man asked me what we do for entertainment. I just say, "We farm." He understood what I meant. He was intelligent. You see, it is a beautiful sight to see our Creator's nice brown earth being smoothly turned upside down in long strips back and forth through the field with the anticipation of producing good food for some hungry person. This is entertainment.

It is thrilling to turn nine horses and mules and a pony out into the pasture when they haven't been out for a while and to see them burst forth at full speed and kick and snort and carry on. This is entertainment.

It is charming to see our smiling fifteen-year-old boy jump on the pony and go and round up the cows at ease and bring them in. This is entertainment.

It is a beautiful sight to see my wife and daughter out in the garden hoeing weeds and picking some fresh mouth-watering organic vegetables. This is entertainment.

Source: Eli Stoltzfus (1969): 40–42

━━━━━━━━━━━━━━━━━━

Pushed into the Headlines

GIDEON L. FISHER

That the Amish feel uncomfortable with publicity is not understood by many news reporters. This account explains how they were drawn into a publicity stunt to aid tobacco lobbyists.

News reporters from all over the United States make large headlines when something unusual occurs among the Amish people, such as the school situation of years ago, or the Social Security Act in Washington. When a labor dispute occurred at one of the local factories, the news reporters made it appear that the Amish had called a strike against their employers. Large headlines appeared in the leading newspaper, and thousands of people saw it. They made it appear that the Amish were all involved in the commotion, but at the same time only a small fraction of them knew anything about it until it was published in our local newspaper.

When legislation was in the making for an act to add an extra thirty-five percent tax increase on Pennsylvania tobacco products, the tobacco companies were very much opposed to the act. They appeared unable to do much about it. So they hatched a plan and by smooth talking they got a number of Amish and Mennonite men interested in helping to throw the new tax act overboard. The tobacco companies were willing to furnish bus transportation to a scheduled meeting in Harrisburg when the members of the legislature met to discuss their views on the act. The protest signs were already made when the Amish arrived. As they descended from the bus, the Amish were made visible for photographers and reporters to take pictures and write a story about the Amish and Mennonites being opposed to the tax act. Even though there were a number of Mennonites in the protesting group, the Amish made the headlines. In the next few days a long and fantastic story was shown on television and published in most of the leading newspapers all over the nation. Here again, only a small portion of the Amish knew what was going on until it was seen in our local newspaper.

If any other class of people would have done the same thing in protesting against an act of the legislature, the news media would probably have published a small article in the local paper. But because the Amish name could be attached to their story, it went down in history as showing how the Amish cooperate with the tobacco companies.

Because our commonwealth was desperately in need of money at the time to meet certain demands, the officials felt that to impose a tax on tobacco products was the proper thing to do. But now that the tax act was thrown overboard, the tax had to be met from some other source. They added another cent to the already high sales tax. This tax of one cent interfered with more people than the tobacco tax would have.

Source: Gideon L. Fisher (1978): 366–67

12

JOINING AND
LEAVING THE FAITH

Although the Amish make no
attempts to proselytize others to their faith, a few converts have joined
them. The patronymic family names of the converts, such as Anderson,
Cross, Flaud, Helmuth, Huyard, Jones, Lee, Luthy, and Whetstone, stand
out in the community against the many traditional Germanic family names.
In Lancaster County, Pennsylvania, these names are predominantly Beiler,
Fisher, King, Lapp, and Stoltzfus; in Ohio, they are Hershberger, Miller,
Raber, Troyer, and Yoder. Presently there are about 126 family names of
Amish in North America. About 40 of these derive from North America,
and the rest are European in origin. In the three largest North American
settlements, over half the population is accounted for in 5 family names.
But despite the scarcity of converts, the Amish population has grown from
about 33,000 in 1950 to over 130,000 in 1989. The increase is due to large
family size and to effective child-rearing patterns. Most converts have either
lived and worked in Amish homes or have become members by adoption.
They were attracted to the Amish by consistent patterns of living rather than
reasoned verbal discourse. Although numerous counterculture members

sought out the Amish in the late 1960s and early 1970s, they soon turned away in disappointment. The greatest barriers for them were hard manual labor and the subtle, nonverbal requirements for inclusion in the community.

People who leave the Amish faith do so for various reasons. The Amish themselves attribute the loss of their children to the weak example or adverse influence of the parents. A few children have been exposed to the values of higher education. Others are influenced by persuasive fundamentalist religious groups. The cultural gap between the modern high school and the Amish way of life is so great that the Amish have virtually no temptation to join the secular world of work and leisure. Those Amish who are attracted to the outside world typically wait until they have performed their moral obligation to their family and, after the recognized legal age, pursue higher education or a profession of their choosing.

JOINING THE FAITH

-⇶-⇶-⇶-⇶-⇶-⇶-⇶-⇶-

I Came to Like Their Quiet Manner

NICHOLAS STOLTZFUS

O*ver 25 percent of the Amish in Lancaster County, Pennsylvania, are named Stoltzfus. All are descendants of Nicholas Stoltzfus (1718–1774), a young man of Lutheran background who lived with an Amish family before coming to America in 1766.*

Nicholas found employment among the Amish in the Zweibrücken area of the Palatinate. In his own words, he was "attracted to their quiet manner of conduct and converted to it." He wished to marry one of the daughters in the family with whom he lived and thus petitioned the Court of Zweibrücken for permission to do so. The court at first refused the marriage of a Lutheran to an Anabaptist (Amish) person but later relented, provided that Nicholas and his bride leave the area. At his death in 1774, Nicholas left behind a wife and four children. His petition for a marriage license reads as follows:

179

Relative to the application for permission from the excellent high office to proceed with the planned marriage to the daughter of the Rinckweyler farmer, an Amish-Mennonite girl, I have been referred to the office of the first prince's government, and this is because my parents have not been of this faith, but from Saxony, where I was born. My deceased father Christoffel Stoltzfus and my mother Frieszen Belleums, wife of the Evangelical Lutheran religion, and I on the return of my mother into the land after my father's death had to go to strangers for a time for employment. From the first time of my employment, I was, during my stay among strangers, on the farms of Cron Weiszemburg, where I had opportunity to stay with Mennonites, because the area was owned by them and no others. I came to like their quiet manner of conduct and was converted to it. And while I stayed there for some time longer and came to be an employed young person of this group around Rinkweyler, I decided upon marriage now that I am twenty-five years of age. I have no parents and cannot expect inheritance from them, and through such a marriage I could come to the means of a livelihood. I am now living in the hope that my desire will be assisted, rather than hindered. In this purpose I request most humbly, of the princely ruler, that my request be considered and that the marriage may be most graciously permitted. Most respectful and obedient to your royal majesty.

Zweibrücken, January 14, 1744

Nicholas Stoltzfus

Source: Unpublished Stoltzfus Family papers

➤➤➤-➤➤➤-➤➤➤-➤➤➤-➤➤➤-➤➤➤-➤➤➤-➤➤➤

Isaac Huyard Joins the Amish

DAVID E. HUYARD

D*avid E. Huyard is the only surviving son of Isaac (1865–1940), who joined the Amish. David and his wife, Lydia, occupy the "grandfather house" on the New Holland, Pennsylvania, farm acquired by his father. David likes to tell how a Lutheran boy joined the Amish.*

My ancestors came from Switzerland and France and from a colony of Huguenots. Their family name was Huyett. My grandfather Moses Huyett was a respected person. As the story goes, he had a brother who lived a life very embarrassing to my grandfather. So strong were his feelings that he decided he could not go through life with the same name as his good-for-nothing brother. So he had his name legally changed from Huyett to Huyard. My grandmother Lydia was a midwife. She vaccinated children against small-pox. At that time, it was called "planting pox germ."

My grandparents were very poor. There were times when the neighbors would take some of the children and care for them. An Amish couple, Jonathan Lapp and his wife, Barbara (they were called Yonie and Bevely), who had no children of their own heard about the poor family. One day Yonie told his wife that he would like to contact the Huyards and perhaps "get a cheap hired boy and also help out the family by raising one of the boys." Yonie approached Moses Huyard, saying that he would give a boy a home, plenty of good food, a good bed, and good clothes to wear. The father turned to his two sons and said, "Boys, what do you say?" When Isaac, the oldest boy, heard "plenty of good food" he was ready to give it a try. He knew what it meant to go to bed hungry.

The lad climbed into the carriage. The Amish man seemed strange to him, but he was cheerful. After the evening prayers, Yonie took the boy to his bedroom. Feeling the separation from his family and brothers, he cried himself to sleep. There were many nights like that, but he was pleased that Yonie and Bevely were nice to him. The farm activities interested him.

One morning Yonie said, "Today Bevely and I are going to visit my brother. You can sweep the spider webs in the entire downstairs of the barn and clean out the hog pen. When you are done, go to the house, read a chapter from the Bible, and when we come home I want you to tell me what you read."

Isaac completed his work in a short time, for he was minded to plan his work and work his plans. He quickly finished the work and went into the house and got the family Bible. On opening the Bible, he was shocked. The Bible was loaded with genuine paper money. There were ten dollar bills, fives, and ones. He was not tempted in the least to take any money. But he was afraid some of it might get lost and he would then get the blame.

When Yonie and Bevely returned home they asked, "Did you find time to read the Bible?" He told of the passage he read and recited some of it. He never mentioned the money, nor did Yonie. The lad was sure the money was placed there for a reason. Young Isaac had proved himself faithful.

Isaac was given a horse and buggy to attend his own (Lutheran) church. Here he had been baptized in infancy. He also sang in the choir and was a Sunday school teacher.

One day Isaac explained to his foster parents that he wanted to get an education, and go into business or become a teacher. Yonie said, "That is no problem." Yonie paid for his education at Millersville State Teachers College. Because the Lutheran church had service only every two weeks, he attended the Amish church every other Sunday. He began teaching in the country schools and taught all eight grades. He worked for Yonie on the farm in the summertime.

There was one girl in the community who was very special to the schoolteacher. Her name was Mary, the daughter of David and Rebecca Zook. In busy seasons the farmers helped one another, for they worked together. Isaac and Mary learned to know each other. Mary was very attractive and had a sweet personality. She was special. One day Isaac got the courage to ask Mary if she would accept him as her husband and life companion. Mary replied that she sure would accept him as a life companion but that she would not leave the Amish church. She said: "This would break my mother's heart, and I would not have a clear conscience to make such a change."

Now it was Isaac's turn to speak. He said: "Mary, I sincerely appreciate your respect for your church and your parents. I certainly would not ask you to leave. I will leave my church for yours. I can worship God in the Amish church. I will certainly join the Amish if they accept me." Mary's parents approved, as did also Christ Beiler, the respected father of Bevely.

Isaac tried hard to do his part. He let his hair grow extra long, and also let his beard and mustache grow. Isaac used to dress up quite a little, often wearing a white cowboy hat. But no more. He got a bottle of black ink and dyed his white hat and telescoped it. He also gave up his earlier desire to become a businessman. Now he would be an Amish farmer.

All went well until the Amish bishops said, "Isaac, we will not marry you, you are not a member of the Amish church." Isaac and Mary then had John Graybill, pastor of the German Baptist Church, perform the marriage ceremony on December 8, 1891. Because Mary married a nonmember, she had to be excommunicated. Then both Isaac and Mary were received into the Amish church together. Although Isaac had been baptized as an infant, he was rebaptized in keeping with the teaching of "believer's" baptism.

The couple worked on the farm of Mary's mother, but later took over Yonie and Bevely's farm, which became "home sweet home" for them. They enjoyed their new home, where Yonie and Bevely also lived in the grandpa house. They were blessed with five children, two girls and three boys.

My parents were conservative and saved wherever they could. They demonstrated that grandfather Christ Beiler was wrong when he told them before their marriage, "You are poor and will always stay poor." But they were cheerful givers and highly respected as honest and upright persons in business both with their neighbors and with the public. My father was chosen to be in the "lot" when a minister was selected, though he was never ordained.

He enjoyed his sausage and eggs. After the death of my mother, he often came and helped us boys on the farm. When he walked home he often repeated the poem "Alone and yet Not All Alone":

Alein, und doch nicht ganz alein
Bin ich in meiner einsamkeit.
Dann wann ich ganz verlassen schein
Vertreibt mir Jesus selbst die Zeit,
Ich bin bey ihm, und er bey mir
So kommt mirs gar nicht einsam für.
(Alone and yet not all alone
Am I in my loneliness.
Although I do seem forsaken and lonely
Jesus is near and helps me pass the time,
I am with him, and He is with me
Then to be alone doesn't seem too hard to bear.)

Source: Huyard (1987)

⟫-⟫-⟫-⟫-⟫-⟫-⟫-⟫

The Peight Family

DAVID LUTHY

Т*he Peight name entered the Amish culture by adoption, although a knowledge of the ancestors remains obscure.*

Isaac Franklin Peight and his wife, Juliana, lived in Mifflin County, Pennsylvania, in the area commonly called Big Valley. They did not belong to the Amish church, even though Mrs. Peight's maiden name was a common Amish name, "Lapp." It is believed they were Lutheran, since they are buried in the Lutheran cemetery and three of their children belonged to the Lutheran church. They had a number of children, one of whom was Samuel, who was born October 13, 1878. When Samuel was six years old his mother died. The Abe Peacheys, who were Amish, opened their hearts and home to this little boy. His brothers and sisters were also placed in homes, but Samuel was the only child that went to an Amish home.

Samuel grew up and joined the Amish church. On February 2, 1905, he married the neighbor's hired girl, Rachel Bawell (her father, Henry, had also come to the Amish from the "English"). In 1906, when he was twenty-eight, Samuel was ordained a minister in the Amish church. In 1911 the church divided into the Peachey and Zook churches. Samuel remained with the Peachey group, which is known today as the "Renno Amish". . . .

Samuel and Rachel set up housekeeping at the foot of Jack's Mountain. On this farm they raised eight children (three others died in infancy). There were six girls and two boys, Daniel and Samuel Junior. Daniel's son, Daniel Junior, was ordained an Amish minister in 1964. Today . . . all reside in Mifflin County, Pennsylvania.

There is an interesting belief that there is Indian blood in the Peight "freundschaft." Although there is no definite proof, it is commonly held by the Peights that one of their ancestors was married to an Indian. One family member writes concerning this: "I asked my father at one time just how this was or came about that we were related to the Indians. He said he had been told that way back (he didn't know how many generations) a hired girl was working for Indians or vice versa and that later they were intermarried. So that was all he had to tell me. . . . Really, it seems we have never found out the facts for sure. . . ." Another descendant writes: "We think it is more than tradition though. We have no written proof or records about the Indian blood more than what the old-timers used to say. But the black hair and high cheekbones in Sam's children and also some of the grandchildren seem to point that way."

Source: Luthy (1972): 21–22

-->>-->>-->>-->>-->>-->>-->>-->>

Rosanna of the Amish

DAVID LUTHY

Rosanna of the Amish *is a book of exceptionally widespread sales. It is an account of an Irish infant who was reared by Elizabeth Yoder, an Amish woman. The book was written by Rosanna's son Joseph Yoder. The condensation is by David Luthy.*

Rosanna of the Amish is not fiction. It is a true happening. Elizabeth Yoder, a maiden lady who lived in the Halfmoon Valley settlement, rented a room in her house to Patrick McGonegal, a recent Irish immigrant, who was working in the ore mines in Centre County. After boarding at Miss Yoder's home for a little more than a year, Patrick married Bridget O'Connor, who he had known in Ireland and who was now living in New York. Elizabeth Yoder offered that the newlyweds could live with her until they found a home of their own. And in so doing, the two women—one Amish and the other Catholic—became close friends. After a few months, the McGonegals moved into a home of their own which was not far away, and the two women continued to visit each other during the next years. But then tragedy struck—Bridget died five days after giving birth to her fourth child, Rosanna, in 1838. It was a terrible blow to Patrick, who was left with four small, motherless children.

Patrick decided to place his three oldest children among relatives in Philadelphia and to move there himself, but could he take a week-old baby that distance? He asked Elizabeth Yoder to care for Rosanna until she was a little older, at which time he would come for her. Months passed, but Patrick never came. Meanwhile, a bachelor, Christian Kauffman, asked Elizabeth to marry him, which she did. More months passed and then years. When Rosanna was four years old her foster parents, Christian and Elizabeth Kauffman, moved from Halfmoon Valley to the Lost Creek settlement in Juniata County. As Elizabeth climbed onto the wagon to leave for her new home, she looked down the familiar road and thought of Patrick McGonegal: "He has never come for the baby. I wonder why. I am sure something happened. Will we ever know?"

The mystery was finally solved five years later when Rosanna was nine. Her brother William, who had been old enough to remember having had Amish neighbors as a child, was clerking in a produce store in Philadelphia. In those days the farmers hauled their grain to that large city. Whenever William McGonegal saw an Amishman, he would ask if he knew his sister, Rosanna. Always the Amishmen would shake their heads no. But then one day Joseph Yoder of the Lost Creek settlement entered the store, and when asked if he knew Rosanna McGonegal, said, "Yes, I know her well." After receiving directions to the home of Christian and Elizabeth Kauffman many miles away, William prepared to go and visit his sister.

When William several weeks later entered the Kauffman home, he related how his father had worked only a short time in a gravel pit near Philadelphia when he and several other men had been killed in a landslide, being buried under tons of gravel. William had visited the Kauffmans with hopes of taking Rosanna back with him to Philadelphia. Regardless of the fact that William was her blood brother, Rosanna had never seen him before. He was a complete stranger to her, and she refused to go with him, nor did the Kauffmans encourage her to go. She had lived with them for nine years and was their "daughter."

Thus it was that Rosanna McGonegal was born in Halfmoon Valley and raised both there and in the Lost Creek settlement. When she grew to maturity she was baptized into the Amish Church and married Christian Z. Yoder of Mifflin County, who later was ordained a minister. . . .

The touching story is told in the biography *Rosanna of the Amish*, which was written by Joseph Yoder, one of Rosanna's sons, and privately published by him in 1940. Not only did the book sell well during its first year of publication, it has sold well ever since.

Source: Luthy (1986): 418–19

LEAVING THE FAITH

➤➤➤➤➤➤➤➤➤➤➤➤➤➤➤➤

They Were Sure I Was Foolish

C. HENRY SMITH

T*he son of Alsatian Amish-Mennonite immigrants, C. Henry Smith (1875–1948) was born near Metamora, Illinois. His curiosity led him to attend institutions of higher education. He was the first American Mennonite to earn a Ph.D. (University of Chicago, 1907).*

Few of my relatives sympathized with me in my life ambitions. Some thought I was lazy; all were sure that I was foolish. Uncle Joe, especially, who thought of values largely in terms of dollars and cents, after finding out some years later that I was earning less money with all my college preparation than his Henry, who had quit country school as soon as he was able to hold a plow handle, once told me he hoped none of his children would ever waste their lives like that. Of course, I did not tell him that I left the farm not to make more money elsewhere but to live a more satisfactory life. He would not have understood. I believe Henry's sister expressed the family estimate of the value of an education when she said, "If I know enough to count my eggs and figure up the amount of my butter I have all the education I need. What more does anybody want?"

But while most of my uncles and aunts may have thought me foolish in wasting my time in an occupation that brought such meager financial returns, I think I retained their respect and affection through all these years. I deliberately set myself the task of avoiding any break in the ties of affection that bound me to my family and my relatives. Although the world of my chief interests was far removed from theirs, that did not prevent me from sharing with them our far more important family heritage and traditions. For years I never returned home from college or from teaching in the city without a visit with them. They were always glad to see me and especially pleased that I was not "stuck up" as college boys were supposed to be when they visited the folks back on the farm. On such occasions I simply stepped out of my world and lived with them in theirs, forgetting for the time being that I had ever been anything but an unsophisticated farm boy.

With Uncle John, I argued the futility of waiting for the right sign of the moon to plant potatoes; with Uncle Pete, who remained a staunch Republican to the end, I talked politics, and to his delight usually agreed with him; while to Aunt Lena, who had taken up the collecting fad in her declining years, I would bring a rock or fossil from some strange place I had visited. This bit of recognition of her pet hobby on my part always gave her great pleasure, even though the contribution may have been nothing but an ordinary pebble picked up from a creek bed in a neighboring state. These visits I continued for years, until one after the other had all silently passed into that better land where neither wise nor foolish, high nor low, are known. It has always been a matter of sweet satisfaction to me that I was able to keep alive this spirit of comradeship and fellowship to the end with the brothers and sisters of my father and mother.

Source: C. Henry Smith (1962): 157–58

-»»-»»-»»-»»-»»-»»-»»-»»

I Tried Being Mennonite

NANCY FISHER

Nancy Fisher (1933–), who was brought up in the Amish faith, near Gap, Pennsylvania, writes of her transition from being Amish to being Mennonite. Today she is a social worker, as well as a practicing member of the Society of Friends.

At one point in my life I tried to be a Mennonite but somehow I just didn't fit. I've internalized Amishness so thoroughly that trying to be Mennonite was like trying to put a square peg in a round hole. I think that part of Mennonitism which made me most uncomfortable was the pressure I felt in Mennonite circles to verbalize that one was "saved," and to tangibly "witness" (hand out tracts, etc.) to others in an effort to lead them to "salvation."

I remember my college days (Eastern Mennonite College), when one earned extracurricular credits to heaven by spending Sundays "witnessing to the lost," the prisoners, the mountain folks and others. I usually stayed in the dorm involved in relaxing, writing letters, or in serious rap sessions with my dorm neighbors. However, periodically I would feel guilty for being somewhat irreligious. To friends I would give the flimsy excuse that I didn't feel comfortable "witnessing" to the people in my oversized Amish bonnet. (College regulations at that time strongly encouraged bonnet-wearing for witnessing and other such activities.)

No longer does such irreligiosity provoke guilt. When I decided that, to a greater theological degree, I was Amish and really valued the Amish attitude toward the specific theological question of salvation, then I could let the Mennonites do their thing without feeling conflict and guilt. The Amish attitude, as radiated by my parents during my upbringing, seems to be that salvation is more a process than a simple act of "being saved." That seemed to make more sense to me when I seriously evaluated the two attitudes. Salvation, I feel, is a heavy thing, a serious thing, a continuing soul-searching thing. Christ-likeness seems to be more focused on relationships. The Amish emphasis on brotherhood rather than on salvation means, to me, to be more in keeping with this whole theme of Christ-likeness.

Source: Nancy Fisher (1971)

➹➹➹➹➹➹➹➹➹➹➹➹➹➹➹➹

My Father Saw Himself as a Runt

BARBARA YODER HALL

Barbara Yoder Hall (1940–1988) *writes of her alcoholic father and his search for recovery, and she also discusses why her parents, with eleven children, left the Amish church.*

There is a saying, "Life begins at forty"; and my father, Mose Yoder, found that to be true. One week before his fortieth birthday, he said to my mother, "Mom, I've got to get help. I can't go on drinking like this. I feel so awful."

Although these were the words my mother had been waiting to hear, she knew that finding help for my father's drinking problem was not going to be easy. . . . That very day that my father made his plea for help, an Amish man came to visit my grandfather on our farm. As the friend was hitching up his horse and preparing to leave, my father asked the man for some money to get help for his drinking problem. My father had heard that there was a program that helped people sober up, although he didn't know where to go to find help. . . .

The friend suggested that he go to Wooster, Ohio, a town about ten miles from our farm, to a blacksmith who had received help for his drinking problem.

My father hitched up the horse to the buggy and made that trip to Wooster. The Amish friend was right. The blacksmith had just been through a hospital program for his drinking and he recommended the same program very strongly to my father. He told him that the hospital was located in Columbus, Ohio, 150 miles from Wooster.

Leaving my oldest sister, Cora, in charge of her eight brothers and sisters, my parents made the trip by train to Columbus to find the place that was going to help my father give up alcohol—the alcohol that had controlled his life since he was in his teens, the alcohol that covered up the loneliness he experienced as a child. . . .

My father was so much younger than his brothers and sisters that he felt like an only child. He was also very slight of build and often saw himself as a runt. In his early years tragedy struck his family. When he was nine, his mother died unexpectedly of measles, and little Mosie's heart was broken. He loved his mother very much and couldn't picture life without her.

When Mosie was thirteen, his father sold the farm where they lived. For several years Mose worked for his married sisters before he started farming for people who were not his relatives.

At the age of sixteen he was sled riding with some of his friends one Sunday afternoon, and the young boys brought out the hard cider. Young Mose liked the effects of this drink. After the second drink he did not feel like a runt, and he was a lot less shy. His friends could see that Mose was not going to quit drinking cider on his own, so they took it away from him. The next morning he awoke with a headache like he had never experienced before. But that headache did not stop him from wanting the cider again. He drank it as often as he could get it. Before he was eighteen years old, he had added beer and whiskey to his diet.

He could still hold down jobs on the farm where he worked. However, it wasn't long before an employer discovered that his supply of good homemade wine was dwindling and had to be put under lock and key.

At the age of twenty-two Mose married Mary F. Miller. The children started to arrive the following year. He knew he was not the husband and father he should be, but he had lost all control of his life.

He discovered by then that the best way to get rid of a hangover and a headache was to have something to drink the morning after.

He worked hard and he drank hard. He hated farming, so he got a job at the pottery four miles from home. He walked that distance every day and drank on the way to work. He threw his whiskey bottle in the weeds by the side of the road near town. After work he retrieved the bottle and resumed drinking on his walk home. He remembered one specific time when he threw his bottle into the weeds, heard a crash, and knew that his bottle had hit a rock. There would be no whiskey on the way home that night.

He would pull himself together on Sundays to take the family to church; but, nevertheless, the Amish community knew that Mose Yoder had a problem.

Mose was sick when he was drinking and sick when he wasn't drinking. This vicious cycle caused him to have bouts of very deep depression. At times my mother was afraid to go to the barn, fearing that she would find him hanging from the rafters.

Although money was scarce, the family never went hungry. The children learned at a young age to work hard under my mother's direction and carry their share of the workload.

Although the children were not aware that their father had a drinking problem, they did know that he was unhappy and gruff most of the time.

There were some things that my two older brothers were not able to understand until later years. They often wondered how empty brown jugs appeared in the haystack. When they were younger, they thought perhaps they grew there. They also wondered why the drinks in their glasses were different in color from the drink their father was having when he took them along to the local bar.

My father's drinking not only caused problems in his marriage; it also created many hard feelings with his in-laws, with whom he lived. They did not understand that the problem that was controlling my father was more than a sign of irresponsibility, that it was something that could not be shed as easily as a cumbersome overcoat. From the age of sixteen until the age of thirty-seven, he had grown more miserable with each day. From the age of thirty-seven until his fortieth birthday, life was almost unbearable for him.

So Mose and Mary made that trip to Columbus, to a hospital that would help him give up the bottle for good, so he was told. The man who met them at the door of the hospital asked my father some questions. My father later said, "I told him part truth, part lie, and the man pronounced me an alcoholic, which is just a fancy word for a drunk."

After my father was settled in the hospital, my mother returned the 150 miles on the train to tend to her children at home. He was to stay five days. He said those were the sickest days of his life. There were twenty-two other men at the hospital, and it wasn't until the fourth day that he heard the term "Alcoholics Anonymous" [A.A.].

Suffering intensely, he asked the manager one day, "How long will I feel like this? When will the craving for alcohol leave?" The kindly manager replied, "Someday it will come easier." Those were the five words that my father hung on to for life.

After five days, Mose traveled home by bus, where my mother was waiting for him with the horse and buggy. It was quite a shock for her to see this sickly man coming home. She was expecting a quick cure that would make him well, not looking like he had been put through a washing machine wringer.

At the hospital he had been told about meetings that were held regularly in Wooster, and that he should attend those meetings for his own good. He paid no attention to that advice. He wouldn't need any meetings; he was sober—and he intended to stay sober even if he was miserable. He kept hanging on to the words of the manager at the hospital, "Someday it will come easier." It was his lifeline.

Ten days after he returned home from the hospital, he went to visit a neighbor who was ill. When he came back from the visit, my mother told him that the blacksmith from Wooster, who had recommended A.A. to him, had come to invite him to a meeting. My father was so touched that someone would go out of his way to pay attention to him that he decided to go to the meeting to see what it was like.

Little did he realize that what he found that night was what he had been searching for all his adult life. He found there a sincere welcome and a look on the faces of the people that was exhilarating. These were people with the same problem that he had, and yet they were smiling. And, most of all, they didn't look like they were sick anymore. Mose wanted that. He said, "I don't remember who spoke that night or what he said. All I know is that I went home with a new hope. I had found a group of people who spoke my language."

New problems surfaced. In our very strict Old Order Amish church involvement in outside activities was frowned upon, so he had to be careful not to offend his friends and relatives with his new-found enthusiasm about A.A. Not wanting to cause trouble within the church, he decided our family would join the Mennonite church, a denomination he thought would be more open to his A.A. involvement. He also needed a car to attend the meetings that were his lifeline.

At the A.A. meetings my father watched as people got up and talked about their experiences with alcohol, and he thought to himself, "I'll never do that." This inhibited, quiet Amish man knew he would never get up in front of people and share his story.

Seven months after he sobered up, my father gave his first "lead"; and for thirty-seven years he told his story to people from all walks of life all over the United States and Canada.

Traveling great distances did not matter to my father. He did not mind driving to Michigan one night and then to Kentucky the following night while still holding down a full-time job at a sheet metal shop. He often came home at four in the morning from a meeting and got up at seven in the morning to go to work. Even in his seventies, he traveled long distances to lead meetings. He averaged between 40,000 and 50,000 miles a year on his car.

He was driving a blind horse until he was forty years old, and the art of driving a car never did come easily to him. No one taught him how to drive a car. He learned by observing others as he rode along with them to meetings soon after he joined A.A.

There was one trait that my father kept from his horse-and-buggy days. It's very unsafe and definitely not recommended for anyone. He would sleep and drive. The reason that my father never had a head-on collision is that my mother kept him awake. Oh, not the usual way, by nagging. She would sing to him while he drove. The more erratic his driving would be, the louder she would sing. Her favorite song to wake him up was "How Great Thou Art." She would start out softly on the verse, and, if that didn't wake him up, she would sing the chorus at full volume. It would usually wake him up.

Just like the blacksmith who had come to his rescue, my father wanted to repay that debt, and he did so by pointing others to A.A. and the program that saved his life.

In the latter years he often apologized to his eleven children for neglecting us. He knew that the first half of his life was consumed by alcohol, and the last half of his life was consumed by Alcoholics Anonymous. He tried very hard to make it up to all of us during the years that his heart slowed him down.

Source: Hall (1985): 1–15

⇛-⇛-⇛-⇛-⇛-⇛-⇛-⇛

Social Activities Were Lacking

NAME WITHHELD

This autobiographical account illustrates the difficulty of a young man who could not accept the standards of his Amish peer group and was thus rejected by them. He sought acceptable social activities, which he could not find among his Amish peers. The author is pastor of a Mennonite congregation.

My childhood days were happy days. Dad and Mother loved and took good care of their children, and they taught us to read the Bible when we were small children. Sundays we had to lay aside storybooks, as only religious literature was read. Since the Amish church used the German Bible, we were taught to read German. Although we received enough knowledge to read the German Bible, we used the English Bible most because we understood it better. Many happy hours were spent visiting the neighbors or having them visit us. We attended church services every two weeks, which is the custom of most Amish churches.

We attended school in the same country schoolhouse that Dad attended when he was a boy. Most of the pupils were either Amish or Mennonite. Two of my teachers, who taught me seven of my eight years of school, were Mennonite ladies. They had a large influence in leading me to a saving knowledge of Jesus Christ. When I graduated from the eighth grade I quit school to help Dad at home on the farm. What little education I received beyond the eighth grade I acquired by reading and through experience.

When sixteen years old, I started to attend the social activities of the Amish young people. Sunday evenings we would gather together for a singing. We left home about seven o'clock and came back around midnight. Assembling at a home where preaching services had been held in the morning, we would gather in a room around a large table and sing from German hymnals for an hour or two; then everyone would go to the barn or shed and play old-time party games until time to go home. If it was too cold to travel with horse and buggy, we would stay home. Saturday evenings we mostly gathered in the barn or tobacco shed to sing.

This was about all the social activity that the Amish church offered her young people. I was not satisfied with these few social activities, so I went to fairs and farm shows to satisfy my social longing. Also, without my parents knowing it, I attended the theater; and about the same time I took my first drink. This led to card playing and gambling. I pretended to be a Christian when I was home, then I would go away and seek the pleasure of the world to satisfy my own desires. Thus, I lived deceiving my parents and the church.

When a minister preached about future life, heaven and hell, conviction would seize me. I knew I was not ready to meet God. I said no to the voice of the Spirit more than once, each time getting farther and farther away from God and the teachings of my loving parents.

After two years of this double-faced life, I thought I couldn't live that way any longer. One morning while working alone, I decided to leave home. I went in the house, packed a small suitcase without anyone knowing it, and left. I walked a few miles to Route 30, where I hiked a ride. That night I slept under an apple tree in a pasture lot in western Pennsylvania. After traveling for several days, I did find a job on a farm in Ohio. While living there I wrote home, telling my parents where I was and what I was doing.

Dad and Mother were heartbroken because their son had left them and their teaching of Christ. Offering a prayer to God, they sent two of my brothers to come and bring me home. I went home with them, but I was as hard-hearted as ever.

After this experience I lived at home again but refused to attend any Amish social activities or church services; then one evening several months later a neighbor came to buy some milk. He talked with me and in the course of the conversation invited me along to services at the Maple Grove Mennonite Church. I accepted the invitation and went along to Sunday School and preaching service. I sat in the back of the auditorium and saw several teachers stand in front of their classes and teach as if they really meant what they taught. I felt they had something I did not have but needed.

The young people of the church accepted me as one of the group. Associating with young people of my own age, who were consecrated to Christ, had a big influence on me. I found real happiness through serving Christ by taking part in the activities of the Mennonite young people.

Source: Name withheld, unpublished manuscript [1961]

13

CONTROVERSIES
AND DISPUTES

Ohe of the social malignancies of the Amish community is envy. Jealousy can divide families, neighbors, and church districts, as well as weaken the spiritual bonds of community. Although the Amish aspire to attain unity, peace, and harmony among members, controversies do arise. Disputes that persist and are unreconciled not only polarize the community but also may destroy it.

Individuals may be excommunicated from the church if they do not show contrition, for at least three reasons—if they live in open sin, cause divisions, or teach a false doctrine. Because the church must maintain a state of purity and unblemished character, the obdurate and disobedient must be excluded. If transgressions are clearly established and the accused person accepts the severity of the offense, there is usually no further problem. However, if the accused person feels that he or she is a victim of unjust accusations and discrimination, or has been dealt with in an arbitrary manner, there is no further recourse. The church has the power to bind or to loose (Matt. 16:18).

->>> ->>> ->>> ->>> ->>> ->>> ->>> ->>>

The Unsigned Letter

DAVID LUTHY

Long *before it disintegrated, the
Amish community in Union County, Pennsylvania, had suffered from grudges
and internal family jealousies, as indicated by these two selections.*

The years 1873–1880 were trying times for the Buffalo Valley [Pa.] congregation. During those seven years only one semiannual communion service was held. Disunity—originating among the ministers but soon spreading to the lay members—prevented the communion services from being held.

Since the people held grudges against one another, events which would have caused only a minor disturbance in other congregations widened the gap between the Union County factions. One such happening was when a romantic letter was sent unsigned to an unmarried Amish maiden. The unsigned letter became the center of a spirited controversy and investigation. Since Bishop Elias Riehl's son had previously sent several such letters and had been disciplined in church for it, he was the obvious suspect. But this time he declared he was innocent.

The people did not let the matter drop but sent away samples of a dozen young men's penmanship to a handwriting expert. He reported that none of their writing matched that of the letter. The matter should have been dropped, surely, by this point, but some people persisted in blaming Elias Riehl's son and demanded that he confess he had written the letter. But he continued to deny any involvement with the letter, and his father supported him in pleas of innocence.

Many years later, long after the congregation had disintegrated, the mystery of the unsigned letter was solved. The young woman who had received the letter confessed that she had written it to herself in an attempt to impress her friends with her popularity!

Source: Luthy (1986): 425, based on Umble (1933b): 163

Disunity in Buffalo Valley

DAVID LUTHY

Samuel Kauffman, an expert carpenter, is said to have constructed the first tower for a windmill on the roof of John Stoltzfus's barn southeast of Vicksburg in 1880. On it he placed a Halliday windmill, for which three of Deacon Christian Stoltzfus's sons—John, Simeon, and Jacob—had a dealership. One of Bishop Elias Riehl's sons, learning that their dealership was only a verbal agreement, went to the company and secured a written contract granting him exclusive rights to sell the Halliday windmill. He toured the surrounding counties, accompanied by some of his brothers, driving a wagon bearing a sign: "Riehl Brothers, Sole Representatives, The Halliday Windmill."

The storm which resulted from the Riehl brothers' action was the darkest day in the settlement's history. John Umble reported the following:

> Members of the congregation demanded that the bishop discipline his sons for the way in which they secured the contract. He took no action in the matter. Practically the entire congregation, including Bishop Riehl's brothers-in-law, took sides with the Stoltzfus brothers and demanded church action.
>
> Finally one Sunday after meeting when it was announced that services would be held at the home of Jacob Stoltzfus (eldest surviving son of the deacon) in two weeks, Jacob emphatically asserted in the hearing of everyone present, "Elias Riehl won't preach in my house." Bishop Riehl absented himself from services after that.
>
> Deacon Stoltzfus yielded to the demands of the congregation and took the voice of the church relative to calling in an investigating committee. The result, as everyone foresaw, was an overwhelming vote in favor of calling ministers from Mifflin County. Tradition reports that full-deacon Samuel Yoder and Preacher David Zook were chosen to settle the difficulty. Feelings had become so strong that many in the congregation demanded not only the silencing of the bishop, but his excommunication as well. . . .
>
> The committee called a members' meeting, which, however, Bishop Riehl and his friends refused to attend. After a perfunctory trial the congregation, with the

exception of some of the bishop's sisters, voted to silence Bishop Elias Riehl and to excommunicate the bishop's brother, Joel, and the latter's wife.

Source: Luthy (1986): 426, based on Umble (1933b): 163

-⫸⫸-⫸⫸-⫸⫸-⫸⫸-⫸⫸-⫸⫸-⫸⫸-⫸⫸

The Silenced Preacher

C.I.B. BRANE

Abraham Draksel *(also rendered as Troxell), born in 1753, was an Amish minister in Lebanon County, Pennsylvania. He came under the influence of Protestant revivalists, for which he was "silenced" by his church. This account was written in 1903 by C.I.B. Brane.*

Soon after the town of Lebanon was laid out, and when most of our fair and fertile farms were covered with forests . . . the work of soul-saving evangelism was organized and entered upon, . . . the movement being pioneered by a company of plain but pious preachers, chiefly of the Mennonite Society, but including members of every other Protestant persuasion. At that time the trend of church life, in spite of the faithfulness of the few ministers then employed to preach the Gospel, was largely negative and neutral, affording little or no stimulation to spiritual exercise. Moreover, this was the period immediately preceding the Revolutionary War, which was additionally demoralizing and detrimental to religion. . . . The period of religious indifference to which I refer was broken by a great Pentecostal meeting at Isaac Long's near Lancaster, in 1767, on which occasion people of high and low degree, and representing almost every phase of belief known to the Commonwealth of Israel, came from far and near and sat under the spell of Gospel unity in a large barn where Martin Boehm, a Mennonite Minister, preached the Word with such power and unction that scores were then and there led to forsake sin and embrace the Saviour. . . .

Lutherans, Presbyterians, Methodists, Amish, Reformed, Dunkards, Moravians and Mennonites came together "in the unity of the faith, and of the knowledge of the Son of God," and there wrought to His glory the salvation of souls.

Of the six men who originally pioneered the cause of United Brethrenism in Pennsylvania, four were natives of Lebanon county, namely Martin Kreider, Abraham Draksel, Casper Sherk and Felix Light.

Next to Martin Kreider, Abraham Draksel stood most helpfully identified with the revival movement in Pennsylvania, and especially in Lebanon County. He was called "the silenced preacher," because his Amish brethren, among whom he was a minister, thought he made too much of the doctrine of regeneration in his preaching. But he insisted that the Christian religion is a matter of new life and enjoyment in the Holy Ghost; so he was "silenced"—notified that he must stop preaching.

Of course, Mr. Draksel continued the work of an evangelist, and was distinguished for his abundant labors, sweet spirit, Gospel sermons and blameless life. It is said that his beaming countenance, which was always lit up with an optimistic faith in God and the Gospel, was an index to the spiritual joy and sunshine that reigned within. He lived two or three miles northwest of Lebanon.

A sacramental meeting of great power and far-reaching influence was held at Mr. Draksel's home on the first day of May, 1796.

Source: Brane (1903): 322–27

>>>->>>->>>->>>->>>->>>->>>->>>

A Dangerous Belief

JOHN R. RENNO

The Amish are often accused of not teaching the "new birth." Although they do teach regeneration of life and practice believers' baptism, they expect these teachings to lead to submission and "walking in righteousness" rather than "a lot of religious talk." Excessive talk about "assurance of salvation" is regarded as pride, "a strange belief." John R. Renno, who was excommunicated for his "strange belief," relates his experience.

In 1952, a new and unheard-of trouble developed in the Old Order Amish groups. It first developed at Belleville, but soon spread all over, in every community. It was the doctrine of the assurance of salvation. Now the Amish hold to the belief that no one knows for sure whether he has been accepted by God or not. They hope so, but it is impossible to know. Such Scripture passages as "His Spirit beareth witness with our spirit, that we are the children of God, and if children, then heirs" remained ambiguous for them. It was said that the Apostles were much better men than we are and they could possibly know, but not us. We are too sinful. And it was reasoned that if a man knew he was right with God, there would be no more effort. His eternal destiny was fixed and settled. The Mennonites were a bit different; they believed that a person could know whether he was right with God now. This doctrine of assurance was strongly adhered to by the Mennonites and they tried to get converts, but the Amish called it dangerous and a doctrine of devils. They argued that we must just do as good as we know how and obey our spiritual leaders and hope for heaven, hope that the Lord will look at all our honest efforts, and if that did not reach, God would supply the grace to get us into heaven once we die.

The bishop, my father, John B. Renno, although a wise man, was not quite equal to this task, for it was so new he never had to combat it before. It looked good and sounded scriptural, and he finally said he could not call it a devilish doctrine, but he just did not know. Those who believed it were obedient to the church rules, although they confessed these rules do not save them, or help them to gain the favor of God. My father said if it were a case of sin and pronounced wickedness it would be easy to deal with it. The guilty ones would soon be placed in the ban, but here were people who were not troublemakers and did nothing morally wrong. Their belief just did not measure up to what we were always taught, and he had his office to protect, so he did the best he could, although it did not seem right. He himself could have borne and tolerated the doctrine, but there were some who were violently opposed to it, insisting that those who believed such heresy must be expelled, and soon, for it was beginning to spread. So the Ministry counseled together, and earnestly requested that nothing more be spoken about this doctrine by anyone, and that the book of the Revelation should not be read at all for the duration, for some were even believing the doctrine of the thousand-year reign of Christ upon the earth and declared in Revelation. He said that the best members of the church do not know much Scripture themselves, they just know what they are told, and they are quiet and do not trouble anyone with what they believe. The new doctrine could be tolerated if the proponents thereof would just be silent, and read the Sermon on the Mount spoken by Jesus, and not concern themselves about the eternal future. Nobody knows what will be anyway, God will be the final judge and cast to hell or heaven whatever he decided.

But all the admonitions did not help, for the more they were told to be quiet, the more they spoke. So now they were disobedient to the church authority, and there is only one remedy for that. If a man will not listen to the church, "let him be to thee as a heathen man and a publican." So he very reluctantly started putting people in the ban. I was the first one. I did not want to leave the Amish, for they were my people. I loved them, and leaving them was the very last resort, and I took instruction all summer trying to be received back into the fellowship again, only to be left alone concerning what I believe. I could not gain entrance, and my wife did not believe that she should avoid me; she was expelled, too, for disobedience. One other family, who were friends of ours, were expelled for associating with us. Now it was hoped that peace could be obtained, but it did not last long, for the doctrine worked in the minds of people, and those who studied the Scripture knew there was something wrong. So to avoid being caught, it was best to stop reading the Scripture, and this did not seem right either.

Although I had many good friends, and my father was always friendly and treated me nice, he had his office to protect. It did not seem right to him to place me with the disobedient and rebels, yet what could he do! I was sorry for them, for I lived on the homeplace where I was born and raised. So I sold the place to my oldest brother and moved out of the community.

Source: Renno [1976]: 21–22

➤➤➤➤➤➤➤➤➤➤➤➤➤➤➤➤

Tobacco

ANONYMOUS

The Amish in Lancaster County, Pennsylvania, and their branch colony in Saint Mary's County, Maryland, are the only Amish who have raised tobacco. At one time over 80 percent of the Amish in Leacock Township grew it. Stripping tobacco leaves from the stems provides work for the family in the winter. Although the crop is profitable, the raising of tobacco is diminishing today. Those who favor the raising of tobacco and those who oppose it advance many arguments, as indicated by these two anonymous letters in Family Life.

Dear Brother:

Concerning farming and the use of tobacco, I will answer to explain my beliefs. First of all, I want to tell you that I am in the process of reducing my farming and restricting myself in its use. Not because I call it bad or unclean, for who am I to call something bad that the Lord called good (Gen. 1:12) or unclean that the Lord cleansed (Acts 10:15)? But that I might be found to be one as Paul recommended (Rom. 14:21) that it is good neither to eat flesh or to drink wine, nor any other thing whereby thy brother stumbleth or is offended or is made weak.

Also, you have said that Christ, when he was here, would not have used tobacco. Let us in this case consider his stand concerning wine (which you will admit is far more violent and deadly). Did he not make wine? (John 2:1–11). Was he not called a wine bibber? (Luke 7:34). Likewise, Paul recommended its use (Tim. 5:23). I am persuaded that the overuse or abuse of tobacco could well be added to the list of wine (alcohol) or excessive eating (reveling), that they which do these things shall not inherit the kingdom of Heaven (Gal. 5:21).

Concerning the opinion of them that believe not, I will not try to appear wise or prudent to them, for the way of truth is foolishness to them that believe not (1 Cor. 1:27, 2:14).

And so, my brother, if I use tobacco or do not use it, if I farm tobacco or do not farm it, if I drink wine or do not drink it, I hope to remain as the Apostle Paul recommended in his Letter to the Romans in the fourteenth chapter, the third verse, "Let not him that eateth despise him that eateth not, and let not him that eateth not judge him that eateth."

This much have I written of my beliefs since you inquired about them. There would be many more details but, since space does not permit, I will close. With a hope and prayer that we can remain of one mind and in peace and love travel together to that eternal abode.

Your Brother, Pennsylvania

I Grew Up with Tobacco

As a parent myself, I know how often we have to say no to our children's wishes and wants. And now that I am an adult, I'm glad our parents taught us to live and eat simply. But I was a child who grew up in a home where tobacco was raised and used. I do not remember at what age I first became aware of the fact, but I was quite young when we first noticed that Father could call gum or candy unnecessary or too extravagant, while at the same time he had money for tobacco. And he bought the tobacco despite Mother's wish that it be laid aside.

Even as a child, I vowed I'd never marry a man who used tobacco, and I hoped never to farm it. This wish was not granted at first, as we farmed on half-shares and this was part of our landlord's agreement. In time we got away from it, and I am thankful, even though I know we could be better off financially today if we had kept on farming it. While some of the other crops we are raising do have their own problems, at least we can sleep at night about them, knowing they at least are doing no one any harm.

I recently read that doctors say over 300,000 people a year are dying from cigarette-related causes. Think it over. Over a period of five years, that is 1,500,000 people! Yet we are a people who would rather go to prison than to go to war or bear arms. Is this consistent?

Sources: Anonymous letters, in *Family Life* (July 1984): 3, and (October 1984): 16

14

MEMORABILIA

The Amish speak in three distinctive tongues. First, children learn a Pennsylvania German dialect sometimes known as Pennsylvania Dutch. "Dutch" derives from *Deutsch* (German) and does not refer to the language of the Netherlands. The dialect, which is used in domestic situations, was also spoken by Amish immigrants. Second, the Amish learn to read, write, and speak English with considerable ease in school. Third, they acquire a passive knowledge of High German by reading the Bible and by recitation. Their worship and formal ceremonies are conducted in modified High German.

Children use English when speaking with non-Amish people. An Amish person will shift his or her conversation from the dialect to English, whichever is more comfortable for the occasion. Because the Amish are bilingual at an early age, they do not have a noticeable accent. The custom of calling the non-Amish person "English" (the equivalent of outsider, or alien) stems from colonial times, when people were identified by their linguistic community, such as French, Spanish, German, and English. This usage does not imply either loyalty to England or disloyalty to America.

Events worth remembering in the Amish community include a large variety of topics, some of which are introduced in this chapter. The earliest printed matter consisted of religious beliefs and was followed by advice of fathers to their children, with some poetry and history, all privately published. The classic religious books, such as Bibles, testaments, and hymn books, are simply reprinted without changes. But most of what the Amish read today is in English. Letters among themselves are in English. Letter writing is rampant between relatives and between Amish communities. Circle letters exist for almost any kind of group. A group of ministers who were ordained in the same year is one example. There are also circle letters among age groups, interest groups, the handicapped, childless couples, dwarfs, "little people" who are not dwarfs, and numerous other groups.

Many Amish are avid story readers, and Amish periodicals publish a variety of stories whose moral tone reflects a deep concern with making the right choices. Many readers are interested in history pertaining to their faith or ancestors. The largest number of books published by the Amish are of a genealogical nature.

⇾⇾⇾-⇾⇾⇾-⇾⇾⇾-⇾⇾⇾-⇾⇾⇾-⇾⇾⇾-⇾⇾⇾-⇾⇾⇾

Heart-Yearnings for Home

JOSEPH W. YODER

*H*ome-yearnings, homesickness, and *nostalgia are popular themes in Amish lore. There are formulas for drawing wayward young people back to their homeland. Joseph W. Yoder (1872–1956) articulates such drawing power in this selection. He lived in Huntington, Pennsylvania, and had grown up in an Amish home in Mifflin County, Pennsylvania. He was the author of several books, an orator, and a noted song leader at teachers' institutes.*

My boyhood friend Simon M. Kanagy came back to the Valley after an absence of about eleven years, in which he taught school and later worked his way through the academy and the college at Northwestern University. He was glad to come back to his boyhood home, and see his old friends. I took our horse and buggy, and Simon and I drove about over the country to see his old friends. We visited many places where we had spent pleasant times together some years before, and, when we approached one of these familiar scenes, Simon would say, *"Oh, des hähmelt mir ahn."* This is a Pennsylvania German idiom, and can hardly be translated, but it calls to mind olden times and pleasures with such vividness that the memories are akin to pain. Several years later while teaching at Lock Haven Teachers' College, in my room one Sunday evening, I determined to put this little teaser into verse. I call the effort *"Es hähmelt mir ahn."*

There's a word that often comes to my mind,
Its meaning is wondrously beautiful;
But I cannot fully explain it,
And make its meaning clear and plain:
But an illustration comes oft when I'm walking
At home, and I often come to the thought:
And now the expression I will write here,
It's just this: "Es hähmelt mir ahn."

"Es hähmelt mir ahn," what a proverb,
Full of love, and homesickness, almost pain;
Full of loneliness for father and mother,
Full of sorrow, and to this, a full heart:
It tells us of childish contentment,
Of this saying everything reminds us,
One looks around, then stands and studies,
And then says, "Es hähmelt mir ahn."

How oft we go back to the old home,
Where we played with childish glee
(Of all the treasures that God gives,
None stays in the bosom like Home);
How full of good times is the old barn.
The haymow just rattles with fun;
Come, let us all here play Bloom-sock,
My gracious! this hähmels mir ahn.

In the barn the overshot was the best place,
When one was long away from home;
Just to sit and listen to the horses,
As the chains rattled at the halters (bridles),
Many are the times that we all sat there,
And sometimes the work was not all done;
But it was raining, and we were tired working,
That old overshot! it hähmels mir ahn.

That was the place that father
Would sit with us and tell us at length,
How they worked when he was still a boy,
And told us how we often make mistakes:
There he taught us to break colts,
And the age of a horse by his teeth;
And the very best way to hold a grain cradle
That old overshot—it hähmels mir ahn.

In the wagon shed the old reaper
Tells us of hay field, and harvest field, and heat,
Of tricks that the boys used to play,
When one was too exalted and tricky;
The ten o'clock piece in the harvest field,
We were all half-crazy to get at
When we think back, it makes us a little homesick.
These things, they hähmel mir ahn.

Every corner in the house tells us plainly,
Of years full of labor and fun;
Full of laughter, and weeping and thinking,
And childish tantrums and hate:
The bedroom with trundlebed and cradle,
Is a reminder with much meaning plain
It tells us of restful sleeping,
No sorrow—Sie hähmelt mir ahn.

Of course, the old cradle is broken,
And the trundlebed has only three legs;
But the joy of mother's singing,
Can never leave the little bed:
When sickness laid us low here,
With pain in body or tooth;
When mother was always with us,
This little trundlebed, Es hähmelt mir ahn.

Yes, I believe we all like to go home,
And just be along somewhere outside;
And walk around slowly and look,
From the barn into the house;
Our eyes grow misty with tears;
As we stand and look at each reminder,
The heart grows heavy and with yearning,
We just say, "Es hähmelt mir ahn."

Source: Joseph W. Yoder (1948): 310–15

BIBLE BOOKPLATE 1, 1845
Benjamin Beiler.
Lancaster County, Pennsylvania. 7¹/₄ × 9³/₄.

This Bible belongs to me David Beiler [1791–1866].
With God let all things begin.
With God let all things come to rest.
So shall the labor of your hands
Proceed and be blessed.

[This bookplate and the two that follow appear in sequence
in the front pages of the Beiler family Bible.]

Private collection.

BIBLE BOOKPLATE 2, 1894
Anonymous.
Lancaster County, Pennsylvania. $6^3/4 \times 9^1/2$.

This Bible belongs to me David F. Beiler (1822–1907). East Lampeter Township, Lancaster County, Pennsylvania. Received from my father David Beiler. Written on the 9th day of April in the year 1894.

Private collection.

BIBLE BOOKPLATE 3, 1916
David C. Hoke.
Lancaster County, Pennsylvania. 6⁷/₈ × 9¹/₂.

*This Bible belongs to me Aaron S. Glick. Received
as a gift from my Mother Rebecca Glick, 1916.*

Private collection.

BOOKPLATE FOR ELIZABETH, 1858
Attributed to Barbara Ebersol (1846–1922).
Lancaster County, Pennsylvania. 4¹/₄ × 7.

This book belongs to Elizabeth Ebersol. 1858.

Private collection.

HYMNAL BOOKPLATE, 1858
Anonymous.
Lancaster County, Pennsylvania. $3^{1}/_{2} \times 5^{5}/_{8}$.

*This hymnbook belongs to me Maria Beiler, in East Lampeter Township,
Lancaster County, State of Pennsylvania. Written on the 5th day of March,
in the year of our Lord 1858.*

*God grant us great fortune and blessings.
And lead us by your ways
That bring us to glory
After the end of our days.*

Courtesy Pennsylvania Farm Museum.

TWO PEARS, 1869
Barbara Zook (1839–1920). *Bookplate.*
Mifflin County, Pennsylvania. 3¹/₂ × 5.

I Barbara Zook give this to Levi Detweiler
as a remembrance. 1869.

Private collection.

BOOKPLATE FOR JONATHAN LANTZ, 1882
Barbara Ebersol (1846–1922).
Lancaster County, Pennsylvania. $9^{3}/_{4}$ x $11^{1}/_{4}$

This book belongs to me Jonathan Lantz,
which I received from my father Benjamin Lantz in the year 1882.

Private collection.

BLUE DOVE *(undated)*
Anonymous artist. *Drawing.*
Mifflin County, Pennsylvania.

Private collection.

-»»-»»-»»-»»-»»-»»-»»-»»

Indian up a Tree

LES TROYER

T*he elderly Amish still relate stories about the frontier and their experiences with Native Americans. Les Troyer, of Amish ancestry, is a linguist and a collector of Amish lore who lives in Ohio.*

Hans was deathly afraid of Indians. Long before he left the high Alps in Switzerland, Hans had read of the massacres and brutal killings of the settlers in America. He had heard of the Red Men shaving off scalps of the White People like the filleting of a Sunday dinner chicken. And when he found himself dreaming of someday going to "The States," it was always as though a tomahawk-swinging Indian stepped right into his mind.

However, after he was grown, opportunity suddenly came; and he sailed for America to join his mother's cousin in Auburn Township, in the foothills of eastern Ohio. When Hans arrived at the Joe Gerber farm in Pleasant Valley on a bright spring morning, the first question he asked was whether or not there were any Indians still around.

Joe and his brother Bill, who lived across the Valley, laughed: "Naw, reckon they ain't no Indians around here much anymore. Them Indians know better'n hanging around the Valley. Bill here'll run 'em off with his hound dogs and his Remington. He'll run 'em off like skeeters out'n the smokehouse." Joe spat a stream of amber tobacco juice skillfully into the weeds along the yard fence.

Bill had a hired hand, a hard worker but as ornery as a bear cub in a wild honey tree. When neighbors found their door latches smeared with apple butter or their boots nailed to their porch floors, the hired man always got the credit. So it was only natural for him to begin hatching a plot when he heard of Hans' fear of Indians.

Hans and the hired hand soon became friends. Since Joe and Bill Gerber's farms joined across the Valley, they often did their plowing and harvesting together. One day as Hans and the hired hand were getting the ground ready for spring planting, he showed Hans barefoot prints in a silt-pad along a small creek at the bottom of the hill. The fact that the print was the same size as that of the hired hand never entered Hans' rather slow mind. Hans turned pale and he didn't sleep well for about a week.

The balmy spring days turned into the more mature summertime and cherry-picking season in the Valley. Bill had several tall blackberry trees on a hill by the house. These hung full, ripe and waiting to be picked. So on a Sunday evening Joe, Bill and the hired hand got their heads together.

Early the next morning just at dawn, dressed only in a pair of red underwear and with a band of turkey feathers around his head, the hired man sneaked up into the top of the largest tree. Hiding himself in the thick foliage, he settled down to wait.

"Hans, I want you to go over to Bill's this morning to that large cherry tree and pick cherry until dinner time," said Joe, with a smile on his face.

Soon Hans was on his way, merrily whistling a tune, swinging a wooden bucket and lugging along a wooden ladder. Joe had told Hans to climb to the top and begin picking downward; so he propped his ladder across the rail fence at the bottom of the tree and climbed up toward the top. Large, succulent berries hung all around.

He had the bottom of the bucket lined with cherries as he approached the top. Then suddenly he stopped. What in the world? A foot! A bare foot in the top of a cherry tree on a Monday morning. Then his eyes shot up through the branches and to his horror there stood a Red Man, an Indian, feathers and all.

Hans whooped and then he screamed. Throwing his bucket in a wide arc and out into space, Hans didn't take time to climb down the tree. He half-slid, half-scraped and fell the rest of the way down and landed on the rail fence. The bucket landed in the field in an explosion of spilling cherries.

Down the hill Hans raced, across the ditch and out into the road. Will and Joe, who were watching and laughing themselves sick behind the woodshed, insisted later that only one of Hans' feet hit the fourteen-foot wooden bridge as he flew across it. Dashing into Joe's barn, Hans burrowed himself deep into the haymow, where no Indian (or white man, for that matter) could find him. It took poor Hans a long time to get over that fright—even after showing him the red underwear and the turkey feathers.

Source: Les Troyer [1987]

Christmas

BARBARA YODER HALL

Barbara Yoder Hall, *born to a large family in one of the strictest Amish groups in Wayne County, Ohio, was an author and lecturer.*

The Year of the Sled

Amish Christmas . . .
no trees, no trimmings, no toys, no Santa, but,
no sympathy needed.
Different world . . . secluded and sheltered.

No electric . . . so no stereo, TVs, radios, cassette
recorders, electric trains.

Christmas was simply—
the birth of the Christ child,
a day of rest.
I loved resting on Friday, or Tuesday, or Saturday. For no
apparent reason.

Oh but, Christmas WAS different.
Breakfast was better . . .
No mush, no oatmeal.
Instead,
fried potatoes, sausage, eggs, fresh butter, biscuits,
buttermilk . . . AND one gift,
unwrapped, beside our plate . . . a practical school item.
Sometimes a ruler, or Eversharp, or a box of Crayolas.

Christmas really WAS special,
Our only candy of the year . . . a block of chocolate . . . a
knife stuck in the middle to chip off pieces all day, and
the next,
if there was any left over.

Oranges too . . . juicy, run down-your-arm kind.
Chocolate and oranges all day,
what a delight.

Oh yes, the year of the sled.
"It stood in the smokehouse between the hams and sausage
for two weeks," Dad said.
"Where did you get the money for it?" an older and wiser
sibling asked.
"I sold a cow," he said simply.
"Good," I said.
"One less to milk."
"Smaller milk-check," Mom said.

Boys rode first while girls did dishes, naturally.

Ten children and a sled.
Two at a time . . . plus baby.
Baby squealed. Babies don't know you're
supposed to be quiet.

Long cumbersome dresses on a sled, but still happy.

Brother Ferdinand said to me, "I knew it was in
the smokehouse."
"No, you didn't," I told him. "YOU would have told me."

Today I went shopping . . . bumper to bumper traffic . . .
tired clerks, rude people rushing.
I say to myself, but ONLY to myself,
"I'm going back to the year of the sled."

   Source: Hall (1982)

⟫-⟫-⟫-⟫-⟫-⟫-⟫-⟫

European and Holy Land Tour

MONROE A. WEAVER

*A*lthough air travel is off-limits to
the Amish, ocean-liner travel is not. A few Amish people with a strong interest
in the land of their forefathers and in the Holy Land toured Europe and the
Middle East in 1978. Monroe A. Weaver, the leader of the group, composed
these verses while en route.

Last fall through friends we got a tip,
That someone was planning a fantastic trip.
To Illinois we dashed, in a hurry one day,
To meet this man, from Makanda by the way.
We heard some good news and some bad,
If thirty people would go, he'd be glad.
We called a meeting at the Triple A's.
Invited our friends, we were in a daze.
Routes were planned and brains were racked,
Passports issued and suitcases packed.

Picked up our passengers along the way,
And headed for New York on a bright sunny day.
Sailed from America on the *QE II,*
What a ship we had to sail the ocean blue!
Five days later, our voyage complete,
On British soil we set our feet.
Piccadilly Circus was quite an event,
Next by bus and Hovercraft we went.
To Calais, France, to meet der Hans,
For Presley Tours he makes many runs.

The best driver/guide, Europe has known,
In the next five weeks this was shown.
Thus we began a fantastic tour.

In and out, throughout Europe.
To Holland we traveled to see the flowers.
Hans showed us his country, the pleasure was ours.
We met Hanni, who served tea and cake.
We asked her along to give her a break.
We took a tour and sang songs of the Rhine,
Saw beautiful castles and tasted their wine.

Next to the Emmental and visited a farm,
The Alps held us spellbound with all their charm.
In Pisa we saw the leaning tower,
Roman ruins were caused by earthquakes' destructive power.
They say when in Rome, do as the Romans do,
But that little boy's example was a real lu-lu!
The Pope gave his blessing that bright sunny day,
We saw the Catacombs and ruins of Pompeii.
From Brindisi to Corfu by ferry we went,
Just one day in Athens we spent.

Went to Israel with great anticipation,
Yuval met us with lots of information.
Visited Tiberias on the Sea of Galilee,
Jesus trod here, this was a thrill to see.
Ezra took us on an Israeli bus,
To see all of Israel, which was a delight to us.
Mt. Beatitude was peaceful and serene,
One of the loveliest spots we've ever seen.
Capernaum, the river Jordan and Cana too,
Nazareth, Jerusalem, Mt. of Olives, what a view.
Gethsemane with the old olive trees,
Where Jesus prayed with his disciples three.

On to the Kibbutz to spend time with them,
And then the next day to Bethlehem.
The star marked the place where Jesus was born,
The shepherds rejoiced on that early morn.
Across the desert to Masada we drove,
Then into the Dead Sea two of our girls dove.
Next was Jericho, it was 108°.
The poor Bedouins have tents, it's their only shade.
Back to Jerusalem for the market to see,
Kids, cats, donkeys and raw meat, *whoo-ee!!*

At the Ritz Hotel, a lady in white,
Knocked on the doors and gave us a fright.
Returned to Athens, the Acropolis to view,
Here Karla joined us, we welcome you!
In Yugoslavia we traveled through traffic thick,
Saw a stork on a chimney with her little chick.
Headed for Venice; the hour got late,
The canal boat had left, it just couldn't wait.
We found a boat that took us to No. 7 pier,
Picked up our suitcases and thought, "Oh, we're almost here!"

Across bridges, through alleys, and over the stair,
Our arms got tired, we thought we'd never get there.
Then Hans and Mr. Presley found our hotel,
If people weren't sleeping, we'd give out a yell!
The next day we went walking to St. Mark's Square,
The bell tower, church, and Palace were there.
We heard the men strike the clock tower bell,
And fed the hundreds of pigeons as well
That evening our group took a gondola ride,
With beautiful music and singing by our side.

Going to Innsbruck, as we came over the ridge,
In front of our eyes appeared this huge bridge.
This lovely place has a charm all its own,
With its Austrian dancers and its Alpine horn.
Through Austria and Switzerland we drove with care,
The scenery was breath-taking, and we're glad they share.
Their snow-capped Alps, tumbling falls and streams,
Villages, valleys and charming chalets, all beyond our dreams.
Hans loves the cows as they graze on the hill,
Of this wondrous beauty we could never get our fill.
The lakes were so blue and splendidly made,
It is something only our God could create.

In Lucerne we hurried our shopping to do,
Because Mr. Presley told us we might get to fondue.
The covered bridge so quaint and old,
We walked across to find our boat.
We took a cruise on Lake Lucerne,
The native dances and customs to learn.
The Alpine horn we tried to blow.

Some were successful and others just so-so.
We look forward to Paris and the Eiffel Tower,
The lights on the fountains which give forth a shower.

By woods or streams or on a mountaintop,
Hans always picked such a beautiful spot.
Our picnics to eat, and the weather was fine,
No King or Queen in greater splendor could dine.
With Hans as our driver and Mr. Presley our guide,
We made many new friends and hope, kept the old,
These memories to us are more precious than gold.
And so as our beautiful trip comes to an end,
We need to get home and tell our friends.
Of the wondrous beauties this world doth impart,
All we say is "My God how great thou art."

Source: Weaver (1978): 103–6

⇒⇒⇒-⇒⇒⇒-⇒⇒⇒-⇒⇒⇒-⇒⇒⇒-⇒⇒⇒-⇒⇒⇒-⇒⇒⇒

The Doll

BARBARA YODER HALL

Barbara Yoder Hall *wrote several stories based on her childhood experiences. The following two appear in her book* Born Amish.

Summer days often began in the strawberry patch or in the garden, depending on what was ripe. We Yoder children knew to start early in the morning picking what was ready to be canned that day. That way we could be out of the hot sun by noon. But our work was far from over even then. We still had to help wash jars, clean the fruit or vegetable and complete all other tasks that go with cold-packing food for winter. Amish children learn very young to work hard, since they are taught that idleness is a sin.

"Dinner is on," Mom said, when we came in from the strawberry patch. The Amish always call lunch "dinner." That day, dinner was strawberry soup, which simply means sugared strawberries drenched with milk and bread broken into it. We knew we'd have the same thing for supper that night. Whatever we were canning was always served for the meals on that day . . . nothing else. A person can fill up on roastin' ears if they're really hungry . . . or green beans or peas.

About mid-afternoon, Mother would say, "If some of you want to go after the mail now, you can go." We never needed a second invitation. All of us "middle" children would go. Not that it took that many to bring in the mail; it was just one of the few breaks we would get in a summer's day of work.

An Amish mailbox usually holds very little. In fact, I could just about tell what would be in the box before I opened it. *The Ohio Farmer* came once a month and I loved it because it had one cartoon in it which we were not supposed to read. I always read it anyway coming down the lane before Mother had a chance to tell me not to look at it.

Another item in every Amish mailbox is *The Budget,* published in Sugarcreek, Ohio. This paper is devoured by the Amish, especially my grandmother, who would go into her room after it arrived and not come out for days, except to eat. Except for an occasional letter from *freundshaft* (kinfolk), the only other mail was the milk check and a bill from the local doctor for some of the last Yoder babies that he had arrived in time to deliver. We did get the *Sears and Roebuck* catalogue, which we used in many ways.

As we got near the end of the lane on this particular summer day, we could tell the mailbox held more than usual because the lid didn't close all the way. We all took off running, trying to be the first to see what the package was.

Brother Ferdinand said, "It's probably my boots that Mom ordered from the catalogue. She told me I needed boots worse than the rest of you."

He always knew just what to say to make all of us mad, but we didn't argue with him. He was bigger than any of us. But he got what he deserved that day. The package was addressed to Barbara Yoder. That was me, and I could not believe my eyes. Surely there must be some mistake. An Amish child does not receive mail, much less a package. The return address said "Ada Hess," who was a distant cousin who was not Amish and had come to visit recently from Indiana. Why she had singled me out of the seven Yoder girls to send a gift to is something I'll never know. But I was not going to argue with fate. I ripped open the package with the undivided attention of my two brothers and sisters.

I don't imagine anyone could describe the shock and amazement on our faces as we stared at the doll, lying in the shoe box. It was a hard plastic doll like one I had seen in the catalogue.

The only doll I'd ever seen was my friend Naomi's Amish doll. Her mother had made it out of cloth and dressed it in Amish clothes so that it looked almost like Naomi herself. The only thing different was that Amish dolls do not have faces because it makes them look worldly. I'd always envied Naomi for having a real doll. All we ever had was blankets rolled up, which we pretended were doll babies.

Just wait till Naomi sees this, I thought to myself. For once she'll be jealous of me! . . .

I entered the kitchen carrying the only store-bought toy I had ever owned, except for the sled that we all shared. "Look what Cousin Ada sent me!" I said, showing my prize to my sisters, Mom, and Grandma. If I hadn't been so wrapped up in my delight, I would have seen the looks on their faces, but I didn't. Dad wasn't home but there was one more person in the family who had not seen my beautiful doll.

"Where is Grandfather?" I asked Grandma. I took off for the basement, where she had said he was. I had gone only about halfway down the steps when I met him coming up. I thrust the doll right into his arms, blabbering excitedly, "Look what Cousin Ada sent me!"

His hair was white and so was his long beard, but all that hair could not hide the lightning that came to his eyes at the sight of the doll. He never said one word, but with a deliberate aim crashed it to the cement, where it broke into many, many pieces. It was hard plastic and shattered immediately.

"A worldly doll you do not need!" he said, as he brushed on past me.

Annie and I were both crying as we stared at the heap of plastic. I held up the hem of my dress like I usually did to gather eggs, while Annie picked up the pieces and deposited them in my makeshift basket.

"Why did he do it?" I asked Annie between sobs as we dumped the pieces on the burn pile.

"Barbara, you know Mom wouldn't have let you keep the doll either. It is a worldly toy and it would have only made you want more things that you don't need. You know what they say, 'Today a doll, tomorrow a car.' Don't hate Grampa. You know he's a kind man."

We stayed outside for a long while that afternoon, and Mom didn't call out for us to get back to work. She knew we would as soon as we could. When we did walk back into the kitchen, there was a silence I had never heard before . . . almost like death. Annie and I picked up a bowl of strawberries and started cleaning them. I never knew that a clock could tick so loud.

After we had worked in silence for a long while, Mom said, "Barbara, Grandma and I are going to make a doll for you."

Smiling through my tears, I asked her, "This one won't break, will it, Mom?"

Source: Hall (1980): 25–33

Our Own Cute Baby

BARBARA YODER HALL

B arbara, you take Fannie's hand and I'll bring Lizzie," sister Annie said. "We're going to Tobe's for awhile, maybe even overnight."

As soon as she said that "maybe even overnight" I knew what was going on. Somehow another baby was going to come into our home. I had no idea where these babies came from, but the only time we ever stayed overnight at anyone's house, it was at our nearest Amish neighbor's, and then only when a new addition was added to our family.

As the four of us walked out the lane I wondered why we could not have stayed home. I really wanted to find out where the next baby came from. Annie said the doctor came sometimes, so I figured he must bring it. I just could not understand how he knew to bring an Amish baby . . . and then *if* he did bring it, why was Mom sick for awhile? It sure did not make sense.

When we arrived at the neighbor's house Annie said to the kindly old gentleman and his wife, "Mom said we should stay here until Dad comes and gets us." I watched them both smile. They knew something too and I was sure *they* wouldn't tell me any more than my parents did. I knew better than to ask questions. The only one I ever asked questions of was my sister and she didn't know much more about babies than I did.

After supper, I watched as our hosts put blankets on the floor and I knew we were not going home. Fannie was fussy all night so we didn't get much sleep. She was only two years old and I'm sure she missed Mom even more than the rest of us did.

After breakfast the next morning, the door opened and there stood Dad.

"I've come to take the children home. They have a new baby sister," he said to our kind neighbors who had cared for us overnight. "Thanks for watching them. I hope you won't have to do it too many more times."

Although I watched the adults exchange smiles, I didn't understand what Dad meant by that last statement.

That made number ten . . . three boys and seven girls. They named her Katie. The Amish name their first four children after the two sets of grandparents, and the rest after the aunts and uncles on both sides of the family. There are only about twenty names that the Amish use for the first names, and there are also only about twenty last names [in this community].

First names for girls are usually Cora, Mattie, Annie, Lizzie, Barbara, Fannie, Katie, Mary, Naomi, Emma, Jemima, Ella, Sarah, Levina and Mandy.

First names for boys are John, Mose, Ferdinand, Dannie, Sam, Amos, Albert, Emanual, Levi, Rudy, Enos, Eli, Jacob and Joseph.

When we arrived at our house that morning, there lay our new sister, Katie, all dressed in Amish clothes. Sure enough, the doctor knew to bring another Amish baby. He sure was smart.

For several weeks our older sisters, Cora and Mattie, became our substitute mother while our Mom stayed in the bedroom.

When the older ones in the family were born, a young teenage cousin would come and be our "Maude" (hired girl). She stayed for a number of weeks, taking care of the house and babies while our Mom recuperated.

The morning after Katie was born, I told Naomi on the way to school that I thought it was kinda dumb that Mom had to go to bed, when the doctor did all the work.

Source: Hall (1980): 80–84

-⋙-⋙-⋙-⋙-⋙-⋙-⋙-⋙-

Mottoes in the School

ANONYMOUS

The interiors of Amish schools are fre-
quently decorated with drawings and mottoes made by the children. Mottoes or wise sayings teach ideals and character. The following sayings were collected from several Pennsylvania schools.

I am only me, but I'm still someone.
I cannot do everything, but I can do something.
Just because I cannot do everything does not give me the right to do nothing.
It is my duty to do what I can and I must never say I can't until I try, then if
    at first I don't succeed I must try again.

Remember when you talk you only repeat what you already know; but if you listen you may learn something.

Let us pray not for lighter burdens, but for stronger backs.

The longer you put off doing a job, the harder it becomes.

Do not rush over your work in school or at home.

Naturally, you will always try to do your best, but do not feel sad or discouraged if you cannot make a perfect score.

Even though our minds may work slower than some children's, let us bear in mind that it is only a blessing that they work at all.

Start each day with a fresh beginning; as if this whole world was made anew.

School is a good place to get along with other people; this will help you when you grow up.

We are known by our actual deeds and not by what we boast that we can do.

Be contented, and do not worry or try to catch up with the world's uneasiness and speed.

Never, never be afraid to do what is right, even if all the others are doing what is wrong.

Do not count the mistakes of your parents or teacher; rather, help them along in life's strife, and your own will become sweeter.

People who are always in a hurry, seemingly, get very little satisfaction out of life.

A person who lives only for himself never knows the real joys of life.

You can be pleasant without talking a lot. Think twice before you speak once.

Singing is a pleasant pastime, good exercise for the lungs and a nice way of giving praise to God.

Source: Anonymous ([1965], unpublished)

Riddles

ANONYMOUS

R*iddles are typically memorized and passed on orally in the context of the family, school, and in groups of visitors.*

What changes name on shortest notice? A woman in marriage.

What does a farmer see every day, a king seldom, and God never? His equal.

What kind of stones are found in water? Wet ones.

Why does a rooster close his eyes when he crows? He knows it by heart.

Which candles burn longer, those of tallow or those of wax? They burn shorter, not longer.

What is finished, yet made every day? A bed.

Where did you sit when you went to school? When I went I walked.

If a rooster lays an egg on top of the barn, on which side will it fall down? None, because a rooster doesn't lay an egg.

Why did the man throw the clock out of the window? Cause he wanted time to fly.

What will come but never will arrive? Tomorrow.

Which side of a chicken has the most feathers? Outside.

How many eggs could Paul Bunyan eat on an empty stomach? One; after that his stomach wasn't empty.

Why do geese fly south? It is too far to walk.

What is the hardest thing about learning to skate? The ice.

How is a game of baseball like a pancake? They both need a batter.

What is the difference between here and there? The letter *T.*

Why did the fireman wear yellow suspenders on the first day of February? To keep his trousers up.

What kind of dog can tell time? A watchdog.

What is the surest way to double your money? Fold it in half.

Where is the best place to get fat? At the butchershop.

Source: Anonymous ([1965], unpublished)

The Autograph Album

Many Amish youth of courting age keep an autograph album in which sentiments are exchanged. Some verses are free expressions, but most are stylized. The owner of this album, Joseph, was twenty-one years old in 1901. Contributors to his album were not only members of his own community at Belleville, Pennsylvania, but also visitors in other settlements and places he had visited as a young man: Lancaster County, Pennsylvania, western Pennsylvania, Ohio, and Michigan.

To Friend Joseph, December 11, 1901

The leaves are green
The roses are red
And here is my name
When I am dead.

> From a friend, M. P. Riehl, Gordonville, Pa.

Friend Joseph, January 23, 1902

A place for me in your album
A place for my love in your heart
A place for us both in heaven
Where the good and true never part.

> Well-wishingly, your friend, Abe S. Yoder, Bertrand, Nebraska

To a Friend, February 2, 1902

The older the tree
The thicker the bark
The older the girl
The harder they spark.

Daniel J. Guengerich, Johnson County, Amish, Iowa

To My Friend

Long may you live
Happy may you be
Blessed with forty children
Twenty on each knee

Joe Hershberger, Burton, Ohio

To Friend Joseph

In battle or business whatever the game,
In law or in love it is ever the same.
If you struggle for power or scramble for pelt
Let this be your motto, "Rely on yourself."

Jacob Miller, Mascot, Pa., Lanc. Co.

To a Friend

Some roses are red
And some are yellow.
You are the girl
That stole my fellow

Yone D. Kauffman, Belleville, Pa.

Source: Anonymous (c. 1901–2, unpublished)

15

LEGENDS

Legends are stories transmitted by word of mouth and are told as if they were true. They frequently have a didactic function in teaching the young. They grow by accretion, by mingling history with fiction. Legends typically combine a heroic character, or a geographic place, with myth and folktale. There is often a nucleus of historical truth, though the details may be fictional. Legends are distinguished from ghost stories, which are acknowledged as fabrication. Most Amish legends have remained oral and also obscure. They have rarely been published.

There are no known legends about Jacob Ammann, but there is at least one legend about Menno Simons. During my adolescent years, my Amish peers were obsessed with attempts to invent perpetual motion. It was widely held that an elderly bishop, Stephen Stoltzfus, had successfully made such a contraption in his farm shop. "God gave him the wisdom to make it, but then told him to destroy it." The invention, it was said, would lead to terrible consequences for humanity. Books containing miracles and allegories are deeply embedded in Amish tradition. *The Wandering Soul* is a book that has been printed in many editions. *The Martyrs Mirror* contains an account of the martyrs which sometimes borders on the legendary. Extra-biblical writings, such as the Apocrypha, are additional sources of legends.

The following selections combine the historical with the imaginary.

➤➤➤·➤➤➤·➤➤➤·➤➤➤·➤➤➤·➤➤➤·➤➤➤·➤➤➤

Jesus Never Laughed

HENRY BEER, ED.

A *letter discovered in the library of the Lazarist Fathers in Rome, it is said, was written by Publius Lentilus, a member of Pontius Pilate's court. Addressed to the Emperor, the letter gives an unusual description of Christ at the beginning of His preaching in Judea.*

I have learned, O Caesar, that you desired some information regarding this virtuous man called Jesus the Christ, whom the people consider a prophet and who is regarded as the son of the Creator of Heaven and Earth.

It is a fact that everyday one hears many things told about him. To be brief, he makes the dead rise and he heals the sick. He is a man of medium size, whose appearance indicates both great sweetness and such an amount of dignity that one feels in looking at him that one must love him and at the same time fear him.

His hair down to his ears is the color of ripe walnut and hangs down on his shoulders as a light blend and clear mass. It is parted in the middle, according to the fashion of the Nazarenes. His beard, of the same color as his hair, is curly and, although not very long, parted in the middle like his hair.

His hands and arms are well-proportioned and attractive. His speech is earnest, and reserved and not overtalkative.

His eyes are rather severe and shine like the sun. It is impossible for anyone to look him long in the face. When he scolds, he inspires fear, but very soon he himself begins to shed tears. Even in his most severe moods he is affable and benevolent. It is said that no one has ever seen him laugh and that he sheds tears very often.

His conversation is agreeable and appealing. He is not seen very often in public and when he appears he carries himself modestly. His manners are very distinguished. He is even beautiful. It is possibly because his mother is an attractive and virtuous woman?

Source: Beer (1979): 68–69

-≫≫-≫≫-≫≫-≫≫-≫≫-≫≫-≫≫-≫≫

Hans Haslibacher

Hans Haslibacher was an Anabaptist preacher of Sumiswald in the Emmental, Bern, Switzerland. He was exiled for his faith and executed on October 20, 1571. His imprisonment and death are described in a thirty-two-stanza poem composed by a fellow prisoner. The poem states that after torture by the Reformed preachers to persuade him to apostatize, Haslibacher dreamed that he would be beheaded and that three miraculous signs would accompany his execution: his severed head would jump into his hat and laugh, the sun would turn crimson like blood, and the town well would yield blood instead of water. The poet claims that all three happened. The entire poem appears in the Amish hymnal (Ausbund). Fourteen of the thirty-two stanzas are given here.

Give ear, kind friends, and help who can,
To sing about an aged man,
    Who hailed from Haslibach;
Hence, Haslibacher was he called,
And lived in parish Sumiswald.

And though he was imprisoned here,
And tortured with torments severe,
    For holding to his faith;
Yet did he steadfast still remain,
In torture, anguish, and in pain.

Our Haslibacher then and there,
Gave all their babbling to the air,
    For thus he straightaway said:

"My faith I never will forsake,
Though life and body you should take."

On Saturday these learned men
Came to his prison-hold again,
   And thus with threats they spake:
"Thou must renounce thy heresy,
Or else thou shalt beheaded be."

"From this my faith I'll ne'er let go,
The Word of God full well I know;
   My cause to God I give;
Yet deep regret doth fill my heart.
That innocent, I must depart."

He further said: "The Lord will show
Three signs, to let you plainly know
   That innocent I die
For when my head's struck off, 'twill fall
Into my hat, and laugh withal.

"The second sign upon the sun
You'll plainly see when it is done;
   And of the third take heed:
The sun will, like my blood, be red,
The town well likewise blood will shed."

When he had finished his repast,
They took his hands to tie them fast;
   When Haslibacher said:
"Pray, Lorenz, listen to my plea.
And leave my hands from fetters free.

"I'm ready now and do rejoice,
That you have let me have my choice
   To die and pass from hence.
But Lord show mercy unto them,
Who me this day to death condemn."

Down comes the sword, when lo, the head
Springs in his hat, as he had said;
   And all the signs were seen—

The sun was red and looked like blood,
The town well shed a crimson flood.

With one accord the people said,
"Henceforth no Baptist's blood we'll shed."
    Then said an aged sire:
"Had you not acted 'gainst my will,
This Baptist would be living still."

The hangman too was heard to say:
" 'Tis guiltless blood I've shed today."
    Then said a yeoman old:
"The Anabaptist's mouth did laugh,
Which surely indicates God's wrath."

He who composed this little hymn,
Received his death in prison dim,
    A sinful mob to please.
They brought him pen and ink to write,
And thus he bade us all "Good night."

Source: Braght (1951): 1128

The Legend of Nancy Zook

PAUL I. SPEICHER

In 1833, in the vicinity of Oakland Mills, Juniata County, Pennsylvania, a little girl was born whose parents were unknown. Several stories about her have been passed down by oral tradition. Here are three.

1. She was left on the doorstep of the people who then raised her. At the time she was dressed in fine clothing and raised by the people who found her as their own daughter.

2. A young woman passed a certain farmhouse carrying a small baby. She asked permission to leave the child until she came back. She never returned, so the child was raised by these people as their own.

3. Jacob and Katie Zook of Juniata County, Pennsylvania, were visiting at a home where a small baby had been found on the doorstep. Barbara, daughter of the Zooks, became so attached to the little baby that she begged her parents to take the baby along home. With the consent of the family who found the baby, the Zooks took the baby home, adopted her, and named her Nancy.

Barbara and Nancy grew up as sisters, and Jacob and Katie Zook were the only parents that Nancy ever knew. Many of the descendants of Nancy believe this to be the most plausible version of the three stories. Nancy always believed that her name was McFarland—Frances Agnes McFarland. While Nancy was a growing girl, a well-dressed man came to see her and asked her if she was happy, and if the people treated her well. Nancy's answer to both questions was "yes." Years later two of her uncles came to see her but were not permitted to interview Nancy. They returned to see her when she was eighteen, and by that time she had already been married.

Nancy Zook married Michael Speicher of Mifflin County and moved to Lawrence County, where they raised a family of ten children.

Source: Speicher (1970): 27

➤➤➤-➤➤➤-➤➤➤-➤➤➤-➤➤➤-➤➤➤-➤➤➤-➤➤➤

Hertzler Legends

DAVID LUTHY

Does the telling of legends, dreams, and the sensational run in the family? In Amish life, storytelling seems to make liberal uses of memory, imagination, and the unpredictable.

An interesting story centers around one of the early settlers—Christian Hertzler. In April 1837 he had married Caroline Hertzler of Mifflin County. They began their married life in his home settlement in Berks County but soon moved to the new settlement in Tuscarora Valley. Their first child,

Nancy, was born there on February 21, 1838. Then on December 22, 1839, another daughter was born to them, but the young mother died in childbirth. The baby was named Caroline after her mother. Snow was rapidly falling and someone had to take the death message to the dead woman's parents, John and Catherine Hertzler, in Mifflin County. The following tale is related:

> Father and mother were much concerned about their daughter's home in Juniata County, as they discussed their dreams of the previous night. Strange indeed they should both have had the same dream. Anxiously they kept watching and, with evening approaching, the mother again goes to the window and sees a rider in the distance. Here comes somebody now, but who can it be? The father said, "Surely no one with good tidings. It rides like Crist Yoder, but that's not his horse." As the rider came closer, they saw it was Crist Yoder, just as they had seen him in their dreams.
>
> Father opened the door, and Crist said, "I have a sad message for you." Mother said, "We know what it is, Caroline is dead." Being much surprised, Crist said, "Yes, but how did you know? I have been wondering and praying how to deliver this sad message." Mother answered, "We knew you would come; you had to come; the day of revelation by dreams is not yet past. We knew, too, you would come on a white horse, but that you had no white horse of your own." "No," he said, "I started on my horse, but the snow was so deep I had to change with a man by the way."

The snow continued to fall for days, so the body could not be buried until the seventh day after death. Caroline Hertzler was laid to rest on her husband's farm. Later others from the Amish community were also buried there. At first it was called the Hertzler Burial Ground but later the Spruce Hill Cemetery.

Another remarkable happening centers around the Hertzler baby, Caroline. Her paternal grandparents, Christian and Nancy Hertzler, Sr., of Berks County, had raised ten sons but no daughters. Christian was sixty-eight and Nancy fifty-eight when they decided to raise their baby granddaughter, Caroline. Riding horseback, they went to fetch her from her maternal grandparents in Mifflin County. On their way they had the following experience:

> Mile after mile was covered in silence as they rode along the mountain trail. It is a beautiful valley in summer in which to behold the handiwork of God; but now it was bleak and cold, covered with a deep blanket of snow. The milk was diminishing alarmingly fast, when Nancy said, "Where can we get more milk? We will need it soon."
>
> I wonder what you or I would have done under similar circumstances? Didn't God say, "Call upon me in time of trouble." And "God shall supply all your need." After asking to supply this need, they traveled on. They soon came to a wooded spot along the way where they found a cow fast in the underbrush. Christian said, "This is nothing else than an answer to our prayer, for why should

this cow be out here when there is so much snow on the ground?" Christian milked the cow, released her, and she immediately turned around and walked back into the woods. This called for a prayer of thanks. The remainder of the journey was made in safety.

Sources: Luthy (1986): 431, based on Sadie R. Mast (n.d.): 68–70

>>>->>>->>>->>>->>>->>>->>>->>>

A Letter from Heaven

Acopy of the so-called Himmelsbrief *(Letter from Heaven) was found in an old family Bible. The original letter, it is maintained, was written by God in letters of gold and dropped by an angel near Magdeburg, Germany. Belief in the letter was encouraged by the Irish monk Clement. He was later summoned before a synod and condemned as a heretic. The persistence of the legend in Germanic folklore shows how ingrained it has become.*

Whosoever labors on the Lord's day, or Sunday, is accursed. For this reason I command ye do not labor on Sunday, but reverently go to church; and do not adorn your faces. You shall not wear false hair, and practice pride or vanity. Of your treasure ye shall give to the poor, give abundantly and have faith and believe that this letter was written with my own hand, and sent out from Christ Himself, and that ye do not as the unconscious brutes. Ye have six days in the week and in these ye shall do your work, but the seventh day, "namely Sunday," ye shall keep holy. If ye will not do this, then I will send wars, hunger, pestilence and famine among you, and I will punish you with many plagues. I also command you all, whosoever ye may be, young or old, great or small, that ye do not at any time work late on Saturday; but ye shall mourn over your sins that they may be forgiven you. Do not covet silver or gold; do not give way to the lust of flesh or to your carnal desire. Remember that I created you, and that I can again destroy you. Do not rejoice in the poverty of your neighbor, but much more have compassion on him, and it shall be well with you. Children, obey fathers and mothers, that it may be well with you upon earth. Whosoever does not believe and do this is condemned and lost. I, Jesus, have written this with my own hand; whosoever shall oppose and despise it, that same person may not expect any help from me, and whosoever has this letter and does not reveal or publish it to others, shall be accursed by the Christian Church, and if our sins be ever so great they shall nevertheless, if you sincerely mourn over them and repent of them, be forgiven you. He that does not believe this shall die and be punished in hell, and at the Day of Judgment I will ask you about your sins and ye will have to answer me. The person who shall carry this letter with him, or keep it in his house, shall not be harmed by thunder and lightning, and shall be secure from fire and flood, and he that shall make it known among the children of men shall have his reward, and shall have a blessed and peaceful departure from this world. Keep my commandments which I have sent to my angel. I, the true God from Heaven's throne, the son of God and of Mary.

Source: Elizabeth M. Miller (1963): 25–26

⋙⋙⋙⋙⋙⋙⋙⋙⋙

"Strong" Jacob Yoder

C. Z. MAST AND ROBERT E. SIMPSON

Jacob Yoder (c. 1726–1790), a native of Switzerland, immigrated to Pennsylvania in 1742. Numerous accounts of his extraordinary physical strength have persisted, and, to distinguish him from other Yoders, he acquired the appropriate nickname "Strong" Jacob.

Once upon a time "Strong" Jacob Yoder and his two sons loaded a wagon with bags of wheat and hauled it to the mill. The grain had to be carried up several flights of stairs. "Strong" Jacob set the grain sacks, containing three bushels each, at the rear end of the Conestoga wagon. The boys were to carry them up the stairway to the third floor. At the head of the first flight of stairs, a mischievous young fellow reached out from a hidden place and pulled the beards of the boys while they were carrying the sacks of wheat. The boys complained to their father, who said he would carry the next sack. Just as the father got to the head of the stairway, the young fellow reached out and pulled his beard. Jacob caught the mischief-maker, held him around his waist and carried him up the remaining two flights, along with the three bushel bags of wheat. The more the young fellow pulled, kicked, and struggled, the tighter the old man held him. On arrival at the third floor, Jacob dropped him on the floor. The young fellow lay docile and quiet for a long while as the boys carried the remainder of the wheat.

On another occasion, "Strong" Jacob was hauling a load of wheat to Philadelphia. He came to a stream of water where the bridges had been washed away. Only a foot log remained across the stream. He unhitched his four horses and made them swim across the stream. He carried the wheat across in sacks, and took the wagon apart and carried it across. After reassembling the wagon, he drove to Philadelphia as though nothing had happened.

Source: Mast and Simpson (1942): 267

16

MISFORTUNES

Natural disasters of unusual magnitude, such as tornadoes, fires, and floods, have a special significance for the Amish. These disasters intrude into the Amish time frame, marking the calendar with important events. They remind the Amish person that no human being controls his or her life span and that all people are totally dependent on the mercy of God for their existence. The telling of these stories from generation to generation strengthens the communal memory of the group.

➤➤➤-➤➤➤-➤➤➤-➤➤-➤➤-➤➤-➤➤-➤➤

A Train Accident

AMOS L. FISHER

T*he famed "Fisher Book," authored by Amos L. Fisher (1920–1986) and his extended family, contains not only the genealogy of virtually all Amish married couples who lived in Lancaster County, Pennsylvania, in 1957 but also outstanding events that affected the community, such as a tragic train and buggy accident.*

A most appalling accident occurred [in 1887] at a crossing a short distance east of Ronk's Station on the Pennsylvania Railroad this afternoon, when the fast line west, due in this city at two o'clock, struck a wagon containing two middle-aged ladies, instantly killing a neighbor lady and the horse, and the other lady died in a few minutes.

The victims were Mrs. Jacob Stoltzfus (nee Kauffman), of Leacock Township, and Mrs. Barbara Stoltzfus (nee Kanagy) of Kansas. When the train reached Lancaster the train was found to be spattered with blood, and the ghastly spectacle was seen by many persons who were at the station when the train arrived.

The wagon, a covered one, similar to those used by all the Amish people, was badly broken, and the horse, which was carried for about 75 or 100 yards, was disemboweled.

The news of the accident spread rapidly and a large crowd was on the scene of the awful catastrophe before the bodies were taken to the Stoltzfus farm, which was so full of life only a few short hours before.

Mrs. Jacob Stoltzfus was a daughter of Samuel Kauffman, deceased, formerly of near Paradise. She was about fifty years of age, and leaves seven children, the youngest two years old. Three are married.

Mrs. Barbara Stoltzfus, the other victim, was the wife of Isaac Stoltzfus, formerly of this county, but now in Kansas. She was the daughter of Absalom Kanagy, of Union County. Mrs. Stoltzfus was here on a visit, none of her immediate family accompanying her. Relatives in the west have been telegraphed of the sad affair.

The ladies were going to a corn husking at Jonathan King's when the accident occurred. Mr. King had been sick and his friends and neighbors resolved to husk his corn for him. The men had gathered for this purpose on Tuesday and the women were to join the party in the afternoon. It being the custom for the women of the households to gather toward the close of the day and enjoy a repast with their husbands, fathers and male relatives. It was such a meeting that the unfortunate women were about to attend.

The double funeral was held at the residence of the late Mrs. Nancy Stoltzfus, whose husband, Jacob Stoltzfus, farms the old Stoltzfus homestead, which is located within a half-mile of the Old Road, a short distance below Weavertown, in Leacock Township.

Vehicles of every description, Amish wagons, carriages, buggies and open wagons, lined the fences all about the premises, and by actual count there were 270 vehicles on the spot, in addition to at least 50 at the neighboring farm of Christian Stoltzfus. These means of conveyance brought an average of at least three persons, and many walked to the farm, so that a close estimate made put the number present at twelve hundred. The house was jammed almost to suffocation, and the grounds were crowded.

According to the rule of the Amish faith, the bodies were dressed in plain white cap and shoulder kerchief, and encased in walnut coffins of the severest plainness, lined only with a linen sheet. These coffins were half-opened by a double lid, which exposed the features of the dead.

After the remains were viewed, they were borne to two open spring wagons, no hearses being used by the Amish people, for conveyance to the burial grounds. At about eleven o'clock the funeral cortege began to form, and as far as the eye could reach was the long string of vehicles. It was fully twelve o'clock before the last team got started for the burial place, Beiler's graveyard, near Ronk's Station. Here the bodies were consigned to the earth with only the ceremony of the reading of a chapter of Scripture by Rev. Stoltzfus and another hymn by Elder Christian Stoltzfus.

During the services at the house the Amish custom of the women removing their bonnets and wearing only the plain white caps was observed, and they stood there while the bodies were viewed in the yard, hundreds of their black bonnets and shawls being hung upon the fence.

After the funeral hundreds of people returned to the house by invitation and were fed, following out the custom usual in the county, everybody being invited to do so, and nearly all the afternoon was so taken up. Besides this, the teams of the relatives and immediate friends of the deceased, were stabled and fed.

Mrs. Jacob Stoltzfus had premonitions of the sad accident which befell her, as related by her own family. Three weeks ago she told her son that her end would be short and she marked and showed to him two hymns in her hymn book, one of which she wished read at her funeral services and the other at her grave. These were the two hymns read by Elders Beiler and Stoltzfus, and thus her wishes were carried out.

Source: Unidentified newspaper clipping, in John M. Fisher Family (1957): 187–89

›››‒›››‒›››‒›››‒›››‒›››‒›››‒›››

Solomon Cried Like a Child

HARVEY HOSTETLER

*I*n *closed communities where deep personal loyalties and kinship ties prevail, jealousy and revenge frequently come to the surface. Deeply held prejudices do their pernicious work. A genealogist relates how an accused murderer, Solomon Hochstetler (1785–1865), was proved innocent after fifty years of accusations.*

Susan, the seven-month-old daughter of John Hochstetler of Somerset County, Pa., died March 4, 1810. Her mother found the child at the lower end of her crib, obviously smothered. Foul play was suspected. Barbara Lehman, a sister of Susan's mother, fixed the blame on Solomon, John Hochstetler's brother. He had a drinking problem, and he had never been baptized in the Amish church, even though he was married and well advanced in years.

Solomon's wife insisted it could not have been him, for he had been at home all evening on March 4. Solomon demanded that the child be exhumed, and he would prove his innocence by touching the body of the dead child in the presence of all. (It was a widely held belief at that time that if a murderer touched his victim, some sign of blood or other manifestation would occur.) However, this was never done.

Fourteen years passed and Susan's mother died. Her father remarried and moved to Holmes County, Ohio, as did his brother Solomon. But the two avoided each other. Eventually John Hochstetler died.

Fifty years after the event, an old man in Wayne County, Ohio, on his deathbed confessed that he had murdered the child. His name was Henry Yoder. When Solomon Hochstetler heard the news, he wept like a child. But Yoder, who had not expected to live, recovered.

What was Yoder's motive? Henry Yoder wanted to court Barbara Lehman, a sister of John Hochstetler's wife, but she did not reciprocate and avoided him at every opportunity. Yoder had blamed John and his wife for alienating Barbara against him. In this he was not mistaken.

At that time Henry Yoder was a single man in his early twenties. One evening after supper, when the adults had returned to work in the sugar camp, Henry entered the house and smothered the child.

A jury of twelve had been summoned to investigate the murder and make a report. No shred of evidence could be found of the guilty party. Although Barbara Lehman herself had served on the jury, she did not mention Henry Yoder as a suspect. Did she not suspect him, or did she want to protect him? No one will ever know.

It was during his illness that Henry Yoder told his misdeed to Jacob Mast, who had been his childhood playmate. Yoder intended that his close friend keep the secret, but Mast felt that he himself might be found guilty if he kept the secret. Mast finally persuaded Henry to confess the murder to his minister, Levi Miller.

Yoder was immediately placed under the ban. Being old and troubled, he begged to be restored as a member of the church. But minister Levi Miller refused, saying a court must first hear the case. Both appeared before a Wayne County judge, who said he could do nothing because the crime was committed in another state. They would need to go to Pennsylvania. There were only three living persons who could testify, and all were old, and all lived in Ohio. The judge informed them that a confession made to a minister would not likely stand as evidence in court. So the matter was dropped.

Source: Abstracted from Harvey Hostetler (1912): 63–65

➤➤➤ ➤➤➤ ➤➤➤ ➤➤➤ ➤➤➤ ➤➤➤ ➤➤➤ ➤➤➤

The Boiler Explosion

MRS. ATLEE HERSHBERGER

Steam locomotives were widely used *for threshing grain in the early twentieth century. Several explosions are still remembered and retold to younger generations.*

The Dan T. Miller family was up early, for it was threshing day. Dan [known as Dan T.] and his son Albert were the operators of an old steam engine threshing rig. It was August 27, 1918. The engine had been in need of repairs, so it had been overhauled. The inspector was there the day before. This morning they would start threshing on their own farm, which was located one mile east of Maysville, Ohio.

Dan, who was fifty-four years old, seemed extra-happy that morning as he went about his work of firing up the engine. His wife, Mary, was busy helping with the chores around the barn. She went by close to the engine to feed a cluck with little chicks, and stopped to talk to her husband. The steam engine was an old one, and Mary had some misgivings about it. "Do you think it is safe?" she asked her husband.

"Yes, it should be safe. The inspector said it was all right," he assured her. She finished tending the chicks and then started for the house. . . .

Albert was helping his father with the engine, and a younger son, Andy, was standing outside the milk house by the barnyard fence.

It was decided to connect some water pipes and hose to the water trough in order to save hauling water with the water tank. Albert and Jacob Swartzentruber had been working with the hose. Jacob had been on the engine with Dan when Dan told him, "You go over to the water trough and let Albert come here to help me with the injectors."

By this time the fire in the engine was burning hot and, unknown to the men, the water in the boiler had evaporated into steam. The boiler was soon very hot.

Dan was standing on the front wheel fixing something on the governor, and Albert was on the step on the side of the engine trying to get the water pumps working.

There was a terrible explosion that was heard for miles around.

Several miles to the west, Ben Sausers, another experienced thresherman, who was firing up his engine on a farm near Applecreek, heard the explosion and exclaimed, "There goes Dan T.'s old pot!"

Two men were sitting on some feed bags on the den floor in the barn, waiting for the wagons to come. Terrified by the explosion, they hurried down the hay hole, raced through the barnyard, and left the farm as fast as they could go.

They claimed that they saw Dan up in the air over the woods. They ran to see what had happened. . . .

When Dan came down, he came though a small roof that had been built over the barn bridge. He landed on the den floor. His right leg was torn off above the knee. His right foot flew over the barn and got caught in the fence on the east side of the barn. The other part of his leg was never found. . . .

Eli Hershberger told him that his leg was off and Dan asked what had happened. When Eli told him there had been an explosion, he asked, "Where's Albert?"

"Albert is dead," Eli told him.

"Send word for all the children to come," were the last words he said.

When the neighbors arrived they told Fannie to start ringing the bell. But she did not respond, as she was in a state of shock. Then Andy was asked to ring the bell, but he did not understand either. But in a short time many bells were ringing in the neighborhood.

A blanket was brought for Dan to lay his head on and a doctor was sent for, but before the doctor arrived Dan was dead. He lived about forty-five minutes after the explosion.

W. M. Hostetler said he saw Dan's foot come over the barn with the shoe and sock still on.

Albert was found north of the barn in three pieces. His body had been torn off at the waist and the legs torn apart. One leg was seventy-five yards from where the engine stood. . . .

When more people had arrived a close search was made, and both men's watches were found. They were still running at the time.

The boiler was under an apple tree seventy-five feet away, and the firebox was turned end for end. The boiler had been ripped open lengthwise in line with the men's feet, where Dan and Albert had been standing.

At Dave K. Troyer's, two miles to the south, the house shook so that the windows rattled and the dishes in the cupboard moved.

The bodies were gathered up and cleaned as best as could be done. Albert's body was laid out in the little orchard close by the chicken house. The undertaker accidentally got Albert's legs on wrong. But since it would be quite a job to change them they were left that way.

The bodies were put on boards and carried to the house. Because of the heat and the condition the bodies were in, they were kept on ice until they were taken to the cemetery.

Mary, Dan's wife, was in bed most of the time until after the funeral. Her son Mahlon had died that spring on May 9. She said, "I have not forgotten Mahlon yet, as he was always so good to me. Now it's Dan and Albert."

The funeral services were held at the Dan P. Weaver home. Bishop Noah Bontrager of Howard County, Indiana, and Samuel Yoder preached in the barn, while Daniel D. Yoder and Daniel M. Wengerd preached in the house.

Source: Mrs. Atlee Hershberger (1971)

⇝-⇝-⇝-⇝-⇝-⇝-⇝-⇝

Her Last Breath

ELI J. BONTRAGER

In his unpublished autobiography, *Bishop Eli J. Bontrager describes the tragedy and the grief of losing his life companion.*

I memorized a short prayer which I devotedly repeated every evening upon retiring. However, I often brought my trials and problems to the Lord while at my work. I remember while still quite young that the words of Paul, "Quench not the spirit," lingered in my mind, and I deemed it as quenching the spirit if I would not pray whenever the thought of prayer entered my mind.

I prayed over many matters and received definite answers to many a prayer, but in my younger years I never could more earnestly pray for any other matter than this, that the Lord might so lead and provide for me a wife with whom I could live in perfect harmony and peace. A wife, a true Christian, and that he would carry us through life into a goodly age. . . .

I prayed the Lord for guidance. I resolved to watch for his guiding hand. One day at the wedding of a cousin of mine I met her. It seemed we were mutually interested in each other at once. However, for several years we only occasionally met each other. Later, however, the Lord brought us into closer friendship, and finally on December 18, 1890, we were married. I soon discovered that the Lord had indeed given me a wife who was a treasure. Our honeymoon lasted not only for a month, but for nearly twenty-eight years. Our love for each other never waned, and our last month together was just as much a honeymoon as the first month.

I never heard her utter an unkind word to me, to her children or to anyone else. The thought of losing her by death was too awful for me to consider it for a moment. I imagined the Lord knew that I could not bear up under such a trial and would never take her away from me. But that fatal day came when she, in the act of helping me, was taken in an instant. Her last breath was a healthy breath. O! The awfulness of that moment, that hour, and the

242

days to follow! I have said nobody ever had a better wife and no children ever had a better mother. . . .

On September 24, 1918, the fatal day came. The little girls were in school, and the boys were helping neighbors with their work. After dinner I had a big load of clover seed to get out of the barn to take to a neighbor to get it hulled. We had to hitch the team to the rear end of the wagon to get it out of the barn. My dear wife, always ready to help me, at my suggestion came to drive the team, while I took the wagon tongue to steer the wagon out. For some reason she lost control of the team and they ran for the corner of the barn, drawing the load after them and catching her, my wife and mother of my children, between the load and the barn, crushing her life out of her in an instant. That was the darkest moment of my life. Changed in a moment from the happiest of families to the most unhappy. . . .

The death of my dear life partner was an awful shock to me. I felt that I had nothing more to live for and expressed the wish that the years might pass as days, so that my dreary life would soon be over. However, the Grace of God is sufficient and able to sustain us in every circumstance. I came to realize her blessed state. She did not have to live through a siege of sickness, or suffer for even a moment. She was well up to her last breath, and then instantly transferred to that better home above—a home so much better than any that I could give her here. These thoughts helped to tide me over these sorrowful days. Besides this, my dear children were, as I often said, just as good and kind to me as they possibly could be.

Source: Eli J. Bontrager (1953): 9, 18

‑≫‑≫‑≫‑≫‑≫‑≫‑≫‑≫

Tragic Self-Destruction

DAVID LUTHY

T*he occurrence of Amish suicides suggests that the victims, like those in other cultures, suffer from social impoverishment and alienation. Although suicides occur, they are infrequent and none has been reported among youth under age eighteen.*

Jacob Nisley, aged thirty and unmarried, had shown up in the settlement and was staying at his cousin Daniel E. Nisley's home. Jacob, who was not Amish, apparently was quite unsettled in his personal life. Former residents have referred to him as a cowboy. His sudden violent death shocked the community and was reported in detail by David J. Troyer in the May 31, 1906, issue of *The Sugarcreek Budget:*

> A sad affair occurred at the house of Daniel E. Nisley on Sunday morning, of which I will give a short description. Several weeks ago Jacob Nisley, son of Joseph Nisley, formerly of Fulton Co., Ohio, came to the home of Dan E. Nisley and worked there since, till last Saturday night, May 19th. On May 17th he received a letter from his brother, somewhere in the east, and was very restless after that and refused to sleep in the house. But Sunday morning he came in for breakfast and seemed to be all right again and said he was going to church, but wasn't quite ready when the rest left, but said he would come pretty soon, the church being about a mile and a half from there. The family left, expecting him to follow, but in about an hour we saw that the house was on fire. We all hurried over and tried to save something but could not.
>
> The house burned down with all its contents, and it is plain that it was set on fire by Jacob Nisley in order to destroy himself. He got the trundle bed and placed it in front of the stove and carried about a quarter-ton of coal on it and poured about four gallons of oil in the house, set it on fire, laid himself on the coal pile, and shot himself. His idea must have been to burn up his body so no one would know what became of him.

Source: Luthy (1986): 144, based on David J. Troyer's account in *The Budget* (May 31, 1906)

Palm Sunday Tornado

ELI E. GINGERICH

A resident of Elkhart County, Indiana, Eli E. Gingerich describes the terrible tornado that suddenly appeared on a Sunday evening.

Without a doubt, nothing in the history of the community has been so moving as this mighty spectacle of nature on the Sunday evening of April 11, 1965. . . . Hundreds of people lost their homes and farm buildings, many were injured and some lost their lives as three or more tornadoes swept through the community in a general northeasterly direction, within several hours time, just before sundown. The last one followed in the path of a preceding one at times. The trailer court at Midway, north of Goshen, suffered the greatest disaster in property and lives. By the time it got to the Shore community south of Shipshewana, it was a half-mile wide and leveled practically everything in its path. . . .

Excepting for a very few people, a tornado was something remotely heard of or only seen in a picture. But that evening when those big swirling clouds bore down from the southwest, many, in a matter of minutes, saw and experienced a time of their lives. People who never seriously thought of such a thing before now sought refuge, most of them in the cellar, if they had one. When the awful freight train sound and the terrific whistling noise of whirling objects were over, only the sky was over them where their house had been.

Many breathed a prayer of thanksgiving that they were alive, and their first thoughts were of their neighbors. Most everything was covered with mud and water. People were hard to recognize, because they were covered with dirt and blood, as well. The able helped the helpless. Outside help began to come in. Roads were almost impassable. Things were in a turmoil. Police came to the scene. People worked together. Ambulances came but there were not enough. The injured and dying were taken to hospitals the best way. Hospitals were filled to overflowing, and emergency space in churches and other public places was set up. Doctors and nurses and many others came to the rescue. Search parties continued into the night for the missing. Temporary morgues were set up as friends tried to identify the dead. . . .

Only those who went through such a thing can realize what it is like. Only those who saw it could picture what it looked like. Even then it was hard to comprehend what you were seeing. It did something to you and gave a person an indescribable feeling. You feel like crying—and many did.

After the cleanup, buildings slowly began to take shape again. Some had lost only part of their buildings, some lost all. Workers came from everywhere, not only the surrounding communities but surrounding states as well. Pennsylvania was probably the biggest contributor and sent a school bus of workers every week for a long time, as well as smaller groups of workers with carpenters to supervise the job. Central eating places were set up where the workers were fed. Different churches took turns in furnishing the food. By fall all of the victims had at least the most necessary buildings replaced and had somehow managed to get in their work besides. . . .

Another fact presented itself and this makes a person feel humble. After all the debris was sifted through, there were no Amish found dead or seriously injured. Although there were no radios or television to warn them, and the only real warning was the sight of the approaching storm itself, all of them managed to get to safety or were marvelously delivered otherwise.

This should strengthen our faith and teach us over and again that although manmade inventions may have their value and usefulness, it is best to place our trust and confidence in God. As someone said, "It is better to watch the sky than listen to the radio."

Source: Gingerich (1980): 10

17

MALICIOUS
ATTACKS

From their earliest settlement in colonial America to the present, the Amish have experienced hostile intrusions into their life. The Hochstetler massacre occurred in Berks County, Pennsylvania, in 1757. In 1984 Naomi Huyard, an Amish girl, was killed by two emotionally disturbed and unsupervised youths. The moral lesson learned from these malicious attacks was the practice of nonresistance. Deep sorrows, the agony of parents and friends, and restless nights are a heavy weight on those affected. Resignation rather than revenge is the appropriate attitude. Healing is aided by the deep loyalty and support of the community.

The Northkill Attack

URIA R. BYLER

The story of the Native American assault on the immigrant Hochstetler family has been retold and rewritten many times. Uria R. Byler describes it for Amish schoolchildren.

The evening of September 19, 1757, was a happy one for the Jacob Hochstetler family. The young people of the neighborhood were gathered there for one of those old-fashioned "apple schnitzings" which provided the Hochstetler household with apples to dry for the winter and also gave the young folks a chance to get together for the evening. It was a closely knit little group, boys and girls who had grown up together in the same neighborhood. First they peeled and sliced apples for a few hours, probably laughing and enjoying themselves, as was usual on such occasions. Later, games were played until quite late, then the "good-nights" were said and the guests went home through the peaceful autumn night. When the last ones had left, the Hochstetlers bolted their doors and went to bed.

The French and Indian War was raging then, and during the last year quite a few white settlers in the neighborhood had been murdered and carried off in captivity. So far none of the Amish had been bothered and the Indians seemed friendly enough. Many times they had come to the house asking for food or clothing.

Tired of the evening's activities, the entire family was now in slumberland, unaware of the danger that was stalking in the forest nearby. There waiting patiently were a dozen Indians. Since soon after dark, they had awaited their chance to strike, and now they made ready. They came toward the house. As they were passing the bake oven, the Hochstetlers' dog began to bark. This awakened Jacob Jr., who opened the door to see what the trouble was. A shot rang out and Jacob felt a sharp pang in his leg. He shut and bolted the door and now the entire family were on their feet. In the dimness of night they could see about ten figures gathered near the bake oven.

The two boys picked up their muskets to defend the family. There was plenty of ammunition in the house, and no doubt the Indians could have been detained until daylight and help came. Being nonresistant and not believing in killing, Jacob's religion absolutely forbade such violence as even defending his loved ones. The stalwart sons implored their father to let them use their rifles, but the father believed with all his soul that when the Lord said to Moses "Thou shalt not kill" he meant just that.

The Indians next set the house on fire. When the Hochstetlers saw this, they all went to the basement. Soon the burning embers began falling through the floor. For a while these were kept extinguished by pouring cider on them. Finally it was apparent that they must leave the house or perish with it.

There was a small window on one side of the basement and through this the family began to leave one by one. Because it was getting daylight the Indians had all left except one, who had lingered to eat a few peaches. He happened to see the Hochstetlers as they were coming out of the window and shouted to his companions, who returned, and soon the entire family was taken.

Jacob Jr. and a daughter were tomahawked and scalped. Another Indian raised his deadly tomahawk over the head of Christian but changed his mind and took him prisoner along with the father. The mother was stabbed to death with a knife and also scalped.

We may well imagine what Jacob Hochstetler's thoughts were when he and his sons Christian and Joseph, hands bound behind their backs, were marched westward toward the Blue Mountains. Behind him lay his dead wife and two children, amid the smoldering embers of his buildings. When they emerged from the basement that morning into the hands of the Indians, he had urged his family to submit to any fate that awaited them.

Jacob was told that they were to be separated and taken to other villages. Sadly they bade each other good-by, not knowing if, and hardly expecting that, they would ever see each other again. The father's parting advice to his sons was: If you are taken so far away and kept so long that you forget the German language, do not forget the Lord's Prayer.

Source: Byler (1963a): 191–203, based on Harvey Hostetler (1912): 29–45

→→→·→→→·→→→·→→→·→→→·→→→·→→→·→→→

Shot in Missouri

DAVID LUTHY

Before *the Civil War, a few Amish settled in Missouri, where they suffered for their nonresistant faith.*

The Raber family had lived in Missouri only three years when the Civil War broke out in 1861. Residents of the state were not united in their sympathies, some favoring the North and others the South. Many people kept their opinions to themselves, the Rabers being among those. But hardships came regardless. Daniel, since he was Amish and opposed to war, did not want to become involved. But at thirty-six and six feet tall, he was a prime candidate for either army, both of which periodically came through the area. During those times he would hide.

One time when the Confederate soldiers were encamped not far from the Raber home, they made a bargain with Mrs. Raber for pies, offering a good price. The family worked all night and delivered the pies at the camp the next morning. They rejoiced at the money they took along home but found out later that it was counterfeit.

Grain and cattle were taken at will by the opposing armies. One time the Confederates forced young Christian Raber to drive his father's team and wagon to a mill thirty miles away. The wagon was loaded with a neighbor's wheat. The next day when he had unloaded the wheat, Christian watched his chance and headed for home, arriving there safely. The next day the Battle of Wilson Creek was fought, which was the worst battle on Missouri soil.

One day fifteen-year-old Christian and a young man named Egly were helping a neighbor move. They were driving the team and wagon on the way home and were near Quincy, Missouri, when a drunken soldier stopped them, demanding to know why they had a government wagon sheet on their wagon. Egly argued with the soldier and was fatally shot. A very shaken Christian Raber loaded the dead man onto his wagon and drove home twelve miles. A few months later he had to go to Springfield as an eyewitness to the death.

The soldier was given an honorable discharge. While in Springfield, Christian heard news which shocked the world—President Lincoln had been shot.

Source: Luthy (1986): 241–42

>>>->>>->>>->>>->>>->>>->>>->>>

Troyer's Dead Cows

SUSAN WICKEY

A *mischievous act against the family of Bishop John H. Troyer, near Conway Springs, Kansas, in 1930, "sapped his spirit and broke his health."*

It was during the Depression, and we were milking cows and a man would pick up sweet cream every morning, same as a milkman does now. That was our income to make payments on our farm. Then one summer we had a patch of Higara corn and when it grows, when it's dry, it is poisonous. We had a good fence around it.

One evening soon after my oldest brother was married, a stray dog came to our house. He didn't seem to be any good, but we let him stay. Later one evening we all went to the neighbors across the field. My mother couldn't walk very well, so she took the little ones in the buggy and drove to the neighbors, while Dad and the rest of us walked across the pasture. That is the way we came home after dark. Our doors were not locked, and, as Mom drove in the lane, she heard the living room door bang, just as it did when you went through it. She thought it must be my brother, who, having just married, might have come home to get some more of his clothes. She tied the horse and started for the porch. Then that stray dog came and stood with his front paws on the porch and growled in toward the door. Mother didn't want to be scared, so she went on up on the porch, and the dog went ahead of her and growled into the doorway. So she turned around and came out to meet Dad and the rest of us. She told us how the dog acted, and that she thought someone was in the house.

Dad and my brothers searched all through the house and found nothing.

So we all went to bed and slept and did not know what the morrow would bring. When my brothers went for the cows to milk that morning, they discovered all the cows except three had been herded through the gate and turned into the patch where the Higara corn was. The tracks showed they were crowded through the gate. My dad went along and checked the fence to make sure, as he didn't want to believe that someone would have done that to us. But the fence was tight and no hair caught of any kind.

That morning left a sight in my memory I'll never forget—a dozen cows and heifers lying along the Higara rows, all bloated and dead. My father never saw a healthy day after that. It stopped the payments on our farm, so we lost it and were forced to move on one of Grandpa's farms in Oklahoma.

Source: Susan Wickey, Salem, Indiana, letter (1978), to David Luthy, in Luthy (1986): 158

➤➤➤-➤➤➤-➤➤➤-➤➤➤-➤➤➤-➤➤➤-➤➤➤-➤➤➤

Baby Adeline

SIMON M. SCHWARTZ

An *Amish infant was killed near Berne, Indiana, one night when a group of boys in a pickup truck threw bricks at the horse-drawn buggy in which an Amish family was riding. Simon M. Schwartz (1908–) is a freelance writer.*

It was Friday night, August 31, 1979, the close of a hot and humid day in Indiana.

The air was still stifling as Levi and Rebecca Schwartz and their seven children headed back to their farm in their black horse-drawn buggy. The Old Order Amish family had spent the early evening visiting friends near Berne, Indiana. Already thirsty, the children talked longingly of the lemonade they had been served.

The clacking of the horse's hoofs and the creaking of leather as they headed north on the Adams County road spoke of the simple life of the Plain People.

It was a hard life, but uncomplicated. Because of their strict religious beliefs they had no automobiles or tractors. Their house was heated by coal- and wood-burning stoves; kerosene lamps reflected the shining cleanness of the wood floors and rustic furniture. Their children, ranging from Adeline, seven months, to Margaret, eleven, would go through the eighth grade and then take their places in the closely knit Amish community of 2,000 living in Adams County.

The bed would look good after the long, hot day, Levi remarked to his wife. Even the brown horse pulling the buggy seemed to agree, quickening its pace as they got within three miles of the hundred acres Levi farmed.

Traffic was heavy, with shoppers from Berne slowing as they saw the triangle-shaped red safety reflector Indiana requires on Amish buggies. The Schwartzes waved as they recognized occupants.

At 9:30 P.M., as nearly as the Schwartzes can remember, a battered old pickup pulled alongside. As it passed, Mrs. Schwartz, who was holding Adeline in her arms, felt a sharp pain in her right wrist. "Somebody threw something from the pickup," she said. A quick check of the children revealed no injury, and the Schwartzes continued home.

The modest but well-kept farmhouse was only a white blob in the darkness when the family arrived. As Levi waited patiently to take the horse to the barn, Rebecca handed Adeline to Margaret. "Take her into the house and put her on the bed while I get the others in," she directed.

As Margaret turned up the wick on a kerosene lamp, she noticed blood on the baby's face. Running outside, she cried, "Mother! Mother! Come quick! Something's wrong with Adeline!"

Levi and Rebecca ran into the house, and the mother anxiously picked up the infant. Immediately they saw a large bump on the back of Adeline's head. Blood was spattered on her face, which looked strangely pale and peaceful in the lamplight. Perhaps she's only unconscious, Mrs. Schwartz found herself hoping, as she wiped the blood from the baby's face. But she could detect no breath.

"She's dead! She's dead!" she cried in anguish. Quickly the dazed father ran to the nearest neighbor who had a telephone. "Call the Emergency Medical Service and the police," he begged. "Adeline may be dead."

She was. A piece of clay tile thrown from the truck had fractured Adeline's skull. She probably had died instantly while still in her mother's arms.

Soon city, county, and state police cars were systematically covering town and country roads in a search for the battered pickup. Earlier in the evening police had been notified that youths in such a vehicle had been throwing objects at Amish homes and buggies.

An hour after the tragedy, the truck was spotted in nearby Berne and the four young male occupants were taken into custody, handcuffed, and driven to the Adams County jail in Decatur, twelve miles to the north. There, charges of reckless homicide were filed against the four. Two of the youths, seventeen and eighteen, were from Berne; the others, eighteen and nineteen, were from Monroe, five miles to the south. Within a week, families of the four had posted $10,000 bond, and the young men were released pending trial.

From the first, the reaction of the youths was one of shock and remorse. "We had no idea we had injured, let alone killed, someone," they said. "We were just out for a little fun."

As news of the tragedy made headlines across the nation, hundreds of letters and sympathy cards arrived at the Schwartzes' farm. Others, addressed to the police, mayors, and newspapers in Berne and Decatur, demanded quick justice for the four youths.

Locals too were stunned and horrified by the senseless tragedy. But there was also concern and compassion for the youths and their families, all of good reputation in the community. None of the young men had been in trouble before, and all were popular among their acquaintances. Still, so incensed was public opinion that they had to go outside the county to find attorneys to defend them.

The four had pleaded not guilty when arraigned and had asked for jury trials. But when three were tried ten months later, in Adams Circuit Court, they changed their pleas to guilty and threw themselves on the mercy of the court.

Before sentencing the three, Judge Herman Busse, of Fort Wayne, Indiana, ordered a month-long investigation to help him determine their sentence. Even in their communities, odds were in favor of their having to serve some time.

On July 29, 1980, Judge Busse sentenced the first two defendants, announcing his verdict to a crowded courtroom. He knew that no sentence, however harsh, could return Adeline to her mother's arms. But the crime could not go unpunished. Each youth was given a five-year prison term, but Judge Busse suspended the sentences, put the youths on five years' probation, fined them $5,000 and court costs, and ordered them to make full restitution to the Schwartz family for medical and funeral expenses. In September, Judge Robert Thompson gave the third youth a three years' suspended sentence and a $5,000 fine.

The sentences might have been much harsher had it not been for a plea entered in the youths' behalf by the bishop of the Amish community. His letter, endorsed by the Schwartzes, was read in court.

"We believe," he wrote, "that the four boys have suffered, and suffered heavily, since the crime, and they have more than paid for what they did.

Sending the defendants to prison would serve no good purpose, and we plead for leniency for them."

This remarkable expression of compassion by the Amish community, many of whom had been harassed by the defendants and others, brought tears to the eyes of onlookers in the courtroom and gained additional friends for the Plain People.

Today, Amish buggies around Berne and Monroe seldom draw more than a cheery wave from passing vehicles. Levi and Rebecca Schwartz like to think that each wave is a tribute to baby Adeline. If so, her death was not in vain.

Source: Schwartz (1981): 3

>>>->>>->>>->>>->>>->>>->>>->>>

Where Was God When Naomi Died?

ANN HOSTETLER SMUCKER

When social order and human planning fall short, questions without answers persist. Why did Job suffer the loss of all? Why do bad things happen to good people? The murder of Naomi Huyard is a question we are left to ponder. Ann Hostetler Smucker is a friend of the Huyard family.

Naomi's favorite hobby was preparing a special meal for friends and family. I remember her tiny frame wrapped in a large work apron, her pointed face creased with a smile as she bustled about the spacious, well-scrubbed kitchen—soaking bunches of celery, stirring pots of home-grown vegetables and aromatic meats, preparing the table with blue-and-white-checked cloth and crystal glasses of strawberry jam.

It was just before Merv and I got married, and the Huyard family had invited us for supper in honor of the event.

Together with her sister and niece and several of their friends, Naomi had pieced and hand-stitched a detailed quilt for our wedding, a broken star whose rays spread out across a field of white in blue diamond-shaped patches.

Now I think of Naomi as this broken star, one whose joyous giving touched so many.

She died, but she did not die quietly. Naomi Huyard was strangled and repeatedly stabbed to death one evening when she went, as she so often did, to the neighbor's freezer to put away food for a company meal. Her basket was found overturned in the freezer, her body in a basement room. The violent end of her peaceful life was soon written all over the headlines.

"Naomi never was afraid," her niece said. "She trusted everyone. She wasn't afraid because she couldn't imagine doing evil to anyone." Before we left, she asked another question, one which we had not dared to voice. "I looked out the window at the sun this morning and knew God was in heaven, but where was he last night?"

She asked the question Job once asked, the question all of us posed in our own minds. "Why do bad things happen to good people?" It is an unanswerable question, but one which we are nonetheless driven to answer when our orderly explanations of the world are violated.

First sheer outrage overwhelms us. Why did she have to suffer such a terrible end? What must she have been going through in those final moments of her life? In many deaths we try to see God's plan at work. But to see Naomi's death as part of God's plan seems incongruous.

But in no way can Naomi be blamed for her own death. She was simply a chanced victim, caught unaware while performing a routine activity she had done each week for years. Her death forces me to accept emotionally what my intellect knows—that in this world innocence is vulnerable to evil.

Every crime of violence is an assault against God, not an object lesson of his own devising. When we perceive God as outraged by violence, we no longer feel that we have to defend his "plan." Instead we can turn to him as a source of strength and comfort when tragedy strikes.

In a larger sense I see Naomi as a martyr to the violence of our own times, just as our Anabaptist forebears were martyrs for their vision of living out Christ's teachings on earth. The greatest difference between them is that the religious martyrs of the sixteenth century knew what they were dying for. Naomi probably never had time to think about it.

One old and revered man, when faced with the question "Where was God when Naomi died?" thought long and silently before putting his response in the form of another question. "Where was God when his own son died?"

Source: Smucker (1983): 8–10

18

CRITICISMS

The attitudes of outsiders toward the Amish people are generally of two kinds. One is admiration and respect. This view is expressed in two letters I have received. "As part of the education of my children," wrote a mother in Wisconsin, "I would like to expose them to the lifestyles of others. I am intrigued by the Amish, and their flourishing culture. Their survival of standards in this crazy world is astonishing." A man in California wrote: "Our society is sick with greed for money and real estate. The Amish are true Christians. They have the real true religion."

The other view is contempt or pity for people who have not eased the burdens of life, who live by "oppressive" customs, and who have rejected progress. Some of the harsh attitudes have been moderated over the past thirty years. The Amish are now viewed as meticulous farmers. Instead of blaming Amish parents for exploiting the labor of their children, some parents today wish that their children would find meaning in their work. Other critics are less sure than before that the world is headed toward progress.

The following selections are from different time periods and cover a wide range of topics.

→≫-→≫-→≫-→≫-→≫-→≫-→≫-→≫

We Don't Visit Together

WALTER M. KOLLMORGEN

I*n his 1942 study of the Lancaster County, Pennsylvania, Amish community, Walter M. Kollmorgen gleaned these observations from his informants.*

The conceptions and attitudes of outsiders toward the Old Order Amish community vary greatly and are naturally conditioned by personal ambitions and experiences. A local banker boasted that 90 percent of his loans to the Amish and Mennonites were made on one-signature papers because they are honest, work hard, and pay their debts. A feed mill operator, however, insisted that the Amish are no better than other farmers: "Some pay their debts promptly and others do not. Some try to do you for all they can". . . .

An advocate of higher education criticized the Amish severely for standing in the way of science and progress: "Every time someone wants to improve a schoolhouse we've got a Supreme Court fight on our hands. Lancaster County should be ashamed of its many out-of-date, one-room schoolhouses." A non-Amish citizen living in the township in which the school fight took place deplored the obstructionist school attitude of the Old Order Amish. He spoke with strong feeling about this fight and the fact that some of his children formerly had to attend an old, ill-equipped one-room school with outside toilets. . . .

Some of the non-Amish farmers in the larger community are not well disposed toward these peculiar people: "They want to buy all the land. I could have sold this farm for much more than it is really worth, but I won't sell." Many resent the widespread opinion that the Amish and Mennonites are better farmers than they are. "I could make lots of money too if I worked day and night and worked my children the way they do." A Mennonite affiliated with one of the more liberal branches of the church found himself definitely isolated in the midst of the Old Order Amish community. He said: "Most of my friends are from ten to twenty miles away from here. I used to have close friends around here but they sold out and bought cheaper land. About the only place I see the Old Order Amish is on the road; we don't visit together". . . .

One farmer criticized both the Amish and the Mennonites for not participating more generally in government agricultural programs. "The rest of us join to improve prices and they can plant as much as they want and still get the same prices we do." Some farmers were rather critical of the fact that the Old Order Amish do not own automobiles, telephones and tractors (for field work), but nevertheless feel free to ask their neighbors for a ride to town, for the use of the telephone, or to plow fields with a tractor. . . .

Businessmen in the city of Lancaster and other nearby trade centers frequently see in the Old Order Amish an opportunity to increase the tourist trade of Lancaster County. These rather unique people with their peculiar garb, big farms, and big houses naturally lend themselves well to advertising, and advertised they are. Post cards, leaflets, and booklets, and even dolls featuring the Amish have been designed to catch the traveler's eye.

Source: Kollmorgen (1942): 3, 4, 16, 17

–⫸–⫸–⫸–⫸–⫸–⫸–⫸–⫸–

"The Amish Cry to High Hell"

ANONYMOUS

D*uring the Iowa school controversy in 1967, Harrell R. Rogers, Jr., was conducting interviews for his doctoral dissertation. He reported these unidentified comments.*

The Amish cry to high hell that they be left alone to live as they choose. The problem, however, is that if they were left alone they would die off. They are not by any means self-sufficient; they depend on organized society for their survival. Being left alone to an Amishman means being able to sponge off of organized society for the things they [the Amish] need (hospitals, law enforcement, highways, food and material products), while not having to accept responsibility for support of the community. They need this community but hypocritically refuse to support it.

[The Amish are] just as human as the rest of us, and subject to just as many vices. Why the public persists in thinking of them as saints is beyond me. They aren't, and they simply can't be allowed to do as they please. The modern world exists! They either admit that, or they will be devoured by it. If not today, tomorrow. If not them, their children. It's cruel not to make them face that reality.

Source: Anonymous quotations, in Rodgers (1969): 41, 76

⫸⫸⫸⫸⫸⫸⫸⫸

"Strangely Primitive"

MARC ALAN OLSHAN

As a student of rural American communities, Marc Alan Olshan has observed changing attitudes toward the Amish way of life. When goals of Americans have become less materialistic and more inclined toward quality-of-life issues, the Amish have been invoked as potential models.

The Amish were depicted as leading a "strangely primitive life" in an early twentieth-century magazine article (*The Independent,* 1903). For Norman Thomas (1923), they were a "backward people."

This "backwardness" upon which the Amish have placed such a high value has proved to be source of irritation and resentment for rural neighbors still actively seeking to improve the quality of their lives as measured by a far different standard. In the period immediately following World War II, Indiana farmers looked unfavorably on their Old Order neighbors since "they ruin these farms by removing electric lights, central heating, and bathrooms, thus lowering the standards and general desirability of a neighborhood" (Lehman 1947). Amish resistance to carnivals, agricultural fairs, and modern public educational facilities may lower local revenues and at times is likewise interpreted to be "destructive to community progress" (Elmer L. Smith 1961).

Frugality and self-sufficiency become vices rather than virtues in the context of a rural community that is aggressively promoting economic growth. In Iowa a businessman complained that the Amish "just don't buy things that everybody else buys." A banker in the same community estimated that if the Amish purchased the same goods that everyone else bought, it would add as much as $1.2 million to the local economy (Rugaber 1965). The owner of a restaurant in a small Wisconsin town referred contemptuously to the local Amish population:

> Not even the Amish and their Bible can stop progress. America is the greatest country in the world and now we get people like this who don't get into a world with automobiles and moon rockets and war. . . . Those people don't fit with us. . . . They're different. It's like Negroes coming into your sections of a big city (Janson 1971).

In short, where the American dream is still being sought, the Amish may symbolize a slap in the collective face of the community; a repudiation of the values to which they are devoting their lives.

Yet in spite of the bad feeling that has sometimes developed in rural areas adjacent to large Amish settlements, the attitude of the larger American public has generally become more favorable. In fact, to the extent that goals in American society have become less materialistic or economic in nature and more oriented toward quality-of-life issues, the Amish have been increasingly invoked, either as exemplifying aspects of the good life, or as a potential model to which others will have to turn out of necessity.

Source: Olshan (1980): 161–62

Is There Anything to Be Said for Stopping?

TOM BRADEN

T om Braden is a syndicated colum-
nist who describes an interesting conversation he had with his daughter.

One of my children is doing a school paper on the subject of the Amish.
The following conversation ensued:

"Dad, it seems to me that the trouble with the Amish is that they don't
go ahead. They've stopped. How can I say anything about them except that
they stopped?"

"They are the best farmers in the world."

"True, but only for small farms. They don't believe in machinery. They
don't believe in anything that happened after the eighteenth century. They're
not with it."

"Is there anything to be said for not being with it?"

The knowledgeable reader will instantly reflect that I have given myself
the last line in the discussion above outlined, and I cast myself in the role of
wise questioner. This is a bad habit of which many fathers are guilty.

And yet as I think upon that conversation and upon the peaceful Amish,
going about their business from dawn to dark, doing the Lord's will as they
interpret the Lord's will from their literal translation of the Bible, ignoring
the bustling American society which sometimes threatens their New York,
Pennsylvania, or Iowa farms, I wonder whether in fact there is not something
to be learned from "stopping." More importantly, I wonder whether we are
not beginning to learn it.

Take the Concorde, that British-French airliner which stabs at the speed of
light. We are about decided not to allow it to land in this country, and if we
so decide there probably won't be any Concorde. There isn't any SST.

Yet who can deny that the Concorde and the SST represent all we ever
learned about progress? The Concorde and the SST fly higher. They fly
better. They fly faster.

Aren't higher, better, and faster worthwhile in themselves? We Americans have always believed so. Yet we are about to say in effect, "Stop."

Another example. We don't know what to do about the world's burgeoning knowledge of how to make nuclear power. We are trying to get together with the nations which possess the knowledge and agree upon some means of keeping the knowledge secret so that some nut, whether he be American, Arab, or Japanese extremist, doesn't steal the means of holding us all at ransom.

In short, there are many voices in the world which are saying, "Stop," as the Amish once said it. And suddenly within the lifetime of a father, the voice which says, "Stop," doesn't seem quite so silly any more.

Source: Braden (1975)

19

SPEAKING OUT,
THE AMISH EXPLAIN

There are rare occasions when the Amish volunteer their deeper thoughts to outsiders. The emphasis on right behavior rather than written or spoken eloquence has its basis in biblical sources. The deeper experiences of reality are accompanied by "sighs too deep for words" (Rom. 8:26).

There are, however, times to speak out. One occasion is when human laws conflict with divine commands. "We must obey God rather than man" (Acts 5:29). In testifying before a court of law, an Amish bishop told the judge: "We don't go down on our knees for nothing." He was speaking of the finality of the baptismal promise made by his church members.

Some Amish will speak out in times of crisis or deep reflection. The selections in this chapter, beginning with short quotations, are of the latter type. A schoolteacher expresses his gratitude for the religious liberty in America. In an autobiographical account left for his children, a bishop reflects about changes in his lifetime. And occasionally outsiders will ask the Amish to write about their farm and family life.

264

>>>-->>>-->>>-->>>-->>>-->>>-->>>-->>>

We Are Christian

WILLIAM A. YODER

We are not Amish, we are Christians. Amish is just a nickname. We don't need to be ashamed that people call us that but we shouldn't build on the name Amish.

Source: William A. Yoder (unpublished)

ANONYMOUS

"We want to be the kind of Christians that the world can see are different. We believe you're supposed to lead a life so that anyone can see you're a Christian, so that you don't have to carry the Bible under your arm."

Source: Snowdon (1972): 124

RULES OF A GODLY LIFE

Be friendly to all and a burden to no one. Live holy before God; before yourself, moderately; before your neighbors, honestly. Let your life be modest and reserved, your manner courteous, your admonitions friendly, your forgiveness willing, your promises true, your speech wise, and share gladly the bounties you receive.

Source: Rules of a Godly Life (1984): 80

We Are Grateful for Our Liberty

URIA R. BYLER

*T*his selection appears in a history textbook written by an Amish author for seventh- and eighth-grade pupils.

The complete story of America cannot be written without telling its readers the story of those who have found protection from the persecutions of the cruel despots of Europe. These have been many; Quakers, Pilgrims, Dunkards, Mennonites, Amish, to mention only a few.

Because it's been many years since these minorities have fled their homeland to find a safe refuge in America, we often are too prone to forget and ignore the liberty that is ours. In counting our many blessings, this is not the least of them, and if we ever had gone through the grief that many religious minorities have in other lands, while we enjoyed our liberties here in this country, we might understand it better, and appreciate them more. . . .

When George Washington solemnly said to the other makers of the Constitution, "This document is in the hands of God," he was not speaking idle words. He and the other signers clearly understood their responsibility in writing this document.

There are countries in the world today where all books are censored, looked over by government officials, and if the books do not suit their fancy they are destroyed and the authors imprisoned. Under our Constitution there is absolute protection against that kind of censoring, as long as the book does not advocate the overthrow of our form of government. This, then, is only one of the reasons for feeling grateful. . . . There has been some conflict between public and private school authorities in several states, but there is reason to hope that restraint and common sense on both sides will eventually serve to work out a solution. Common sense and restraint were two virtues used in writing the Constitution. They are as valuable now in any controversy, large or small, as they have ever been. It is the time-tested formula for settling disputes in America, from the halls of Congress down to the small hometown community. Sometimes there is a lot of fuss and feathers flying for awhile but in the end things usually work out as they should; the American way. We're grateful for that, too.

Last, but not least, we are grateful for living in a country where we may worship as our conscience dictates, where private and parochial schools are tolerated, where we may live in peace with our fellow men, who have the common sense to respect the wishes of a minority. . . .

The makers of the Constitution have long been dead, but their great work lives on. It lives on only because there are people who want it to live and not die. By deeds and words, with courage, with the same traits that the Founders of our Constitution had, common sense and restraint, these people are defending the rights of the minorities.

Who are these people? . . .They are practically everywhere, and their numbers are many. . . . We have them in our home community, neighbors, towns-men, local and county school officials, legislators, both state and national.

Source: Byler (1963a): 261–62

➤➤➤-➤➤➤-➤➤➤-➤➤➤-➤➤➤-➤➤➤-➤➤➤-➤➤➤

Reflections on Change

DAVID BEILER

The first large book by an American member of the Amish church was by Bishop David Beiler (1786–1871). The book, Das Wahre Christentum (True Christianity), *was written in 1857 and posthumously published in 1888. It comprises a wide scope of subjects, from biblical exposition to teachings on baptism, marriage, and nonresistance. In this selection, Beiler comments on the widespread changes during his lifetime.*

A great change has taken place in our churches within the past sixty years. One who has not lived though it would hardly believe it possible. At that time there was much more Christian humility than now, and a greater respect for those in authority, especially the ministers and elders. How it is now is known to everybody. It has often seemed to me that the present is like the time of the Judges when there was no king in Israel, and everybody did that which seemed right in his own eyes. That is entirely too much the case with us. It is as the prophet says, "The young man is proud and arrogant against his elders, and the wicked man sets himself against the honest man." I can remember very well the time when it was customary for us to walk to church or meeting, especially the young people, who went barefooted. Of fine shoes and boots there was no thought whatever. Light spring wagons, too, were entirely unknown in our church. The old people who could not walk would either have to travel on horseback or remain at home. Sixty years ago it was not customary among us either to appear in fine Sunday shirts or bosom shirts [dress shirts with decorative front tucks], according to the fashions of the world, as is now too much the case. Fine and strangely colored store clothing was unknown among us. We were perfectly satisfied and contented with homemade wearing apparel.

The wives and daughters spent the winter in spinning. The flaxseed was sown in the spring; and in the autumn it was shredded, broken, strung up and heckled. This was work mostly for the women and girls. In almost every farmhouse one could hear the spinning wheels hum and sing, and in the exceptions it was the common talk that such families did not do their duty. Now there is so much outside material, especially cotton material, in use among us that the homespun clothes have been almost entirely replaced, and our daughters no longer know how to spin. What a great change we have undergone in the last sixty years. . . .

Sixty years ago plows were made without any metal, being entirely constructed of wood. Harrows were unknown. Threshing machines or horse treads were both unheard of. Everything was done by hand. During the winter the grain was trodden out by horses. This was for the most part work for the boys. At this time it was more customary than now to keep the boys at home and at work. And they did not gad about two or three months each year out in the world among their friends and acquaintances wasting the priceless time of grace in idleness, cracking silly jokes, and talking vain nonsense. At this time it was not customary to waste several months each winter in school. It was thought sufficient if boys could learn to read and write. It was commonly held that for people like us, a humble plain people, or for the common man, no more learning was needed. It was not permitted either to build such gorgeous houses and barns as now after the fashion of the world. We were satisfied to live in houses that were meant for shelter. I remember very well when horses were not tied in their stalls. The harness on the horses was not as elaborate as now either. Saddles and reins were not made after the fashions of the world as now. Wagons were unpainted.

At that time there was not so much time wasted in the decoration of houses as now, and our fathers were satisfied with much simpler household furniture. Colored dishes were very rare. Colored and flowery sofas might be found in the leading houses, but were unknown among those who belonged to our humble circles. Writing desks and bureaus, too, were forbidden; long carpets also. I can remember very well when we wore wooden shoes. Leather shoes were regarded as too costly. Our whole dress was much simpler than now. I honestly believe that if many of the church members would have carried on sixty years ago as they do today . . . they would have been excommunicated as unworthy members.

Source: C. Henry Smith (1929): 251–52

The Decline of the Family Farm

GIDEON L. FISHER

After all other wars a depression usually followed ten to fifteen years afterward. But this time, after World War II, the government took the initiative and went into debt by millions of dollars so that the individual person could enjoy prosperity. After all, the government is the people. Therefore the enormous debt which the government is carrying is the people's debt, but the majority don't realize it.

Hence this false prosperity which is being enjoyed by the public is not really a natural product, although it is being handled by the politicians in such a way that it looks rosy to the public as well as to the working class of people.

By 1960, due to the unpredictable prosperity, not only did the town folk go to the factories for a job, but the farm youths also turned an eye toward an easy way to make money. In the last half century the cycle has changed considerably as far as farm labor is concerned. Thousands of farm youths, after going through high school, left the farm for a higher salary, rather than being tied down with responsibilities of farming.

The school laws, which required higher education and longer school terms, tempted many farm youths, both boys and girls, to go to college after high school, and accept the results of prosperity, for more money and time to associate with world activities. A large percentage of the youths who attended high school and college chose office work of some kind. After having the higher education, the youths naturally wished to use the knowledge that they were taught. So they became schoolteachers, doctors, nurses, lawyers, politicians, architects, mechanical engineers, agents, or businessmen. . . .

In many of the non-Amish or Mennonite localities the situation of the younger generation leaving the farm was serious. It was not unusual for a well-to-do farmer with a large family, the man and his wife being alone, to do the farm work, while their children would go through grade school, high school, and college, adding to the expense of their parents. . . . Many fathers and mothers of middle age, who had spent their prime on the farm, dreamed of the day of retirement. They hoped that one of the children would take over the responsibilities of the farm, and made provisions for the others of the family so that when they were grown they could also enjoy a peaceful farm life.

However, the dreams of many of these old-time farmers turned into nightmares. Many an aged man and wife, with years of farming experience, were obliged to do the farm work to the best of their ability until they were too feeble to take care of themselves, let alone do the labor which is required to run a farm. Very often we find that the farm itself was in a more run-down condition than it had been in years past. The buildings were in need of repair, the paint was faded, underbrush was growing along the fence line, the farm machinery was outdated and well-worn. In the early years of farming, before the family was old enough to help, the day-laboring man was considered a very important person to have around to help out. Then in later years, after he was no longer available, and the high schools offered temptation and activities to the students, the parents were just swamped with work. Many farmers lost interest in keeping things in the best of shape.

Quite often the parents would agree to sell the home farm to one of the children at a greatly reduced price. It might have been in the family for two, three, or four generations, and they wished to have it continued in the family name. Sometimes the children would excuse themselves for not buying it because of its run-down condition, compared to what it had been. It would require hard labor to run a farm after having a diploma qualified them for office work. So they felt it would not be the proper thing for them to live and work on the farm. Farm work was by 1950 considered second-class labor. . . .

Many parents and old people, even though it was against their wishes, decided to sell both real estate and personal property at public auction. From 1940 to 1960 thousands of farms across the nation were offered to buyers at bargain prices. . . .

Many old landmarks or family homesteads were squandered away, because of the trend in this modern world of high education, less physical labor, and more progressive attitudes. Very often a young man and his wife both held a job in the same office, and at the same time hired someone to do their housework and baby-sitting. . . .

The children of these aged parents have many excuses for not giving their parents a home. Houses are too small, man and wife both work, or live in a city (the parents would find it difficult to adjust to city life), and for their children they hire a baby-sitter. They can't afford to take time off to attend to their parents, because they feel they can't give up a good-paying job for the sake of doing so. Because of this they agree to have them live at some old peoples' home, and hope they enjoy their time there.

Source: Gideon L. Fisher (1978): 56–59

-➤➤➤-➤➤➤-➤➤➤-➤➤➤-➤➤➤-➤➤➤-➤➤➤-➤➤➤

Some Thoughts on Our Spiritual Life

NAME WITHHELD

Explicit oral and written explanations *of their religious faith are not readily forthcoming from the Amish. Individuals can identify right from wrong but cannot always explain why. In this selection an unidentified Amish person makes many rich associations between the physical and the spiritual world.*

Our spiritual life is a little like a field planted with a crop. Even with good seed and good soil and the sunshine and the rains that God sends, any hoping for a good crop would only be wishful thinking if we neglected the field and let the weeds take over.

God gave us our abilities to use. Salvation was never meant to take no effort or sacrifice on our part. God never expects us to let Him do it all. He did the part that we could not do, but that does not excuse us from doing our part.

All summer and especially when harvest time comes close, we can look over the field that we have planted and taken care of. It is not wrong to have hope if we see the promise of a good crop. We still know that our efforts

271

would have helped nothing without God's miracles of the seeds sprouting and growing and without God's sunshine and rain. If we like the work, there is nothing else that we would rather do than work with the crop that we have planted. Such is also the part that we are to do for our salvation; we can find contentment and fulfillment in our Christian life. The toil will not always be easy, because anything that we will ever get of any worth will have to be worked for. Those who do God's work will get God's pay.

Source: Name withheld, *Family Life* (January 1984): 13

➤➤➤-➤➤➤-➤➤➤-➤➤➤-➤➤➤-➤➤➤-➤➤➤-➤➤➤

What Does It Mean to Be Amish?

MONROE L. BEACHY

Monroe L. Beachy lives near Sugar- *creek, Ohio, and is a member of the Old Order Amish church.*

There are many churches. For example: Church of God, Assemblies of God, Baptist, Church of the Brethren, Christian and Missionary Alliance, United Church of Christ, Church of the Nazarene, Quaker, Mormon, Lutheran, Methodist, Moravian, Presbyterian, Salvation Army, Unitarian, Christian Scientist, Episcopalian, Catholic, Jew, Muslim and so on.

It is interesting to notice that most of these came into being after 1525, which is usually considered as the year when ours started. Now, of course, we dress differently and our lifestyle is different, but are they the only differences between the Amish and all these other churches?

Well, let me tell you a story: Some time ago a group of fifty-two people chartered a bus and came to Holmes County to see the Amish. They had arranged to have an Amishman meet them and answer some of their questions.

The first question was: "We all go to church," and they named some of these churches, "so we know about Jesus, but what does it mean to be Amish?"

The Amishman thought a bit and then he asked a question of his own.

"How many of you have TV in your homes?" Fifty-two hands went up. "Now, how many of you feel that perhaps you would be better off without TV in your homes?" Again fifty-two hands went up. "All right. Now, how many of you are going to go home and get rid of your TV?" Not one hand went up!

Now that is what it means to be Amish. As a church, if we see or experience something that is not good for us spiritually, we will discipline ourselves to do without.

The world in general does not know what it is to do without!

Source: Beachy (1982): 18

-》》-》》-》》-》》-》》-》》-》》-》》

Our Farm

MARY MILLER

In *search of a bicentennial theme in 1976, the* Michigan Farmer *asked an Amish girl to describe her life on the farm. Mary Miller grew up in Michigan and now lives in Indiana, where she is a mother and homemaker.*

I find it a bit difficult to write about what is to me a world within a world. I live in the smaller world, loving the quiet life, but distantly can hear the clamor from the outside world. At times I might pause to envy what looks like an easier life, filled with every luxury, knowing that in the world things are moving at a faster speed. Always my world calls me back as I realize that within my way of life lies the peaceful beauty of unchanged time. . . .

Vividly to my mind comes the remembrance of the times when I was a small girl of three or four. Sitting with Mem (Mother) during church services, having a few small toys to keep me occupied quietly. The first hour wasn't bad. I loved to hear them sing but that wooden bench kept getting harder and harder. Minutes dragged like hours. Sometimes I was allowed to get up for a drink but it always meant sitting down again. My feet didn't touch the floor so I'd swing my legs back and forth, wiggle around trying to ease my discomfort. At times I would lean my head against Mem's shoulder and take a nap. But as soon as that last Amen sounded, us kids were the first ones up and away to our friends and games.

Farm life is hard and often difficult. Patience and endurance are factors much needed for successful farming. No matter what the season, there is always an endless stream of work to be done. In the coldest hours of a winter morning or beneath the blazing sun of summer, man's comfort cannot be weighed against time or labor. . . .

Plowing is done and satisfaction rests in the heart. Six or eight horses are hitched to the harrow as it is dragged over the fields, breaking up the clods of soil. Soon the rich fertile ground is ready to receive the tiny kernels of corn that grow into tall slender stalks during the course of summer. This corn must be carefully cultivated to keep it weed-free and insure a better crop. It means hours spent moving slowly through the field beneath the hot sun, with eyes glued to the row passing under the seat and feet regulating the cultivator with pedals while the hands keep the horses from stepping on the corn with their big feet. The horses find it impossible to resist tasting the corn, so they must wear *mahl-korply* (muzzles made of wire mesh). These enable the horses to breathe freely but still keep them from eating the corn. . . .

Women also have the job of mowing and cleaning the lawn. The hand-pushed lawn mower is enough to wear anybody out, but the grass keeps growing.

It's a simple life full of toil but it holds much joy.

Hayfields, with plenty of rain, have grown pretty high again by mid-August. Haymaking starts again but there isn't as much as there was with the first cutting, so it doesn't take as long. But it's usually enough to fill that last nook in the barn.

With summer gone, a kind of sadness lingers over the farm. Water pistols are laid aside. The cuddly kittens are grown. Wildlife gets ready for hibernation. Even the snakes crawl off. No matter how much work there is to be done, us kids always find time for fun. Each day goes in routine yet is vastly different from the day before. Farm life is adventurous and exciting. It is full of surprises, overflowing with blessings. Farm life is the only life I have ever known. It's a way of life I love and cherish.

Source: Mary Miller (1976): 8–11

-⋙-⋙-⋙-⋙-⋙-⋙-⋙-⋙-

A Letter to Governor Thornburgh

NAME WITHHELD

The filming of the movie Witness *in Lancaster County, Pennsylvania, created apprehension and displeasure among the Amish people and their friends. This letter to Governor Richard Thornburgh expresses some of the reasons.*

Dear Governor:

I am a young girl living with my parents. I am writing for the majority of us Amish people. It is concerning the movie *Witness.*

It is out of character for us to defend ourselves. But in reality the time has come when we must speak up. This is a necessary issue. On most issues we have mainly used faith and prayer as our sources of defense. We have mostly let others (who respect us) speak up for us. We feel they are better qualified. We do not ask others to come to our defense, although we are thankful for what they do to help us.

Our concerns about the movie may seem small to you, but for us it is no small thing. We are disappointed to learn that Hollywood was actually invited to come here by the Commonwealth of Pennsylvania. We realize the state may need money, but we question whether making a movie will pay off in the long run.

First, we Amish feel we are being used to lure tourists to our community. We do not have any resentment against tourists, but it is the tourist attractions that work against us. The making of the movie and then advertising it "As Seen in the Movie *Witness*" (by the Pennsylvania Dutch Visitors Bureau) means that more motels and amusement centers will be needed. Where will these places be built? On farmlands? This makes it very hard for us as farmers. We are gradually being crowded out by commercialization.

Second, we are opposed to having so much attention drawn to us. There are those in our areas who are jealous of us for receiving all this attention. They hate us for it. They imply that we enjoy all this attention, which is very false. Concerning either our bad points or our good points, we do not enjoy all this attention. Those who do come to see us in reality are often disappointed and lose respect for us. All this popularity turns into hate against us. Our hands are tied. We are not living this way to attract attention. We want to be left alone like other humans. We are opposed to having our souls marketed.

Could not greater blessings be brought to Lancaster County if the wishes and religion of the Christians were respected? We are not ungrateful for all your efforts to serve our state and country. But please, if it is within your power, do not allow any more movies to be made about us Amish in the future. Please consider. Thank you.

Source: Name withheld (unpublished letter, 1985)

$$\text{➤➤➤-➤➤➤-➤➤➤-➤➤➤-➤➤➤-➤➤➤-➤➤➤-➤➤➤}$$

More Important than Money

ROBERT L. SUMMER

T*he author is a newspaper columnist.*

This week we'd like to salute an unnamed Amish farmer in North Indiana.

It seems that the Amishman owned some farm machinery which had been loaned to another farmer and it, in turn, had been involved in an accident with a truck. The other farmer had been killed, and the equipment heavily damaged.

Since Amish people take a dim view of going to law, among other things, a friend of the man asked an attorney he knew to see if he could recover some damages for the one who had suffered the loss of vital machinery.

The lawyer visited the offices of the trucking firm and eventually reached an agreement with its officers for a settlement of $13,500. Since an attorney's fee in this type of case is usually one-third of the settlement, the fortunate lawyer had a chance to pick up more than $4,400 for a pittance of involvement.

However, when he reported the offer to the farmer, the Amish brother turned him down flat. Indignantly he insisted, "All I want is $150—what the equipment was worth."

They don't make many men like that anymore in our materialistic society. With him, integrity and character were more important than a monetary windfall which he had not earned and to which he was not ethically entitled. Legally, the money could have been his without question; morally, it was a different story.

Source: Summer (1974)

20

TRIBUTES

Amish communities are an example of how small holistic communities can function within the larger culture, even though the little community holds ideals that may occasionally conflict with those held by the larger society. What distinguishes the Amish from most communities is the unity of their religious faith, the motivation to practice their beliefs in daily life as consistently as possible, and the depth of their community experience.

Through the years, the Amish have made it quite clear, consciously and overtly, that their ways of thought are their very being and that without the possibility of pursuing those ways they would cease to be Amish. For them, living in community is not a preference. It is mandated by a deep personal, individual faith, involving a spiritual or supernatural connection. Living in community is itself an act of worship. Although religion has its formal aspects in Amish society, it is pervasively informal, demanding a pragmatic relationship with earthly affairs, family, and nature.

Divisions within the Amish culture are likely to occur, not from any difference in faith, but by the ability of some Amish communities to cope more successfully than others with the inroads of social and technological change. The Amish have sometimes been criticized as a self-serving group who make little or no contribution to society at large, but it can be argued that at least one positive function of the Amish is to serve as a model. As Turnbull (1984: 112) has noted, tourists come to look at the unusual, as anthropologists would, but they observe that the Amish also feel, think, and compare. The Amish function, consciously or otherwise, as a kind of sacred community in a secular society, reminding the rest of society of its own ideas, as well as the contradictions that develop between beliefs and practice. In this chapter, several selections describe ways in which the Amish function as models.

A Revelation to Europeans

WILLIAM I. SCHREIBER

William I. Schreiber, Professor of German at Wooster College in Ohio, is well known for his book Our Amish Neighbors.

The Old Order Amish community in America may become the last refuge of German peasantry. In Germany the accentuated rate of modernization, communication, and transportation is causing the rapid disappearance of the "Bauer." The so-called *Wirtschaftswunder,* the miracle of economic revival on the Continent, is pervading even the most remote rural areas.

The German "Bauer," who a scant twenty years ago believed that his horse or ox and his fractional parcels of land were his eternal, foreordained inheritance is of a different mind now. The changes and mechanization all about him are strong propagandists, and rural and city inhabitants will not for long show sharp cultural and social differences. . . .

The Old Order Amish are a revelation to Europeans because they have succeeded in maintaining a distinct "group" character in an America renowned for modernity and progress and an apparent homogeneity and conformity in manners and customs. Europeans ordinarily do not suspect that a group like the Amish, free in its hilly surroundings to preserve an age long gone, can exist in America. The Amish must then become increasingly attractive to the student of Old World folkways: what escapes the researcher abroad may be alive in America, not as a festival-day exhibition but as the very core of Amish being. . . .

What will become of the Old Order Amish in Ohio? Without assuming the role of either seer or prophet, the answer is simple. There will always be Old Order Amish, barring international catastrophe. This claim needs no complicated justification. The people of the hilly back roads of east-central Ohio live relatively sheltered and unmolested. Furthermore, as Anabaptists and Mennonites, they have a long history of survival behind them. As the "first sect of Protestantism" with origins in Reformation times, the doctrines of these religious agriculturists have developed deep, tough roots. The large number of Mennonites in modern America attests to their vigor and vitality.

Source: Schreiber (1962): 206–7

→≫-≫-≫-≫-≫-≫-≫-≫

If Life Means Going Without, the Amish Go Without

ARCHIBALD MACLEISH

Archibald MacLeish, *prolific writer on American life, with Lord Snowdon as photographer, produced a noteworthy feature on the Amish people for* McCall's *magazine. Lord Snowdon expresses some thoughts on the many visitors to Amish country.*

Jefferson, though he saw farther into the future than any man of his century, did not foresee Metropolis. There was no example in history of a great people picking itself up from its countryside and crowding into enormous, choking cities incapable of government of any kind and particularly of the government of themselves. But even without this foreknowledge, Jefferson was convinced that a free society required openness to live in—a relationship with the order and the seasons of the earth.

It is here that the Amish, . . . have something of their own to say about the country *in* but not *on* which they live. The usual view of the Amish is that they are an anachronism, a people who got struck in history back with the horse and wagon and an Old Testament God and other chronological oddities, such as the art of husbandry, and domestic skills long unused, and harmonious lives. We regard them as quaint—charming, even—but as curiosities rather than contemporaries. A recent automobile advertisement says it all. The company was apparently persuaded that the reason folks don't go touring as they used to is simply that there's nowhere left to tour. The cities won't serve; you can't see them for the smog or walk in them for the muggers. And as for the countryside—scenery has a disconcerting way of turning into strip mines as you come around a curve in Kentucky or into virgin sewers as you follow a mountain trout stream in California. Which leaves you with nothing to head for but expressways connecting with other expressways. And you can't sell automobiles to go riding just for the ride unless you are willing to limit yourself to customers under seventeen.

So what they needed was a place to go, and some unsung genius came up with the Amish country. It made a beautiful photograph. There you were in your brand-new car, tooling along a country lane with a horse-drawn Amish wagon framed in your windshield. What better reason for driving a thousand miles? Better for you, that is: the Amish farmer cramping into the ditch to let you go by might have a somewhat different opinion. . . . The Amish have reason to believe that they and their fathers and their fathers' fathers have been wiser about the world than the forebears of the gawking tourists.

And the Amish have. Generations before the rest of us had even begun to realize that there is a world under all other questions and that our future depends on our ability to answer it, the Amish had faced up to the question. At a time when we believed, in our trusting innocence, that the cotton gin and the railroad train and the flying machine and the internal-combustion engine knew where they were going (and where we were going with them) the Amish had already decided that they weren't joining the procession. We used to laugh at the Amish when they wouldn't buy Model T's. Now we don't even smile. We're too busy trying to get the railroads back in business and keep the highway lobby from drowning the continent in concrete.

The fact is that the Amish, for whatever reason, had spotted the idea of progress for what it is a long time before the rest of us had learned the clichés—or even learned that they are clichés. It wasn't technological inventiveness that was going to define the future for the Amish. They themselves would do the defining. And what they would define would be their lives; not the means to life but the life itself. If, to live as they proposed to live, they would have to go without, they would go without.

It is easy enough to dismiss all this as religious aberration—primitivism.

What can't be dismissed is the fact that the Amish, for whatever reason, asked the right question: a question we have not been able to bring ourselves to ask even yet. We talk about ultimate values. We talk about rearranging our priorities. All we mean is shifting the priority of items in the federal budget—taking a billion or two out of Vietnam and putting it into housing. What the Amish mean is the nature of human life, the living of human life—everything Metropolis ignores and will go right on ignoring no matter how many miles of apartments are constructed.

Source: MacLeish (1972): 79–86

➤➤➤·➤➤➤·➤➤➤·➤➤➤·➤➤➤·➤➤➤·➤➤➤·➤➤➤

A Uniquely American Phenomenon

LORD SNOWDON

Visiting the Amish community is like visiting a very large agricultural rural monastery. . . .

But nothing had prepared me for the exploitation I would find of these peaceful, enormously hard-working people. And most of all, I never imagined I would come away so deeply moved nor so emotionally involved with and affected by their way of life. . . .

Fourteen years ago, some Lancaster businessmen formed the Pennsylvania Dutch Tourist Bureau to advertise and promote the region. And since then, the serene Amish country has become pockmarked with some sixty motels, with restaurants, amusement parks, museums, service stations, and countless gift shops selling such souvenirs as Amish dolls made in Hong Kong.

While the tourist board has tried hard to romanticize and cash in upon the Amish, the attitude of the Amish people (who rigorously shun publicity) and the philosophy which governs life remain every bit as obscure as before. During my own stay, for example, I encountered maps and brochures of Amishland at every turn, but I could find no literature about their religious beliefs. It is almost as if one is not expected to take them seriously in terms of what they believe but rather only in terms of what they look like. . . .

"Now with this tourist business," one Amish farmer said to me, "well, we feel sometimes it's getting monotonous. But we hope and pray that it won't get too much worse. I figure if I go about my business and they let me alone, I'll let them alone. I feel that if it's wrong God will give them their punishment, not me.

"We want to be the kind of Christians that the world can see are different. We believe you're supposed to lead a life so that anyone can see you're a Christian, so that you don't have to carry the Bible under your arm."

It is ironic and tragic that the Amish, who originally settled here on the basis of William Penn's offer of religious liberty, should ultimately be forced to seek their liberty elsewhere. But, speaking as an outsider, I believe that hope still exists for keeping them together and on their own land. I can't compare the Amish with anything I know in Europe; they are a uniquely American phenomenon. . . .

There is no way of preventing people from staring at things that fascinate them. But when the object of their attention is another group of human beings, it would seem to me necessary to try to "go the second mile"—to approach them not only better informed about their world, but with a sense of honest reverence, the kind of common courtesy and respect for privacy that people normally display towards others.

Source: Snowdon (1972): 88, 124–26

➤➤➤-➤➤➤-➤➤➤-➤➤➤-➤➤-➤➤➤-➤➤➤-➤➤

They Set a World Record

GEORGE R. SMITH

George R. Smith was for many years *the editor of* The Budget, *a weekly newspaper that has served the Amish people since 1890.*

Large families have always been the rule among the Amish people and during my many years of association with *The Budget* I have made a list of some of the exceptionally large family groups mentioned in the obituary columns.

I had recorded two family groups of more than 500 members and thought my list was fairly complete until Mrs. John D. Schmucker, Sr., of Bedford,

Wisconsin, reported the death of Adam Borntrager of that community and stated that he had 707 direct descendants, 675 of them still living.

This was such an astonishingly large total that I wrote to Mrs. Schmucker, asking if that might include any adoptions, stepchildren, or any who were not blood relatives.

Here is her reply: Adam Borntrager, who died at age 96, had 11 children, 115 grandchildren, 529 great-grandchildren, and 20 great-great-grandchildren, all living and all blood relatives. No adoptions or stepchildren. In addition, 8 grandchildren and 24 great-grandchildren of the same family are deceased.

I felt that must be a world record, so I consulted *The Guinness Book of World Records* and, sure enough, the largest family group recorded there was that of Mrs. Joanna Booyson of South Africa, who was estimated to have 600 living descendants in January 1968, and Wilson Kettle of Newfoundland left 582 living descendants when he died in 1963 at the age of 102.

Up to this time, the largest Amish family group I had recorded was that of Bishop Moses Borkholder of Napanee, Indiana, who died in 1933 at the age of 94. He had 17 children by two wives. Eleven of the children survived him, along with 138 grandchildren, 388 great-grandchildren and 18 great-great-grandchildren; a total of 555 living descendants at the time he died.

To the best of my knowledge no other monogamous society in the world has recorded family groups as large as the Amish families mentioned above.

Source: George R. Smith (1987)

⇒⟫⟩-⟫⟩-⟫⟩-⟫⟩-⟫⟩-⟫⟩-⟫⟩-⟫⟩

Always Available to Each Other

GERTRUDE ENDERS HUNTINGTON

G*ertrude Enders Huntington, an anthropologist, was educated at Oberlin, Swarthmore, and Yale. In her studies of human conservation, she was attracted to the Amish, especially their culture and agriculture. The result was one of the most comprehensive doctoral dissertations ever written on the Amish.*

The social structure of the Amish community is based on the availability of all to gather for work bees, for barn raisings, for day-long weddings, and day-long funerals. The Amish share labor within the family, between families and among church members whenever there is extra or special work to be done. This combination of mutual aid and social interaction keeps the community strong and of one mind. This interaction can be relatively easily achieved in a church district in which most of the household heads are farmers; it is almost impossible when most of the men work in factories or on construction crews. The traditional Amish culture is dependent on both parents working in the home, that is, being available to each other and to the children and to the community any hour of the day, on any day of the week. Although the Amish are tied to the American market system, the culture mitigates these ties and functions to isolate the Amishman by circumscribing his economic options in such a way that the Amish family-centered culture can be perpetuated both socially and physically.

During the 250 years the Amish have been in America, they have successfully resisted the lure of mass consumption and mass communication, they have maintained their emphasis on limited gratification and limited consumption, stressing economy, savings, and cash payments. While the urban villagers of Boston argue that money earned should be spent immediately to make daily life more pleasant, the Amish argue that "no one would want such a beautiful home here on this earth if they hoped for heavenly home after this time" (*Family Life* [June 1973]: 11). Life is too short to risk losing one's soul just for comfort or pleasure.

The Amish stress on the individual's total commitment to God, thus his responsibility to live according to the Amish *Ordnung,* has enabled the Amish culture to survive, sometimes at tremendous personal expense to the individual. In the early years of their history, some individuals were martyred, and the total group was strengthened by the payment of the few. In recent times certain individuals have lost their farms and savings; they were in a sense economically martyred, and again the total group profited by the payment of the few. The steadfastness of the Amish as individuals finally resulted in changes in and the enforcement of various laws, for example, Social Security, high school attendance, noncertified teachers in Amish schools, and alternative forms to military service. The Amish culture will continue to change as it adjusts to economic, technological, and social changes in the surrounding culture, but as long as the Amish are able to maintain their basic cultural configuration, their unique world view, and their own social structure, they will persist even though the details of their lives change.

Source: Huntington (1976): 320–21

A Network of Loving, Caring Relationships

SANDRA L. CRONK

Through careful and thoughtful scholarship, Sandra L. Cronk describes the deeper significance of the traditional Amish and Mennonite people.

The Old Order Amish and the Old Order Mennonites remain aloof from many of the values and practices of the general society, but they are not premodern relics of a bygone era. The Old Order movement is a conscious attempt to maintain a style of Christian living based on principles different from those of the larger society. The Old Order movement arose in nineteenth-century North America when both Amish and Mennonite communities were threatened with partial assimilation into the more general North American way of life. In response to this threat, conservative Amish and Mennonites organized separate church-communities to preserve what they considered the Christian way of life. Although the Old Order Amish and Old Order Mennonites are distinct groups with somewhat differing practices, they do have certain common understandings which have been so powerful that they have preserved their separate religious identity in the face of strong pressures to conform to the larger society.

The goal of all the distinctive patterns of life in the Old Order communities is to create a loving brotherhood. As people in the larger society grow discontent with the growing drive for individual success, wealth, and status, many find that the Old Order way of life with its network of loving, caring relationships is a symbol of the healing and wholeness for which they are searching. Thus, the Old Order people have an important message for seekers in the broader society. Friends (Society of Friends) in particular have a special interest in the Old Order movement because it embodies many elements which were traditionally part of the Quaker vision. Some of these elements have been lost in contemporary Quakerism. But Friends may wish to look at these elements with renewed understanding before they chart their course.

Source: Cronk (1977b): 3

An Embarrassment to American Agriculture

GENE LOGSDON

A*friend of the Amish, Gene Logsdon admires their farm management practices.*

The Amish have become a great embarrassment to American agriculture. Many "English" farmers, as the Amish call the rest of us, are in desperate financial straits these days and relatively few are making money. As a result it is fashionable among writers, the clergy, politicians, farm machinery dealers and troubled farm banks to depict the family farmer as a dying breed and to weep great globs of crocodile tears over the coming funeral. All of them seem to forget those small, conservatively financed family farms that are doing quite well, thank you, of which the premium example is the Amish.

Amish farmers are still making money in these hard times despite (or rather because of) their supposedly outmoded, horse-farming ways. If one of them does get into financial jeopardy, it is most often from listening to the promises of modern agri-business instead of traditional wisdom. His brethren will usually bail him out. More revealing, the Amish continue to farm profitably not only with an innocent disregard for get-big-or-get-out modern technology, but without participation in direct government subsidies. . . .

It is in agriculture that the Amish raise economy to a high art. The most amazing part of the Amish economy to me is that, contrary to notions cherished by old farm-magazine editors who escaped grim childhoods on 1930s farms for softer lives behind desks, the Amish do not work as hard, physically, as I did when my father and I were milking a hundred cows with all the modern conveniences in the 1960s. English farmers like to make fun of the Amish for their hairsplitting ways with technology—allowing tractors or engines for stationary power tools but not in the fields. But in addition to keeping the Amish way of life intact, such compromises bring tremendous economy to their farming while lightening the work load. A motor-powered baler or corn harvester, pulled by horses ahead of a forecart, may seem ridiculous to a modern agri-businessman, but it saves thousands of dollars over buying tractors for this work. The reason tractors aren't allowed in the fields is that they would then tempt an Amishman to expand acreage, going into steep debt to do so, and in the process drive other Amish off the land—which is exactly why and how American agriculture got into the trouble engulfing it today.

To satisfy religious restrictions, the Amish have developed many other ingenious ideas to use modern technology in economizing ways. Other farmers should be studying, not belittling, them. When Grade A milk regulations forced electric cooling tanks on dairymen, the Amish adopted diesel motors to generate their own electricity for the milk room, cooler, and milk machines. They say it's cheaper than buying electricity and keeps them secure from power outages. Similarly, they operate commercial woodworking and other shops with diesel-powered hydraulic pumps rather than individual electric motors for each tool. Their small woodworking shops, like their printing and publishing houses and a lot of other enterprises, make money where others so often fail.

Where Amish are active, countryside and town are full of hustling shops and small businesses, neat homes, solid schools and churches, and scores of roadside stands and cheese factories. East-central Ohio even has a small woolen mill, one of the few remaining in the country. Compare their region with the decaying towns and empty farmsteads of the land dominated by large-scale agri-business. The Amish economy spills out to affect the whole local economy.

Source: Logsdon (1986): 74–76

➤➤➤-➤➤➤-➤➤➤-➤➤➤-➤➤➤-➤➤➤-➤➤➤-➤➤➤

They Have Escaped Disintegration

WENDELL BERRY

W*endell Berry is a Kentucky small farmer who has written numerous books, including essays and poetry, about nature, soil, community and responsible stewardship. He has been called "a prophetic conscience to the nation" and "the closest we have to a modern Thoreau."*

To argue for a balance between people and their tools, between life and machinery, between biological and machine-produced energy, is to argue for restraint upon the use of machines. The arguments that rise out of the machine metaphor—arguments for cheapness, efficiency, labor-saving, economic growth, etc.—all point to infinite industrial growth and infinite energy consumption. The moral argument points to restraint; it is a conclusion that may be in some sense tragic, but there is no escaping it. Much as we long for infinities of power and duration, we have no evidence that these lie within our reach, much less within our responsibility. It is more likely that we will have either to live within our limits, within the human definition, or not live at all. . . .

The only people among us that I know of who have answered this question convincingly in the affirmative are the Amish. They alone, as a community, have carefully restricted their use of machine-developed energy, and so have become the only true masters of technology. They are mostly farmers, and they do most of their farm work by hand and by the use of horses and mules. They are pacifists, they operate their own local schools, and in other ways hold themselves aloof from the ambitions of a machine-based society. And by doing so they have maintained the integrity of their families, their community, their religion, and their way of life. They have escaped the mainstream American life of distraction, haste, aimlessness, violence, and disintegration. Their life is not idly wasteful, or destructive. The Amish no doubt have their problems; I do not wish to imply that they are perfect. But it cannot be denied that they have mastered one of the fundamental paradoxes of our condition: we can make ourselves whole only by accepting our partiality, by living within our limits, by being human—not by trying to be gods. By restraint they make themselves whole.

Source: Berry (1977): 95

Holding the New Barbarians in Check

FRANKLIN H. LITTELL

I*n 1967, when Amish values were in conflict with school attendance laws, Franklin H. Littell spoke these words at a conference on public policy for nonpublic schools at the University of Chicago.*

It is the dialogue with the past, practiced in lively fashion, which holds in check the totalitarian ideologies and the accomplished new barbarians who implement them. . . .

Of the various freedoms Americans use and abuse these days, love of bonnets and buggies seems one of the more harmless. But the central concern—the commitment to the wise and ultimately meaningful life—is today in short supply. We could do worse than to learn from the Amish rather than to coerce them into our own undisciplined and violent arts. . . .

The Amish and other sectarian Protestants are not about to blow up the world, even though they may slow up its vaunted onrush of progress. On the other hand, the most dangerous man in the modern world—whether he fancies himself a nuclear physicist or a "human engineer"—is, as Mr. Justice Jackson said at the Nürnberg Trials, the technically competent barbarian.

Source: Littell (1969): 79, 82

CHRONOLOGY OF
AMISH HISTORY

1525	Founding of the Swiss Brethren, Zürich
1693–97	Amish and Swiss Brethren division
1727	Amish-like names appear on several ship lists during September and October
1737	Ship *Charming Nancy* arrives in Philadelphia on October 9 with numerous identifiable Amish immigrant families
——	First New World congregation founded, Berks County, Pennsylvania
1748	*Martyrs Mirror* begins publication in Ephrata, Pennsylvania
1749	Bishop Jacob Hertzler arrives in America
1757	Native American attack on the Jacob Hochstetler homestead
1772	Somerset County, Pennsylvania, settlement founded
1790	Amish of Montbéliard, France, move to Galicia, Poland
1791	Mifflin County, Pennsylvania, settlement founded
1808	First Ohio settlement founded in Holmes County
1815	Alsatian Amish come to America

291

1824 Bavarian Amish settle in Ontario, Canada

1830 Alsatian Amish settle in Lewis County, New York

1831 First Illinois settlement founded in Tazewell and Woodford counties

1834 *Neu Täufer,* or Apostolic Christian Church, founded in Emmental, Switzerland, by Samuel Froelich

1839 First Indiana settlement founded in Marshall County

——— Adams County, Indiana, settlement founded

1840 Elkhart County, Indiana, settlement founded

——— First Iowa settlement founded in Lee County

1850 First Maryland settlement founded in Garrett County

——— First West Virginia settlement founded in Preston County

1852 Allen County, Indiana, settlement founded

1855 First Missouri settlement founded in Hickory County

1862 *Diener Versammlungen,* or annual ministers' meetings, begin. End in 1878.

1864 Henry Egli division, Amish County, Indiana

1869 Davies County, Indiana, settlement founded

1872 Stucky division in Illinois

1874 Russian Amish settlement in Volhynia moves to South Dakota

1879 First Oregon settlement founded in Clackamas County

1880 First Nebraska settlement founded in Gosper County

1886 Geauga County, Ohio, settlement founded

1888 Indiana-Michigan Amish Mennonite Conference organized

1890 Western Amish-Mennonite Conference organized

——— First Tennessee settlement founded in Dickson County

——— *The Budget* begins publication in Sugarcreek, Ohio

1891 First Minnesota settlement founded in Wilmont and Nobles counties

1892 First Oklahoma settlement founded in Custer County

——— First Virginia settlement founded in Faquier County

1894 First North Dakota settlement founded in Pierce and Rollette counties

1895 First Michigan settlement founded in Newaygo County

1896 First Mississippi settlement founded in Monroe County

1903 First Montana settlement founded in Dawson County

1909 First Colorado settlement founded in Elbert and Cheyenne counties

——— First Texas settlement founded in Hale County

——— First Wisconsin settlement founded in Sawyer County

1912 *Herold der Wahrheit* begins publication in Kalona, Iowa

——— Conservative Mennonite Conference founded

1915	First Delaware settlement founded in Kent County
1918	First North Carolina settlement founded in Currituck County
1921	First New Mexico settlement founded in Colfax County
1925	First private Amish school founded in Dover, Delaware
1927	Beachy Amish church founded by Moses Beachy, in Somerset County, Pennsylvania
1927	Amish families begin spending the winter in Florida
1937	Jonathan Fisher completes a trip around the world
1940	St. Mary's County, Maryland, settlement founded
1944	Lawrence County, Tennessee, settlement founded
1957	*Blackboard Bulletin* begins publication in Aylmer, Ontario
1958	First Kentucky settlement founded in Todd County
1964	Pathway Publishing Company founded in Aylmer, Ontario
1965	Palm Sunday tornado in Indiana
1966	"New Amish" denomination founded in Lancaster County, Pennsylvania
1967	National Committee for Amish Religious Freedom organized
1969	*The Diary* begins publication in Gordonville, Pennsylvania
——	*Family Life* begins publication in Aylmer, Ontario
1972	U.S. Supreme Court upholds Amish schools in *Wisconsin* v. *Yoder et al.*
1974	*Die Botschaft* begins publication in Lancaster, Pennsylvania

BIBLIOGRAPHY

Beachy, Monroe L.
1982   "What Does It Mean to Be Amish?" *Family Life* (August/September): 18.
Beer, Henry, ed.
1979   *The Gospel of Nicodemus* (1819).
"Behind Prison Walls"
1968   *Family Life,* part 1 (August): 12–14; part 2 (September): 16–19.
Beiler, Joseph F.
1974   "On the Meaning of Ordnung." Gordonville, Pa.
Bender, Christian W.
1948   *Descendants of Daniel Bender.* Berlin, Pa.: By the author.
Bender, Harold S.
1927   "The Discipline Adopted by the Strasburg Conference of 1568." *Mennonite Quarterly Review* 1 (January): 57–66.
1930   "An Amish Church Discipline of 1781." *Mennonite Quarterly Review* 4 (April): 140–48. Article on Bishop Hans Nafziger.
1934   "Some Early American Amish Mennonite Disciplines." *Mennonite Quarterly Review* 8 (April): 90–98.
1937   "An Amish Church Discipline of 1779." *Mennonite Quarterly Review* 11 (April): 163–68.

1946a   Ed. and trans. "An Amish Bishops' Conference Epistle of 1865." *Mennonite Quarterly Review* 20 (July): 222–29.

1946b   Ed. and trans. "The Minutes of the Amish Conference of 1809 Probably Held in Lancaster County, Pennsylvania" (facsimile). *Mennonite Quarterly Review* 20 (July): 240–42.

Berger, Peter L., and Richard J. Neuhaus

1977   *To Empower the People.* Washington, D.C.: American Enterprise Institute.

Berry, Wendell

1977   *The Unsettling of America: Culture and Agriculture.* New York: Sierra Club Books.

Bible, the Holy

Authorized King James Version. London: Oxford University Press.

Blackboard Bulletin, The

1957–   Monthly periodical published in the interest of Amish schools and homes by Pathway Publishers, Aylmer, Ont.

Bontrager, Eli J.

1953   "My Life Story." Shipshewanna, Ind. Mimeo.

Bontrager, John M.

1967   "The Challenge before Us." In *The Challenge of the Child,* edited by Joseph Stoll, pp. 74–75. Pathway Publishers: Aylmer, Ont.

Bontrager, Levi

1961   "Princess Anne, Virginia." *Budget* (October 26).

Braden, Tom

1975   "On Starting to Say 'Stop.' " *Los Angeles Times* Syndicate.

Braght, Thieleman J. van

1951   Comp. *The Bloody Theatre; or, Martyrs Mirror.* Scottdale, Pa.: Mennonite Publishing House. Originally published in Dutch (Dordrecht, 1660).

Brane, C.I.B.

1903   "Landmark History of United Brethrenism in Pennsylvania." *Pennsylvania German* 4 (July): 322–27.

Budget, The

1890–   Sugarcreek, Ohio. A weekly newspaper serving the Amish and Mennonite communities.

Byler, Uria R.

1963a   *Our Better Country.* Gordonville, Pa.: Old Order Book Society.

1963b   "What about Corporal Punishment?" *Blackboard Bulletin* (February).

1969   *School Bells Ringing: A Manual for Amish Teachers and Parents.* Aylmer, Ont.: Pathway Publishers.

1985   *As I Remember It.* Middlefield, Ohio.

"Confessions of a Hired Girl"

1984   *Family Life* (May): 32.

Correll, Ernst

1925   *Das schweizerische Täufermennonitentum* Tübingen: J.C.B. Mohr.

Cronk, Sandra L.

1977a   "Gelassenheit: The Rites of the Redemptive Process in Old Order Amish and Old Order Mennonite Communities." Ph.D. diss., University of Chicago.

1977b   "Old Order Amish and Old Order Mennonites: Loving Community Based on the Power of Powerlessness." *Quaker Witness* (Spring): 3.

1981   "Gelassenheit: The Rites of the Redemptive Process in Old Order Amish and Old Order Mennonite Communities." *Mennonite Quarterly Review* 55 (January): 5–44.

Detweiler, Virgil

1984   "Melchior Detweiler and Son Rudolph, 1736 Immigrants." *Mennonite Family History* (April): 73–74.

Diary, The

1969–   A monthly periodical devoted to Amish history and genealogy published by Pequea Publishers, Route 1, Gordonville, Pa.

Diener, Menno A.

1970   "Experiences in an Army Camp." *Family Life* (December): 22–24.

Erickson, Donald A.

1969   *Public Controls for Non-Public Schools.* Chicago: University of Chicago Press.

Family Life

1968   A monthly periodical of Pathway Publishers, Aylmer, Ont.

Fisher, Gideon L.

1975   *Alabama Tornado.* Ronks, Pa.: By the author.

1978   *Farm Life and Its Changes.* Gordonville, Pa.: Pequea Publishers.

Fisher, Nancy

1971   "Reflections." *Newsletter.* Philadelphia Mennonite Fellowship.

Fisher Family, John M.

1957   *Descendants and History of Christian Fisher Family.* Ronks, Pa.: By Amos L. Fisher.

Fishman, Joshua

1977   "Language, Ethnicity, and Racism." *GURT* (Georgetown University Round Table on Languages and Linguistics), pp. 297–309.

Fletcher, S. W.

1955   *Pennsylvania Agriculture and Country Life, 1640–1840.* Harrisburg: Pennsylvania Historical and Museum Commission.

Friedmann, Robert

1949   *Mennonite Piety through the Centuries.* Goshen, Ind.: Mennonite Historical Society.

1950   "Anabaptism and Protestantism." *Mennonite Quarterly Review* 24 (January): 12–24.

"Funeral of Bishop John B. Mast"

1941   Article of 1888 reprinted in *Reading Eagle* (June) and *Diary* (October 1969): 9–10.

Gaustad, Edwin S.

1982 *A Documentary History of Religion in America.* 2 vols. Grand Rapids, Mich.: Eerdmans.

Gibbons, Phebe Earle

1882 *Pennsylvania Dutch and Other Essays.* Philadelphia: J. B. Lippincott.

Gingerich, Eli E.

1966 "To Our Public School Officials of Elkhart County." *Blackboard Bulletin* (August): 19–20.

1980 *Indiana Amish Directory.* Middlebury, Ind.: By the author.

Gratz, Delbert

1953 *Bernese Anabaptists.* Goshen, Ind.: Mennonite Historical Society

Grebel, Conrad

1952 "Infant Baptism. An Abomination," translated by Elizabeth Horsch Bender. In *Quellen zur Geschichte der Täuffer in der Schweiz.* Vol. 1, *Zürich,* ed. Leonhard von Muralt and Walter Schmid. Zürich: S. Hirzel Verlag. [Täuferäkten Kommission.]

Hall, Barbara Yoder

1980 *Born Amish.* Randolph, Ohio: Jacbar Publications.

1982 "Christmas." Broadside.

1985 *Moses Yoder.* Hartville, Ohio.

Hark, Ann

1952 *Blue Hills and Shoofly Pie.* Philadelphia: J. B. Lippincott.

Hershberger, Jacob J.

1961 "Lynnhaven Gleanings." *Budget* (September 9).

Hershberger, Mrs. Atlee

1971 "The Boiler Explosion." *Diary* (December).

Hershey, Mary Jane Lederach

1987 "Andreas Kolb (1749–1811): Mennonite Schoolmaster and Fraktur Artist." *Mennonite Quarterly Review* 61 (April): 121–201.

Hostetler, Harvey

1912 *The Descendants of Jacob Hochstetler.* Elgin, Ill.: Brethren Publishing House.

Hostetler, John A.

1980 *Amish Society.* 3rd ed. Baltimore: Johns Hopkins University Press.

1983 *Amish Life.* Scottdale, Pa.: Herald Press.

1985 "The Plain People: Historical and Modern Perspectives." In *America and the Germans: An Assessment of a Three Hundred Year History,* edited by Frank Trommler and Joseph McVeigh, pp. 106–17. Vol. 1. Philadelphia: University of Pennsylvania Press.

Hostetler, John A., and Gertrude Enders Huntington

1971 *Children in Amish Society: Socialization and Community Education.* New York: Holt, Rinehart and Winston.

Huntington, Gertrude Enders

1956 "Dove at the Window: A Study of an Old Order Amish Community in Ohio." Ph.D. diss., Yale University.

1976   "The Amish Family." In *Ethnic Families in America: Patterns and Variations,* edited by Charles H. Mindel and Robert W. Habenstein, pp. 295–322. New York: Elsevier.

Hutterian Brethren

1987   *The Chronicle of the Hutterian Brethren.* Vol. 1. Rifton, N.Y.: Plough Publishing House.

Huyard, David E.

1987   "Issac Huyard Joins the Amish." New Holland, Pa. Mimeo.

Janson, Donald

1971   "Amish Await Final Ruling on Compulsory Schooling." *New York Times* (February 16): 35.

Klaassen, Walter

1971   *Anabaptism: Neither Catholic nor Protestant.* Waterloo, Ont.: Conrad Press.

Kline, David

1984a   "Bluebirds." *Family Life* (March): 10–12.

1984b   "The Adaptable Whitetail Deer." *Family Life* (November): 13–14.

Kollmorgen, Walter M.

1942   *Culture of a Contemporary Community: The Old Order Amish of Lancaster County, Pennsylvania.* Rural Life Studies no. 4. Washington, D.C.: U.S. Department of Agriculture.

Kraybill, Donald B.

1989   *The Riddle of Amish Culture.* Baltimore: Johns Hopkins University Press.

Lapp, Henry

1975   *A Craftsman's Handbook.* Introduction and notes by Beatrice B. Graven. Philadelphia: Philadelphia Museum of Art.

Lehman, Leland

1947   "The Economic Development of the Mennonite Community at Berne, Indiana." M.A. thesis, Ohio State University.

"Letter to Governor Thornburgh, A"

1985   Anonymous. Lancaster County, Pa.

Lindholm, William C.

1974   "An Act of Self-Preservation." In *Controversies in Education,* edited by Dwight W. Allen and Jeffrey C. Hecht, pp. 488–95. Philadelphia: W. B. Saunders.

Littell, Franklin H.

1969   "Sectarian Protestantism and the Pursuit of Wisdom: Must Technological Objectives Prevail?" In *Public Controls for Non-Public Schools,* edited by Donald A. Erickson, pp. 61–82. Chicago: University of Chicago Press.

1971   "Foreword." In Walter Klaassen, *Anabaptism: Neither Catholic nor Protestant.* Waterloo, Ont.: Conrad Press.

Logsdon, Gene

1986   "Amish Economics: A Lesson for the Modern World." *Whole Earth Review* (Spring): 74–76.

Luthy, David
1972   "The Peight Family." *Family Life* (November): 21–22.
1984   "An Important Pennsylvania Broadside of 1812." *Pennsylvania Mennonite Heritage* 7 (July): 1–4.
1986   *The Amish in America: Settlements That Failed, 1840–1960.* Aylmer, Ont.: Pathway Publishers.
1988   "Henry Lapp: Amish Folk Artist and Craftsman." *Pennsylvania Mennonite Heritage* 11 (October): 2–4.

McCauley, Daniel, and Kathryn McCauley
1988   *Decorative Arts of the Amish of Lancaster County.* Intercourse, Pa.: Good Books.

McGrath, William R.
1966   *Christlicher Ordnung or Christian Discipline.* Aylmer, Ont.: Pathway Publishers.

MacLeish, Archibald
1972   "Rediscovering the Simple Life." *McCall's* (April): 79–88. Photographs by Lord Snowdon.

Mast, C. Z., and Robert E. Simpson
1942   *Annals of the Conestoga Valley.* Elverson, Pa.: By the authors.

Mast, John B.
1950   Ed. and trans. *The Letters of the Amish Division.* Oregon City, Oreg.: Christian J. Schlabach.

Mast, Sadie R.
n.d.   *Bishop John Blank and Family.* N.p.

Miller, Abraham B.
1922   "Old Settler Stories." *Christian Monitor* (May): 528–29. Reprinted in Luthy (1986): 149.

Miller, David
1976   "Thomas, Oklahoma." *Budget* (August 11).

Miller, Elizabeth M.
1963   *From the Fiery Stakes of Europe to the Federal Courts of America.* New York: Vantage Press.

Miller, Mary
1976   "An Amish Farm." *Michigan Farmer* (July): 8–11.

Miller, Mrs. S. M.
1961   "Sarasota, Florida." *Budget* (November 2).

"Mottoes in the Schools"
1965   Anonymous.

Newman, Sadie C.
1897   "Church Rules in 1897." Belleville, Pa.

Olshan, Marc Alan
1980   "The Old Order Amish as a Model for Development." Ph.D. diss., Cornell University.

Overholt, William J.
n.d.   *From Conestoga Wagon to Modern Times: The Eventful Life of W. J. Overholt.* Seymour, Mo.: Edgewood Press.

Randle, Bill
1974   *Plain Cooking.* New York: Quadrangle Books of the *New York Times.*

Renno, John R.
[1976]   *A Brief History of the Amish Church in Belleville.* Danville, Pa.: By the author.

"Riddles"
1965   Anonymous.

Rodgers, Harrell R., Jr.
1969   *Community Conflict, Public Opinion, and the Law: The Amish Dispute in Iowa.* Columbus, Ohio: Charles E. Merrill.

Rugaber, Walter
1965   "Iowa's Amish Fight Worldly Schooling." *New York Times* (November 28): 1.

Rules of a Godly Life
1984   *Ernsthafte Christenpflicht* (1793). 3rd ed. Aylmer, Ont.: Pathway Publishers.

Rush, Benjamin
1875   *An Account of the Manners of the German Inhabitants of Pennsylvania* (1789), edited by Daniel Rupp. Philadelphia: Samuel P. Town.

Schlabach, Roy L.
1984   "A Lesson from Our Past." *Family Life* (February): 40.

Schmitt, Barbara
1970   "Log Cabin Days." *Diary* (January): 19–20.

Schreiber, William I.
1962   *Our Amish Neighbors.* Chicago: University of Chicago Press.

Schwartz, Simon M.
1981   "Death of an Amish Child." *Liberty* (March/April): 3.

Séguy, Jean
1973   "Religion and Agricultural Success: The Vocational Life of the French Anabaptists from the Seventeenth to the Nineteenth Centuries," translated by Michael Shank. *Mennonite Quarterly Review* 47 (July): 182–224.

1977   *Les Assemblées anabaptistes-mennonites de France.* The Hague: Mouton.

Shryock, Richard H.
1939   "British versus German Traditions in Colonial Agriculture." *Mississippi Valley Historical Review* 26 (June): 39–54.

Simons, Menno
1956   *The Complete Writings of Menno Simons,* translated by Leonard Verduin and edited by John C. Wenger. Scottdale, Pa.: Herald Press.

Smith, C. Henry
1929   *The Mennonite Immigration to Pennsylvania.* Vol. 28. Norristown, Pa.: Proceedings of the Pennsylvania German Society.
1962   *Mennonite Country Boy.* Newton, Kans.: Faith and Life Press.
Smith, Clyde
1912   *The Amishman.* Toronto: William Briggs.
Smith, Elmer L.
1961   *The Amish Today: An Analysis of Their Beliefs, Behavior, and Contemporary Problems.* Proceedings of the Pennsylvania German Folklore Society. Vol. 24. Allentown, Pa.: Schlechters.
Smith, George R.
1987   "The Editor's Corner." *Budget* (November 18).
Smucker, Ann Hostetler
1983   "Where Was God when Naomi Died?" *Christian Living* (July): 8–10.
Snowdon, Lord
1972   "The Plight of the Amish . . ." *McCall's* (April): 88, 124–25.
"Social Activities Were Lacking"
1961   Lancaster County, Pa.
Speicher, Paul I.
1970   *A History of the Speicher, Spucher, Spyker Family.* N.p.: By the author.
Stoll, Joseph
1962   "Teachers Do a Lot of Self-Study." *Blackboard Bulletin* (May).
1965   *Who Shall Educate Our Children?* Aylmer, Ont.: Pathway Publishers.
1967   Ed. *The Challenge of the Child.* 2nd enl. ed. Aylmer, Ont.: Pathway Publishers.
1976   *Child Training.* Aylmer, Ont.: Pathway Publishers.
Stoltzfus, Eli
1969   *The Serenity and Value of Amish Country Living.* Strasburg, Pa.: By the author.
Stoltzfus, Grant M.
1954   "History of the First Amish Mennonite Communities in America." *Mennonite Quarterly Review* 28 (October): 235–62.
Stoltzfus, Nicholas
1744   "Petition for Marriage to the Daughter of the Rinckweyler Farmer" (January 14). Zweibrücken, Germany. Private collection of the Stoltzfus Family.
Studer, Gerald C.
1967   *Christopher Dock: Colonial Schoolmaster.* Scottdale, Pa.: Herald Press.
Summer, Robert L.
1974   "More Important than Money." *Sword of the Lord.* (August 2).
Thomas, Norman
1923   *The Conscientious Objector in America.* New York: B. W. Heubsch.

"To Our Men of Authority"
1938   Broadside issued by a committee of Old Order Amish and Old Order
        Mennonites. From minutes of November 9.

Troyer, Effie
1961   "Dover, Delaware." *Budget* (September 14).

Troyer, Les
[1987] "Indian up a Tree." Sugarcreek, Ohio.

Turnbull, Colin M.
1984   "The Individual, Community, and Society: Rights and Responsibilities
        from an Anthropological Perspective: The Amish and the Mbuti."
        Washington and Lee Law Review 41 (Winter): 111–16.

Umble, John S.
1933a   "The Amish Mennonites of Union County, Pennsylvania. Part I: Social
        and Religious Life." *Mennonite Quarterly Review* 7 (April): 71–96.
1933b   "The Amish Mennonites of Union County, Pennsylvania. Part II: A
        History of the Settlement." *Mennonite Quarterly Review* 7 (July): 162–
        90.
1941   "An Amish Minister's Manual" [edited by Joseph Unzicker]. *Mennonite
        Quarterly Review* 15 (April): 95–117.

Wagler, Raymond, and Willie Wagler
1939   *A Trip to Europe and the Holy Lands.* Sugarcreek, Ohio: By Ralph
        Yoder.

Weaver, Monroe A.
1978   *Amish Europe and Holy Land Tour via "Queen Elizabeth II."* Holmes-
        ville, Ohio.: By the author.

Wenger, John C.
1950   *The Doctrines of the Mennonites.* Scottdale, Pa.: Herald Press. Dor-
        trecht Confession, pp. 75–85.
1961   *The Mennonites in Indiana and Michigan.* Scottdale, Pa.: Herald Press.

Widow in Kansas, A
1985   "View from the Other End." *Family Life* (January): 4–5.

Williams, George H., and A. M. Mergal
1957   *Spiritual and Anabaptist Writers.* Philadelphia: Westminster Press.

Wiser, Frederick S., and Howell J. Heaney
1976   Comps. *The Pennsylvania German Fraktur of the Free Library of Phila-
        delphia: An Illustrated Catalogue.* 2 vols. Breinigsville: Pennsylvania
        German Society and the Free Library of Philadelphia.

Wisconsin v. *Yoder et al.*
1972   U.S. Supreme Court. No. 70–110. Argued December 8, 1971; decided
        May 15, 1972.

Yoder, Abe S.
1965   *My Life Story.* Belleville, Pa.: By the author.
1968   "The Amish in Nebraska." *Family Life* (January): 11–12.

Yoder, Don
    1974   "Fraktur in Mennonite Culture." *Mennonite Quarterly Review* 59 (July): 305–42.

Yoder, John H.
    1973   *The Legacy of Michael Sattler.* Scottdale, Pa.: Herald Press.

Yoder, Joseph W.
    1940   *Rosanna of the Amish.* Huntington, Pa.: Yoder Publishing.
    1948   *Rosanna's Boys.* Huntington, Pa.: Yoder Publishing.

Yoder, Mary E.
    1971   "Amish Settlers and the Civil War." *Family Life* (March): 26–27.

Yoder, Sarah
    1961   "Galena, Maryland." *Budget* (October 19).

Zehr, William
    1961   "Grabill, Indiana." *Budget* (September 21).

ACKNOWLEDGMENTS
AND PERMISSIONS

Permission to use material from the following publishers is gratefully acknowledged: American Enterprise Institute, Brethren Publishing House, William Briggs, the *Budget,* Conrad Press, Faith and Life Press, *GURT,* Herald Press, Lancaster Mennonite Historical Society, *Liberty,* J. B. Lippincott, *Los Angeles Times* Syndicate, Mennonite Historical Society, Charles E. Merrill, the *Michigan Farmer,* J.C.B. Mohr, Mouton, the *New York Times,* Old Order Book Society, Pathway Publishers, Pennsylvania German Society, Pennsylvania Historical and Museum Commission, Pequea Publishers, Philadelphia Mennonite Fellowship *Newsletter,* Plough Publishing House, Quadrangle Books of the *New York Times, Quaker Witness,* Review and Herald Publishing, W. B. Saunders, *Sword of the Lord,* Täuferäkten Kommission, U.S. Department of Agriculture, University of Pennsylvania Press, Vantage Press, *Whole Earth Review,* and Yoder Publishing.

"Showdown in Iowa" by Donald A. Erickson is from *Public Control for Non-Public Schools,* reprinted with permission of the University of Chicago. Copyright © 1969 by the University of Chicago; "A Revelation to Europe-

305

ans" by William I. Schreiber is from *Our Amish Neighbors,* reprinted with permission from the University of Chicago. Copyright © 1962 by the University of Chicago; "If Life Means Going Without, the Amish Go Without" is from "Rediscovering the Simple Life" by Archibald MacLeish and "A Uniquely American Phenomenon" is from "The Plight of the Amish . . ." by Lord Snowdon; both are reprinted with permission from McCall's magazine. Copyright © 1972 by The McCall Publishing Company; "They Have Escaped Disintegration" by Wendell Berry is from *The Unsettling of America* by Wendell Berry. Copyright © 1977 by Wendell Berry. Reprinted with permission of Sierra Club Books.

I gratefully thank the following people and institutions for permission to use the illustrations: Bruderschaft Library, Ezra and Orpha Hershberger, Hiram and Mary Jane Lederach Hershey, Historical Society of the Cocalico Valley, Muddy Creek Farm Library, Pennsylvania Farm Museum, Rare Book Department, Free Library of Philadelphia, and Schwenkfelder Library.

Thanks to all writers, especially those who have contributed substantially: Uria R. Byler, Gideon L. Fisher, David Luthy, and Joseph Stoll.

Thanks also to others who, for reasons of privacy, wished not to have their names disclosed.

I also thank Ray Dieffenbach for his translation work.

NOTES ON
SELECTED CONTRIBUTORS

Jacob Ammann (c. 1656–?) was a Swiss Mennonite elder and the founder of the Amish group in Switzerland and Alsace.

Monroe Beachy (1933–), an Amish father of six children who lives in Sugarcreek, Ohio, works as an accountant.

David Beiler (1786–1871) was a prominent Amish bishop who lived near Bird-in-Hand, Pennsylvania, and authored two books, one of which was his memoirs. He was a strong advocate of maintaining the older forms of conservatism.

Jacob Beiler (?–1772) was the founder of the Amish Beiler (Byler) family in America. A native of Guggisberg, Switzerland, he immigrated to America, with his wife, Veronica, and their five children, on October 8, 1737. They settled in Berks County, Pennsylvania.

Joseph F. Beiler (1923–) is an Amish minister who lives near Gordonville, Pennsylvania. He publishes books and periodicals for the Amish constituency under the imprint of Pequea Publishers.

Christian W. Bender (1875–1945), an Amish historian, is the author of *Descendants of Daniel Bender* and a resident of Somerset County, Pennsylvania.

Wendell Berry (1934–) is a small farmer, poet, and essayist who lives in Kentucky. His widely read books on wholeness, and the interdependence of people, animals, land, and weather, have led to his title "a modern Thoreau."

Eli J. Bontrager (1868–1958) was a widely known and well-traveled Amish bishop. He helped to pioneer new settlements in Michigan, North Dakota, and Wisconsin.

John M. Bontrager (1924–) assisted in the development of the Amish school movement in northern Indiana. He lives in Shipshewanna, Indiana.

Uria R. Byler (1913–1982) was an active lay leader, teacher, and dynamic speaker. He was a promoter of the Amish school movement in Ohio and a superintendent of the Geauga County, Ohio, Amish schools. He also wrote several textbooks, including *Our Better Country*.

Sandra L. Cronk (1942–), a Quaker scholar, teaches at Pendle Hill, a retreat and adult study center of the Society of Friends, in Wallingford, Pennsylvania.

Virgil Detweiler (1924–) is a genealogist active in tracing the Detweiler Amish immigrant family. He lives in Saugerties, New York.

Christopher Dock (?–1771) immigrated to America from Germany in about 1714. He was a farmer and also taught school among the Mennonites. One of his pupils was Christopher Sauer, who became a noted publisher of Bibles and German books. Dock wrote hymns and a book entitled *School Management*, which contains "A Hundred Rules for Children." He also taught his students how to beautifully illuminate manuscripts. See the plate *Merit Award, c. 1760*.

Donald A. Erickson (1925–) has taught education at several major universities. He organized the 1967 University of Chicago conference "Freedom and Control in Education," which examined state regulation of private schools. The author of *Public Control for Non-public Schools*, he was an expert witness in *Wisconsin* v. *Yoder et al.* (1972).

Amos L. Fisher (1920–1986) was an Amish lay leader, historian, and genealogist, as well as the author of *Descendants and History of Christian Fisher*.

Gideon L. Fisher (1913–), a retired Amish farmer and machine-shop operator who lives in Lancaster County, Pennsylvania, is the author of *Farm Life and Its Changes*.

Jonathan B. Fisher (1879–1953) was the eldest of fifteen children in an Amish family. He and his wife, Sarah Farmwald, were the parents of three daughters and one adopted son. Their home was in Bareville, Pennsylvania. Jonathan was well-traveled, having gone to Europe as well as around the world.

Eli E. Gingerich (1915–) is an Amish minister, author, and genealogist, and a resident of Elkhart County, Indiana.

Conrad Grebel (c. 1498–1525), son of a prominent family in Zürich, was the chief founder of Swiss Anabaptism.

Barbara Yoder Hall (1940–1988) was a lecturer and the author of *Born Amish*, a collection of short stories about her Amish childhood.

Ann Hark (1891–1971), a Moravian and a native of Lancaster, Pennsylvania, wrote several books about the Pennsylvania Dutch and was a feature writer for the *Philadelphia Inquirer* and other newspapers.

Ella Hershberger (1920–) lives near Oakland, Maryland. She is married to Atlee Hershberger. She wrote the account "The Boiler Explosion of 1918."

Jacob J. Hershberger (1908–1965), a bishop in the Beachy, or Amish-Mennonite, church, lived near Norfolk, Virginia. In the last two years of his life, he wrote a weekly column, "Lynnhaven Gleanings," for *The Budget*.

Harvey Hostetler (1857–?) was born in Summit Mills, Pennsylvania, and also lived in Council Bluffs, Iowa. His grandfather was a member of the Amish church, but he himself was a graduate of Iowa State University (1881) and Union Theological Seminary in New York (1884). He was a Presbyterian clergyman and was noted for his compilation of two large genealogies of the Hostetler family.

Gertrude Enders Huntington (1926–), a cultural anthropologist who teaches at the University of Michigan, is the author of books and articles on conservation and on Amish and Hutterite culture.

David E. Huyard (1907–) and his wife, Lydia Smoker, are a retired Amish couple who live in New Holland, Pennvania, where they make beautiful quilts and receive visitors from home and abroad.

David Kline (1945–) is a member of the Amish church. He, his wife, Elsie, and their five children manage their 125 acres of rolling Ohio farmland, "independent of the electrical grid." David not only farms but also writes about nature, conservation, and farm life.

Walter M. Kollmorgen (1907–), a social geographer and researcher, is also the author of a federally funded study, *Culture of a Contemporary Community: The Old Order Amish of Lancaster County, Pennsylvania* (1942).

William C. Lindholm (1932–) is pastor of Holy Cross Lutheran Church in Livonia, Michigan.

Franklin H. Littell (1917–) is Professor Emeritus of Religion at Temple University. A champion of religious liberty, he has written widely on the Radical Reformation, the origins of the Anabaptists, and the Free Church movement.

Gene Logsdon (1931–) is an Ohio small farmer, author, and columnist.

David Luthy (1941–), a member of the Amish church, is the author of numerous works pertaining to Amish life and history. Born in Illinois, he spent much of his adult life in Ontario. He is the director of the Amish Historical Library, near Aylmer, Ontario.

Archibald MacLeish (1892–1982), an eminent American poet, playwright, essayist, and statesman, was a three-time winner of the Pulitzer Prize and Librarian of Congress.

Abraham B. Miller (1861–?) helped to found an early Amish settlement in Custer County, Oklahoma, in 1893. His father acquired 160 acres of land there.

Elizabeth M. Miller (n.d.), an Amish wife and mother in Millersburg, Ohio, is the author of *From the Fiery Stakes of Europe to the Federal Courts of America.*

Mary Miller (1955–) wrote an article for the *Michigan Farmer.* She married David A. Kauffman and moved from Michigan to Indiana, where she is a mother and homemaker.

James L. Morris (1810–1849), a village merchant in Morgantown, Pennsylvania, was active in local religious and political affairs. He frequently served as an executor of wills, was a surveyor, and kept a diary.

Hans Nafziger (1706–?), who married Barbara Hooley, was the elder of the Amish congregation in Essingen, Germany. He assisted small, struggling Amish groups in the Netherlands by writing a bishop's manual for maintaining congregational life.

Hans Nussbaum (n.d.) was an Amish leader who immigrated to America from Switzerland in 1818.

Marc Alan Olshan (1945–) is a rural sociologist who observed Amish settlements in New York and wrote his Cornell University dissertation on "The Old Order Amish as a Model for Development."

Bill Randle (1923–) is a former Cleveland disc jockey and radio announcer. His book *Plain Cooking* contains Amish recipes.

Hans Reist (n.d.), also known as John Reist and Hans Hüsli, was the senior elder in Switzerland at the time of the Amish and Swiss Mennonite division (1693–97).

John R. Renno (1924–), a former member of the Amish church who lives in Pennsylvania, retains a deep interest in his Amish roots and community.

Roy Schlabach (1915–) is an Amish bishop and farmer in Ohio.

Barbara Schmitt (1908–) is the wife of Amish minister Emanuel Schmitt, of Adams County, Indiana.

William I. Schreiber (1906–), Professor of German at Wooster College, in Wooster, Ohio, is the author of *Our Amish Neighbors* and articles about the Ohio Amish.

Jean Séguy (1925–) is a French sociologist and author of *Les Assemblées anabaptistes-mennonites de France,* the definitive study of the social and religious origins of the Mennonites in eastern France.

C. Henry Smith (1875–1948) is recognized as the major historian of the Mennonites, having written five books about them. The son of Alsatian Amish-Mennonite immigrants, he was born near Metamora, Illinois. He taught Mennonite history at Bluffton College, in Bluffton, Ohio.

Clyde Smith (1852–1930) is the author of the first book in North America about the Amish, *The Amishman,* which consists of thirty chapters of a literary rather than a sociological nature.

George R. Smith (1907–) was editor of *The Budget,* a weekly newspaper, from 1936 to 1969. He is now its associate editor.

Ann Hostetler Smucker (1954–) lives in Philadelphia and teaches English at the University of Pennsylvania.

Lord Snowdon (Anthony Charles Robert Armstrong-Jones) (1930–) is a British photographer and filmmaker. The former husband of Princess Margaret, he is a London resident.

Paul I. Speicher (1892–) is a genealogist of the Speicher family and lives in Berks County, Pennsylvania.

Joseph Stoll (1935–) is an Amish farmer, writer, and teacher, as well as a leader of the Amish school movement. For many years he edited *The Blackboard Bulletin,* a journal that he had founded for Amish teachers. Born in Indiana, he has spent most of his life in Ontario.

Eli Stoltzfus (1923–), the author of *The Serenity and Value of Amish Country Living,* was the caretaker of the Amish Homestead, a tourist attraction near Lancaster, Pennsylvania.

Grant M. Stoltzfus (1916–1974), Professor of History at Eastern Mennonite College, in Harrisonburg, Virginia, was a historian of Amish and Mennonite groups. From 1947 to 1954, he was the editor of the journal *Mennonite Community*.

Les Troyer (1924–) grew up in an Amish community in Holmes County, Ohio, and is a free-lance writer.

John S. Umble (1881–1966), who descended from the Amish, was a professor at Goshen College, in Goshen, Indiana. He wrote articles on Amish cultural and social history.

Joseph Unzicker (n.d.), an Amish bishop in Germany, was in charge of the Nassau congregation in Upper Hesse. His minister's manual was used by early congregations in America.

Willie Wagler (1914–1983) lived in Reno County, Kansas. He and his brother Raymond, who were members of the Beachy Amish-Mennonite church, published a travelogue, *A Trip to Europe and the Bible Lands*.

John C. Wenger (1910–) is Professor Emeritus of Historical Theology at Goshen Biblical Seminary in Elkhart, Indiana. He also taught at Goshen College, in Goshen, Indiana, from 1938 to 1969. He is a lecturer and the author of many books on Anabaptist and Mennonite history and theology.

Abe S. Yoder (1878–1968) was the son of homesteading parents in Gosper County, Nebraska. He later lived in Mifflin County, Pennsylvania, where he wrote his autobiography.

Joseph W. Yoder (1872–1956), the son of Rosanna McGonegal and Amish minister Christian Z. Yoder, was born in Mifflin County, Pennsylvania. He was the author of *Rosanna of the Amish* and several other books. He was also a lecturer, a composer, and a teacher of vocal music.

Christian Zook, Jr. (1752–1826) was a minister in the Amish church in Chester County, Pennsylvania.

INDEX